MW00861160

Theology without Metaph.

One of the central arguments of post-metaphysical theology is that language is inherently "metaphysical," and consequently that it shoehorns objects into predetermined categories. Because God is beyond such categories, it follows that language cannot apply to God.

Drawing on recent work in theology and philosophy of language, Kevin W. Hector develops an alternative account of language and its relation to God, demonstrating that one need not choose between fitting God into a metaphysical framework, on the one hand, and keeping God at a distance from language, on the other. Hector thus elaborates a "therapeutic" response to metaphysics: given the extent to which metaphysical presuppositions about language have become embedded in common sense, he argues that metaphysics can be fully overcome only by defending an alternative account of language and its application to God, of such a kind as to strip such presuppositions of their apparent self-evidence and release us from their grip.

KEVIN W. HECTOR is Assistant Professor of Theology and of the Philosophy of Religions at the University of Chicago Divinity School. His essays have appeared in *Modern Theology*, *International Journal of Systematic Theology*, *Scottish Journal of Theology*, *Journal of Religion*, and *Expository Times*.

CURRENT ISSUES IN THEOLOGY

General Editor:
Iain Torrance
Princeton Theological Seminary

Editorial Advisory Board:

David Ford   *University of Cambridge*
Bryan Spinks   *Yale University*
Kathryn Tanner   *University of Chicago*
John Webster   *University of Aberdeen*

There is a need among upper-undergraduate and graduate students of
theology, as well as among Christian teachers and church professionals, for a
series of short, focussed studies of particular key topics in theology written by
prominent theologians. *Current Issues in Theology* meets this need.

   The books in the series are designed to provide a "state-of-the-art"
statement on the topic in question, engaging with contemporary thinking
as well as providing original insights. The aim is to publish books that stand
between the static monograph genre and the more immediate statement
of a journal article, by authors who are questioning existing paradigms or
rethinking perspectives.

Other titles in the series:

Holy Scripture   John Webster
The Just War Revisited   Oliver O'Donovan
Bodies and Souls, or Spirited Bodies?   Nancey Murphy
Christ and Horrors   Marilyn McCord Adams
Divinity and Humanity   Oliver D. Crisp
The Eucharist and Ecumenism   George Hunsinger
Christ the Key   Kathryn Tanner

KEVIN W. HECTOR

Theology without Metaphysics

God, Language, and the Spirit of Recognition

CAMBRIDGE
UNIVERSITY PRESS

CAMBRIDGE UNIVERSITY PRESS
Cambridge, New York, Melbourne, Madrid, Cape Town,
Singapore, São Paulo, Delhi, Tokyo, Mexico City

Cambridge University Press
The Edinburgh Building, Cambridge CB2 8RU, UK

Published in the United States of America by Cambridge University Press, New York

www.cambridge.org
Information on this title: www.cambridge.org/9781107010284

First published 2011

Printed in the United Kingdom at the University Press, Cambridge

A catalogue record for this publication is available from the British Library

Library of Congress Cataloging in Publication data
Hector, Kevin.
   Theology without metaphysics : God, language, and the spirit of recognition /
   Kevin Hector.
      p.   cm. – (Current issues in theology)
   Includes bibliographical references and index.
   ISBN 978-1-107-01028-4 (hardback) – ISBN 978-0-521-27970-3 (pbk.)
   1. God (Christianity)   2. Philosophical theology.   3. Language and
   languages–Religious aspects–Christianity.   4. Metaphysics.   I. Title.
   II. Series.
   BT103.H43 2011
   231.01'4–dc23
   2011026081

ISBN 978-1-107-01028-4 Hardback
ISBN 978-0-521-27970-3 Paperback

For Krista

Contents

Preface

I regularly encounter persons who think it is self-evident that language is inherently metaphysical, that it therefore shoehorns objects into a predetermined framework and so inflicts violence upon them, and that it must accordingly be kept at a distance from God. I have never been convinced that this is the case, much less that it is *self-evidently* the case. This book argues that there is good reason to resist such a view, since there is reason to think that language is not – or need not be thought to be – metaphysical. If I am right about this, the book should contribute to current discussions of theological language as well as of metaphysics. That is my hope, at any rate.

This project began as a dissertation written at Princeton Seminary, and I am grateful to Gordon Graham, George Hunsinger, Wentzel van Huyssteen, Bruce McCormack, Daniel Migliore, and Jeffrey Stout for their invaluable help with it. McCormack and Stout deserve special recognition, since whatever theological and philosophical skill I have is due largely to them. I was blessed to have been mentored by two professors who are not only among the best in the world at what they do, but who earnestly care about – and root for – their students.

The dissertation has since been rewritten from the ground up; hardly a sentence of the original remains. For their contributions to this effort, I owe a debt of thanks to my (current and former) colleagues at the University of Chicago, especially Dan Arnold, Curtis Evans, Dwight Hopkins, Jean-Luc Marion, William Schweiker, and Kathryn Tanner, and to members of the Race and Religion Workshop and my Theology and Metaphysics seminar, especially Jason Cather,

Julius Crump, and Bryce Rich. I am likewise grateful to Steve Bush, David DeCosimo, Rick Elgendy, Keith Johnson, Bruce Marshall, Lisa Powell, Joseph Steineger, and Ted Vial for their comments on earlier drafts. The finished product is much improved for their help.

Special thanks are also due to my editors at Cambridge, Laura Morris and Iain Torrance. They have been as kind as they have been helpful, and I am grateful for their good work.

Chapters 2 and 6 contain revised versions of material previously published as "The Mediation of Christ's Normative Spirit: A Constructive Reading of Schleiermacher's Pneumatology," in *Modern Theology* 24:1 (2008); "Attunement and Explicitation: A Pragmatist Reading of Schleiermacher's 'Theology of Feeling,'" in *Schleiermacher, the Study of Religion, and the Future of Theology*, Brent Sockness and Wilhelm Gräb (eds.) (Berlin: Walter de Gruyter, 2010); and "Grappling with Charles Taylor's *A Secular Age*," Review of *A Secular Age*, by Charles Taylor, *Journal of Religion* 90:3 (July 2010). I am grateful to the editors of *Modern Theology*, Walter de Gruyter, and *Journal of Religion* for their permission to reuse this material.

Finally, like everything else I do, the writing of this book was bound up with the life I share with my family. My son Simeon was born the day after I turned in my dissertation, and my daughter Anastasia a week after I finished rewriting it. They have been a blessing to me in countless ways, among which I would include (nowhere near the top of the list) their providing me with an endless supply of test cases with which to assess my claims about language. My wife Krista, meanwhile, has been an inexhaustible source of encouragement and support, joyfully and effortlessly given, as well as a reliable touchstone by which to test my philosophical and theological intuitions. She has been my constant champion, and I dedicate this book to her.

1 | Therapy for metaphysics

As its name suggests, this book proposes a novel strategy by which to avoid metaphysics. There is nothing new about trying to avoid metaphysics, of course – in the memorable words of Hegel, "metaphysics is a word from which more or less everyone runs away, as from someone who has the plague"[1] – but unlike recent proposals, the chapters which follow pursue a *therapeutic*, rather than *apophatic*, approach to doing so. One of the difficulties facing any attempt to overcome metaphysics, it seems, is that certain metaphysical presuppositions about what it means to be in touch with reality – and about reality itself – have become common sense. A crucial first step in overcoming metaphysics, then, is to render these presuppositions visible *as* presuppositions; on a therapeutic approach, this is accomplished by defending an alternative account of reality, of "being in touch," and so on, thereby stripping such presuppositions of their apparent self-evidence. Not just any account will do, however, since one

---

[1] Hegel, *Vorlesungen über die Geschichte der Philosophie*, Sämtliche Werke, vol. XVII, Glockner (ed.) (Stuttgart: Bad Canstatt, 1965), p. 400, cited as the epigraph to the first edition of Martin Heidegger's "Nachwort zu: Was ist Metaphysik?" *Wegmarken*, *Gesamtausgabe* vol. IX (Frankfurt am Main: Vittorio Klostermann, 1976), p. 304 n1. Naturally, metaphysics – even the variety of metaphysics at which this book takes aim – has also had its defenders; the best recent example of such a defense is offered by Radical Orthodoxy, for which see, for instance, John Milbank, Catherine Pickstock, and Graham Ward, "Suspending the Material: The Turn of Radical Orthodoxy," *Radical Orthodoxy: A New Theology*, John Milbank, Catherine Pickstock, and Graham Ward (eds.) (New York: Routledge, 1999); John Milbank, *Theology and Social Theory: Beyond Secular Reason* (Oxford: Blackwell, 1990, 2006); and John Milbank and Catherine Pickstock, *Truth in Aquinas* (London: Routledge, 2001).

who has long been in the grip of metaphysics may feel as if its loss leaves him or her out of touch with reality, as if condemned to a life among shadows. The therapeutic strategy, then, is to inoculate one against such feelings by explaining that which metaphysics purports to explain – what reality is like and what it means to be in touch with it – in terms of ordinary practices and experience, thereby deflating these notions and demonstrating that one need not appeal to metaphysics in order to do them justice. Before elaborating this strategy, however, we need to say more about the metaphysics at which it takes aim; to this we now turn.

The question of metaphysics

1

Modern thought has engaged in a recurrent rebellion against metaphysics: so, for instance, Kant's critical philosophy aims to make the world unsafe for Leibnizian metaphysics; Nietzsche insists that Kant is still beholden to the metaphysics at which his critique took aim; Heidegger claims that Nietzsche's "will to power" is the culmination, rather than overcoming, of metaphysics; Jean-Luc Marion argues that Heidegger's "ontological difference" keeps us bound within a metaphysics of Being/being; John Caputo maintains that Marion's "de-nominative" theology remains complicit in the metaphysics of presence; and so on. This recurrent rebellion against metaphysics indicates that although we moderns may want to avoid metaphysics, we have a hard time doing so. It would appear, in other words, that metaphysics is a kind of *temptation*: we want to resist it, but find it difficult to do so.

To see why this might be the case – and to begin gathering clues to a way forward – we must consider, first, the metaphysics against which theologians repeatedly rebel. It is important to address this matter explicitly, since the term "metaphysics" can be used to refer to several different things, and I am by no means suggesting that everything that goes by that name is to be rejected. So, for instance, the term is sometimes used to designate any set of claims about that which transcends nature, or any set of claims about what things are like. I am emphatically *not* interested in doing without metaphysics in *these* senses – or, more precisely, I am interested in doing without them just insofar as they are bound up with the variety of metaphysics I *am* interested in doing without. (In light of this remark, some readers may understand this book as defending a revisionist metaphysics, rather than as doing without metaphysics. I have no objection to this interpretation, so long as too much is not made of it.)

Turning, then, to the metaphysics at which this project takes aim, it will be helpful to begin with Martin Heidegger's account of the subject, not least because his account has had unparalleled influence on contemporary anti-metaphysics.[2] To be sure, Heidegger himself defines metaphysics in more than one way, though the main lines of his account are fairly consistent. At the most general level, he defines metaphysics as an attempt to understand beings "as such," that is, "what beings are *as* beings."[3] To this definition, Heidegger then adds a crucial qualification: metaphysics identifies the being of beings as that in and upon which they are *grounded*, and identifies this ground, in turn, with human *ideas* about them.[4] Simply put,

---

[2] It is worth noting that Heidegger's account of metaphysics parallels Karl Barth's account of natural theology in crucial respects, as well as Rudolf Bultmann's account of "objectification," such that a theology that does without metaphysics (in Heidegger's sense) is roughly equivalent to one that does without natural theology (in Barth's sense) and objectification (in Bultmann's).

[3] Heidegger, "Was ist Metaphyisk?" *Wegmarken*, p. 118; "Einleitung zu: 'Was ist Metaphysik?'" *Wegmarken*, p. 378. Two notes on translations: first, here as elsewhere I am following the convention of translating Heidegger's "Seiende" as plural, since the latter best captures Heidegger's sense. Second, apart from a couple of exceptions, translations throughout are mine.

[4] Heidegger writes, accordingly, that in metaphysics "the being of beings is preconceived as the grounding ground. Therewith all metaphysics is in its ground and from the ground up, that which accounts for the ground" ("Die onto-theo-logische Verfassung der Metaphysik," *Identität und Differenz, Gesamtausgabe* vol. XI [Frankfurt am Main: Vittorio Klostermann, 2006], p. 66).

then, Heidegger claims (a) that metaphysics equates the being of beings – their fundamental reality – with our conceptions of them, and (b) that it thus fits beings into a prior conceptual framework. To get a grip on what Heidegger means by this claim – and on what grounds he asserts it – it will be helpful to look at examples of such metaphysics; for this reason, we will consider Heidegger's treatment of two figures whose thought he regards as the very epitome of metaphysics: René Descartes and Friedrich Nietzsche. Not, to be sure, because Heidegger is a reliable guide to these figures, but because his treatment of them sheds invaluable light on Heidegger's own thought.

2

We begin with Descartes, whose philosophy Heidegger describes as "the initiation of the fulfillment of Western metaphysics."[5] Like many historians of philosophy, Heidegger sees Descartes's project as a response to problems posed by the Renaissance and Reformation, the net effect of which were to undermine appeals to tradition and revelation. We will say more about these problems in the next chapter, but for now their upshot is straightforward enough: neither historical precedent, nor the alleged claims of revelation, nor even the deliverances of sense-perception had proven sufficient ground by which to determine what to believe or how to act, since each of these had either been proven wrong (as when scientific investigation had disproven certain traditional beliefs) or, at the very least, as themselves in need of a ground (as when claims about revelation were at issue in debates among Protestants and Roman Catholics). For reasons we shall rehearse in the following chapter, the moral drawn from this story by Descartes and others was that reason alone would have to provide such grounds. Heidegger thus characterizes Descartes's situation as

---

[5] Heidegger, "Die Zeit des Weltbildes," *Holzwege, Gesamtausgabe* vol. v (Frankfurt am Main: Vittorio Klostermann, 1977), Zusatz 4, p. 99.

one in which certain intellectuals, at least, had been liberated from their bondage to churchly and supernatural authorities, but because these authorities had been the foundation upon which beliefs had previously been grounded, it followed that these intellectuals would now have to find a new ground for belief. Given that neither tradition, nor revelation, nor even sense-perception could provide such a ground, the only place left to turn was to the human knower him- or herself.[6] On Heidegger's account, then, "the metaphysical task of Descartes became this: to create the metaphysical ground for the liberation of the human person to liberty as the self-determining that is certain of itself."[7] The old foundations having crumbled, Descartes needed to lay a new, more secure foundation on the basis of liberated human reason.

It is against this background, Heidegger thinks, that one should understand Descartes's famous "*cogito ergo sum*," the upshot of which is that the "I" is necessarily co-posited in all thinking and, indeed, is the rule by which the latter must be measured. The crucial move here, on Heidegger's reading, is Descartes's identification of fundamental reality or "substance" with that which human persons clearly and distinctly perceive – that is, with that which they *represent* to themselves – so that the content of one's representations can be equated with an object's ownmost being.[8] This is crucial, since

---

[6] Thus Heidegger: "Liberation *from* the salvation-certainty provided by revelation," he claims, "must in itself be a liberation *to* a certainty in which the human person secures truth as that which is known in his or her knowing. That was possible only in that the self-liberated person him- or herself guarantees the certainty of the knowable. Such a thing could happen, however, only insofar as the human person decides by and for him- or herself what is knowable as well as what it means to know and to secure the known" (Heidegger, "Die Zeit des Weltbildes," Zusatz 9, p. 107).

[7] Heidegger, "Die Zeit des Weltbildes," Zusatz 9, p. 107. On this point, cf. Heidegger, *Nietzsche*, vol. ii, *Gesamtausgabe*, vol. ii.2 (Frankfurt am Main: Vittorio Klostermann, 1997), pp. 117–30.

[8] So Heidegger claims that, for Descartes, "the true is that which the human person clearly and distinctly sets before him- or herself and thus confronts as that which is brought-before-oneself (represented or 'set-before'), in order to secure that which is represented in such confrontation. The security of such setting-before is *certainty*" ("Die Metaphysik als Geschichte des Seins," *Nietzsche*, vol. ii, p. 389). The key here,

the representing subject then encounters nothing other than that which it represents to itself, and it represents to itself nothing other than that which has been subjected to its own measure. As a result, "only what is secured in the manner just noted – through representation – is validated *as* a being," and "the human person becomes to each being that upon which the manner and truth of its being is grounded."[9] (Heidegger here points, as evidence, to Descartes's assertion that the substance of a corporeal object is that which can be subjected to the rule of mathematics, namely, the object's extension, shape, position, and motion.)[10] Descartes thereby responds to the problems mentioned above: human belief and action are secured, on this account, precisely because the representing subject encounters – and can encounter – nothing other than objects whose fundamental reality corresponds to the subject's predetermined measure. The security of the representing subject is thus guaranteed in advance, since anything that does not fit neatly into its categories is consigned to "mere appearance" and so, finally, to non- (or second-class) being.

As Heidegger reads him, then, Descartes's metaphysics is characterized by an account of being-as-such and of the representations to which such being must correspond. From one point of view, this account is novel, since the priority Descartes accords to the representing subject has few precedents. From another point of view, however, Descartes's representationalism can be seen as the culmination of all prior metaphysical systems, in the sense of

obviously, is the notion of "representation," in which one "brings that which is represented before oneself, of oneself, as something standing over against oneself, relates it to oneself and in this relationship forces it into the normative domain of the self" ("Die Zeit des Weltbildes," p. 91).

[9] Heidegger, *Nietzsche*, vol. II, p. 150; "Die Zeit des Weltbildes," p. 88.

[10] Heidegger, *Sein und Zeit* (Tübingen: Max Niemeyer Verlag, 1927, 1953), especially pp. 95–7; cf. René Descartes, *Meditations on First Philosophy*, in *Oeuvres de Descartes*, vol. VII, Charles Adam and Paul Tannery (eds.) (Paris: Librairie Philosophique J. Vrin, 1983), pp. 43 and 80.

making explicit that which lay hidden at the heart of those systems. Looking back over Descartes's shoulder, in other words, one can now see those systems for what they are, namely, attempts to secure human knowing by identifying the being of beings with human ideas about them. Heidegger traces the beginning of metaphysics, in this sense, back to Plato.[11] Two steps are crucial to the emergence of such metaphysics, the first of which is the drawing of a distinction between the "thatness" and "whatness" of a being.[12] So the being of a stone, for instance, can be understood in terms of its existence – the very fact *that* there is a stone – or in terms of its essence – what makes it the thing it is, namely, its stone-ness or "idea." The second step is to identify whatness as that which is fundamentally real about a being, at which point "all essential determinations of essence as such, i.e. the character of beings, are brought within the compass of *kataphasis*, i.e. of *kategoria*, they are categories."[13] Human knowledge is thereby secured here, too, since the fundamental reality of an object is thought to be identical with that in terms of which humans know it, namely, ideas or categories. Heidegger claims, accordingly, that *"meta-physics begins* with Plato's interpretation of being as *idea,"* and that, ever since, "being is sought in the idea, in ideality and ideals."[14] We can thus see the sense in which Descartes is supposed to represent the culmination of the history of metaphysics, since Descartes's

---

[11] So on one reading, for instance, Plato argues that one's perception of some object counts as knowledge only when it has been "tied down" by a reasoned account (*Meno*, 97e–98a; cf. *Theaetetus* 201d, and *The Republic* 476a–d), and it can be so tied only by something that does not change, namely, the ideal Forms of which the object partakes (cf. *Timaeus* 27d). For Plato, then, one's perception of a particular object-instance counts as knowledge only insofar as one recognizes it as an instance of an unchanging idea, and it is the latter which is taken to be that which an object truly or fundamentally is. (Translations taken from Plato, *Complete Works*, John M. Cooper [ed.] [Indianapolis, IN: Hackett, 1997].)

[12] Heidegger, "Die Metaphysik als Geschichte des Seins," pp. 363ff.

[13] Heidegger, "Die Metaphysik als Geschichte des Seins," pp. 392–3.

[14] Heidegger, *Nietzsche*, vol. II, p. 196.

representationalism simply makes explicit that which was implicit in Platonic metaphysics – namely, the identification of the being of beings with human ideas about them.

That which is implicit in metaphysics is not yet entirely explicit, however. The final step remains to be taken by Nietzsche, whose philosophy Heidegger describes as "the fulfillment" or "completion" of Western metaphysics.[15] The key development is this: whereas Plato and Descartes still see ideas and representations as corresponding to the way things really are – and identify "the way things are" with extra-phenomenal essences – Nietzsche insists that our ideas are measured only by standards of our own positing. Heidegger claims that this insistence marks the birth of a new consciousness, one that "unconditionally and in every respect has become conscious of itself as that knowledge which consists in knowingly willing the Will to Power as the being of beings."[16] To be sure, Heidegger thinks there is nothing novel about identifying the being of beings with something that humans have posited; what is new, rather, is Nietzsche's explicit awareness that this is the case, and his consequent refusal of appeals to that which transcends such positing. Heidegger claims, accordingly, that Nietzsche's philosophy marks the consummation of metaphysics, since here, for the first time, it becomes explicit that human persons answer only to humanly posited values. We could thus understand the fulfillment of metaphysics as proceeding through three steps: (a) Plato identifies the being of beings with ideas, but thinks of these ideas as objectively real – as part of the furniture of the universe, as it were – and so thinks of human knowledge as dependent upon something external to it; (b) Descartes identifies the being of beings with that which fits within the representing subject's predetermined categories, thereby eliminating the assumption that the ideas to which beings conform are

---

[15] Heidegger, *Nietzsche*, vol. II, p. 171; cf. *Nietzsche*, vol. I, *Gesamtausgabe* vol. VI.1 (Frankfurt am Main: Vittorio Klostermann, 1996), p. 431.

[16] Heidegger, "Nietzsche's Wort: 'Gott ist Tot,'" *Holzwege*, p. 257.

themselves external to human subjects; Descartes thinks his procedure is warranted, however, by the fact that these categories correspond to the fundamental reality of objects, and so still thinks of human knowing as dependent upon something external to it; (c) by contrast, Nietzsche asserts that the decision to understand objects in, say, mathematical terms is just that, a decision, and that the resultant knowledge counts as such just because we have decided so to count it; more generally, then, Nietzsche contends that the ideas and values in terms of which we understand the world are irreducibly *our* ideas and values, and that we must have the courage to take responsibility for them. The consummation of metaphysics, therefore, is the insistence that there is nothing outside of human positings to which those positings must – or can – answer. The quest for a secure ground is thereby fulfilled: "In that the Will to Power achieves its ultimate, unconditional security," Heidegger argues, "it is the sole criterion of all securing and thus of what is right … What it wills is correct and in order, because the Will to Will is the only order that remains."[17]

Simply stated, then, Heidegger understands metaphysics as the attempt to secure human knowledge by identifying the fundamental reality of objects – their being as such – with our ideas about them. The bottom line, according to Heidegger, is that "metaphysics is anthropomorphism – the forming and beholding of the world according to the image of the human person."[18] In order to set this understanding of metaphysics apart from other referents of that term, we can label it *essentialist-correspondentist metaphysics*, since what sets the latter apart is precisely an understanding of the being of beings – their essence – as that which must correspond to the ideas of a human knower.

---

[17] Martin Heidegger, "Überwindung der Metaphysik," *Vorträge und Aufsätze*, *Gesamtausgabe*, vol. VII (Frankfurt am Main: Vittorio Klostermann, 2000), p. 86.

[18] Heidegger, *Nietzsche*, vol. II, p. 111.

3

We can spell this out further by considering some of the critiques to which such metaphysics has been thought liable, beginning with those leveled by Heidegger himself. Four critiques are especially pertinent to the present argument, but before turning to them we must consider, if only briefly, Heidegger's own fundamental concern with metaphysics. His worry, simply stated, is that metaphysics precludes being itself from coming into view, since metaphysics pictures Being as grounded in beings rather than vice versa. That is to say, insofar as metaphysics grounds thatness in whatness, it grounds the being of beings within beings themselves, thereby taking Being (as opposed to Nothing) for granted. Heidegger claims, accordingly, that "metaphysics makes it seem as if the question concerning Being has been asked and answered. Yet metaphysics nowhere answers the question about the truth of Being, because it never asks this question. It does not ask it, because metaphysics thinks Being only in that it represents beings as beings."[19] Heidegger's treatment of metaphysics is thus motivated by his concern with the question of Being, yet the latter is of little interest to the present proposal; those interested in a theological treatment of this question can turn instead to the brilliant work of Paul Tillich. We will focus, rather, on Heidegger's analysis itself, not the project in whose service it was set.

Heidegger's central concern *is* related, however, to a criticism relevant to our project, namely, that metaphysics does violence to objects by forcing them into predetermined categories. Heidegger claims, that is, that in metaphysics, "human persons give beings their measure, in that they determine from and by themselves what should be allowed to circulate as being," in consequence of which "the metaphysically stamped manner of human representation finds everywhere only the metaphysically constructed world."[20]

---

[19] Heidegger, "Einleitung zu: 'Was ist Metaphysik?'" p. 370.
[20] Heidegger, *Nietzsche*, vol. II, p. 151; "Überwindung der Metaphysik," p. 71.

Metaphysics ends up doing violence to the objects to which it directs its gaze, accordingly, insofar as such objects are allowed to show up – indeed, to *be* – only as they fit within a prior framework established by one's ideas, words, categories, and so on. The notion that the mind corresponds with reality, in other words, carries freight in both directions: on the one hand, it pictures one's words and categories as corresponding to an object's fundamental reality, but on the other, it ends up equating an object's fundamental reality with that which fits within the bounds of those categories.[21] The danger is obvious: if one thinks that one's preconceived ideas correspond to an object's fundamental reality, one may be tempted to force the object to fit one's conception of it, whether because one fails to see anything beyond one's conception or, worse, because one tries to make it conform to that conception. We see this sort of violence at its most graphic when human persons are its object – when, for instance, a woman or a person of color is allowed to "show up" only insofar as he or she fits within one's prior conception of femininity, blackness, and so on, and when his or her attempts to transcend these conceptual boundaries are met with implicit or explicit resistance.[22] This violence is compounded by the fact that metaphysics can render one insensitive to actual experience, since the essence to which one's ideas supposedly correspond is defined as that fundamental reality which stands at a remove from experience. (More on this in a moment.) Metaphysics thus seems to limit an object's particularity to that which fits within one's preestablished ideas about it, which explains why it is commonly criticized as "totalizing," "calculating," and "instrumentalizing."[23] Insofar as metaphysics identifies

[21] On a *correspondentist* picture of such correspondence, that is; as I explain in Chapter 5, some correspondence theorists resist this problem by insisting that the "direction of fit" moves from world to mind, as it were, but not vice versa.

[22] Of many relevant examples, see Naomi Wolf, *The Beauty Myth: How Images of Beauty are Used Against Women* (New York: Anchor Books, 1991), and Frantz Fanon, *The Wretched of the Earth* (New York: Grove Press, 2004).

[23] As claimed by Emmanuel Levinas, Martin Heidegger, and Theodor Adorno, respectively.

an object's essence with one's ideas about it, it may force the object to fit into one's preconceptions, and this conceptual violence may give comfort, in turn, to other sorts of violence.

This critique is related to a second: because metaphysics identifies fundamental reality with idea-like essences, it pictures such reality as standing at a remove from everyday, phenomenal experience; one is thereby tempted to think that such experience is somehow out of touch with reality (including the reality of one's very self).[24] As Heidegger famously argues in his analysis of "The Worldhood of the World," the metaphysical tendency is to see the objects one experiences, objects of everyday to-ing and fro-ing, as in some respect "mere appearances," and an object's ultimate reality as standing at a remove from such experience.[25] A sense of distance from reality is thus cultivated, and while neither Plato, Descartes, nor any other metaphysician seems to have been troubled by this distance, this is only because each claimed for humans an experience-transcending faculty by means of which to bridge it. This is evident in the fact that whenever a prevailing picture of correspondence has been called into question, skeptical worries have become rampant. (As I suggest below, this is one way of understanding some claims of postmodernism.) The picture of such distance and correspondence contributes, in turn, to the idea that the correctness of one's beliefs consists wholly in one's standing in a certain relationship to objects, which has seemed to entail that one's answerability to objects is incompatible with, say, answerability to one's peers, or that the latter is irrelevant to the former. Hence Richard Rorty, for instance, draws a sharp distinction between approaches which seek "objectivity" and those which seek "solidarity," and because he wants to see human persons as "answerable only to those who answer to us – only to conversation partners,"

---

[24] With respect to the self, consider a claim of Kant: "as concerns inner intuition," he argues, "our own subject is known only as appearance, not as it is in itself," *Kritik der reinen Vernunft, Kants Werke: Akademie Textausgabe* (Berlin: Walter de Gruyter, 1968), p. B156.

[25] For which see "The Worldhood of the World," part III, Division 1 of *Sein und Zeit*.

he concludes that "we are not responsible either to the atoms or to God, at least not until they start conversing with us."[26] If one were to do without correspondentism, on the other hand, one might free oneself from this sense of incompatibility – one might even arrive at a view according to which one answers to objects *by* answering to one's peers. A view along these lines is defended below.

A third critique is more specifically theological. According to this critique, metaphysics fits God, too, into an essentialist-correspondentist framework, such that God, too, is conceived as an object which corresponds to one's preconceptions. That is to say, if God is thought to correspond to one's ideas of God, then God will be cut down to size like any other object. Hence, if idolatry is "the subjection of God to human conditions for the experience of the divine" (as Jean-Luc Marion asserts), it would appear that metaphysical theism is unquestionably idolatrous, since God is here subjected to the conditions imposed by correspondentism and essentialism.[27] In Heidegger's memorable verdict, "one can neither fall to one's knees in awe, nor can one play music and dance before such a god."[28] The ideas with which God's essence is thought to correspond, moreover, are almost always drawn from an idealized picture of human persons, such that "God" turns out to be a projection of ourselves. Metaphysical theism thus appears guilty of a particular sort of idolatry, namely, that of attempting to speak of God by speaking of human persons in a loud voice.[29] We will have much more to say about these matters in the

---

[26] For the former, see Rorty, "Solidarity or Objectivity?" *Objectivity, Relativism, and Truth* (New York: Cambridge University Press, 1991), p. 21; for the latter, see Rorty, "Response to Jeffrey Stout," quoted in Jeffrey Stout, "On Our Interest in Getting Things Right," in *The New Pragmatists*, Cheryl Misak (ed.) (New York: Oxford University Press, 2007), p. 9.

[27] Marion, *L'Idole et la Distance: Cinq Études* (Paris: Éditions Grasset and Fasquelle, 1977), p. 23.

[28] Heidegger, "Die onto-theo-logische Verfassung der Metaphysik," p. 77.

[29] For an influential critique along these lines, see Karl Barth, "Das Wort Gottes als Aufgabe der Theologie," in *Das Wort Gottes und die Theologie* (Munich: Christian Kaiser Verlag, 1924).

sections which follow – and, again, in Chapter 3 – but for now, it is important to note that metaphysical theism is taken to be idolatrous in two respects: it is accused (a) of subjecting God to humanly constructed preconditions, and (b) of projecting a God in our image.

This leads us to a final critique, to the effect that metaphysics is fundamentally an act of self-justification (in the theological sense). As Heidegger argues, metaphysics "justifies (*rechtfertigt*) itself before the claim of justice (*Gerechtigkeit*) that it has itself posited," and such justification is the secular counterpart of a theological doctrine of justification (*Rechtfertigung*).[30] On Heidegger's account, metaphysics is fundamentally the project of subjecting objects to a predetermined measure in order to assure the security of one's knowledge. One thus provides the measure by which to justify all that is, including God, and thereby to see oneself as justified. At bottom, then, metaphysics can be seen as a theological project – specifically, the project of self-justification.[31]

✱✱✱

As the term is to be used here, then, metaphysics is characterized by two features: first, essentialism, that is, a picture according to which an object's ultimate reality is identified with a real, idea-like "essence" that stands at a remove from ordinary experience, such that the latter may come to seem shadowy, second-rate, a realm of "mere appearance," etc. Because fundamental reality is thus thought to stand apart from experience, it might appear that human knowers are in fact cut off from reality, since we are immediately in touch only with the phenomenal realm. This leads to a second feature of

---

[30] Heidegger, "Nietzsche's Wort: 'Gott ist Tot,'" p. 244.

[31] For a career-length elaboration and defense of this point, see the work of Robert W. Jenson, especially *A Religion Against Itself* (Richmond, VA: John Knox Press, 1967), *God after God: The God of the Past and the God of the Future, Seen in the Work of Karl Barth* (New York: Bobbs-Merrill, 1969), *The Triune Identity: God According to the Gospel* (Philadelphia: Fortress Press, 1982), and *Systematic Theology*, 2 vols. (New York: Oxford University Press, 1996 and 1999).

metaphysics, namely, what I am calling correspondentism, according to which the distance between human persons and fundamental reality is supposed to be bridged by dint of our ideas and words hooking up with or corresponding to such reality. Once these features have been made explicit, it is easy to see why one would want to avoid metaphysics, since it seems alienating, violent, and idolatrous. This raises an obvious question: given these reasons for wanting to avoid metaphysics, why has it seemed so hard to do so? Why is it, in other words, that generation after generation proclaims the end of metaphysics, only to be accused by its successors of remaining in its clutches? In the sections that follow, we will consider two very different answers to this question.

Apophatic anti-metaphysics

What I am calling apophatic anti-metaphysics offers a ready explanation of why it would be difficult to free oneself from metaphysics: metaphysics is almost impossible to avoid, on this view, precisely because language itself is complicit in it. Derrida's assertion is typical: "ordinary language," he claims, "is neither innocent nor neutral. It is the language of Western metaphysics, and it carries with it not only a considerable number of presuppositions of all kinds, but presuppositions inseparable from metaphysics."[32] Derrida's contention here is not simply that certain everyday concepts reflect and reinforce metaphysical presuppositions (as when one speaks of seeing an image with "the mind's eye"); his contention, rather, is that language use is *itself* metaphysical. Indeed, the very use of concepts is thought to be complicit in correspondentism, since, by applying a concept to some object, one fits it into a predetermined framework: so when one predicates "redness"

---

[32] Derrida, "Sémiologie et Grammatologie," in *Positions* (Paris: Éditions de Minuit, 1972), p. 29. Heidegger anticipates this claim: "Our Western languages are, in different ways, languages of metaphysical thinking" ("Die onto-theo-logische Verfassung der Metaphysik," p. 78).

of a fire hydrant, for instance, "person" of a person, or "unjust" of a particular social arrangement, one fits the object into a prior category to which the object is then thought to correspond. Subsequent chapters will elaborate this claim in a variety of directions, but for now, it suffices to note that on this view, one could do without metaphysics only by doing without – or at least loosening the grip of – language and concept use. Some theologians have attempted to do just that; this section considers two of the most prominent.

1

We begin with Jean-Luc Marion, one of the most influential of contemporary apophatic theologians. As Marion sees it, a God whom one could conceptualize would be no God at all; such a "God" would be an idol. To see how he arrives at this conclusion, recall, first, that Marion understands idolatry as "the subjection of God to human conditions for the experience of the divine"; hence, if concepts are a kind of "human condition," and if their application to God is thus "a subjection of the divine," it follows that a "God" grasped by concepts would be an idol.[33] Marion claims, accordingly, that "the concept consigns in a sign that which the mind first seized with it (*concipere, capare*); but such seizure measures not according to the amplitude of the divine, but according to the scope of a *capacitas*," in consequence of which "the concept, when it knows the divine in its hold and thus names 'God,' defines it. Defines it, and therefore measures it according to the dimension of its hold."[34] To apply a concept to God, then, would be to turn God into "God," since concepts cut objects to their measure by fitting them into antecedently defined categories. The very attempt to apply concepts to God, in other words, is idolatrous.

---

[33] Marion, *L'Idole et la Distance*, p. 23. Marion elsewhere claims that "equivalence with a concept transforms God into 'God,' into one of the infinitely repeatable 'so-called gods'" (*Dieu sans l'être* [Paris: Librairie Arthème Fayard, 1982], p. 51), and that "only an idol could be identified with the concept" (*L'Idole et la Distance*, p. 103).

[34] Marion, *Dieu sans l'être*, pp. 26, 44.

This claim is reinforced by Marion's understanding of divine incomprehensibility: "Even if we were to comprehend God as such (by naming him in terms of his essence)," Marion reasons, "we would at once be knowing not God as such, but less than God, because we could always easily conceive an other still greater than the one we comprehend. For the one we comprehend would always remain less than and below the one we do not comprehend. Incomprehensibility therefore belongs to the formal definition of God, since comprehending him would put him on the same level as a finite mind – ours – and would submit him to a finite conception."[35] On Marion's view, accordingly, God cannot be conceptualized, since, on the one hand, concepts force objects to fit the measure of their grasp, such that a conceptualized "God" would necessarily be an idol, and, on the other, it belongs to the divine nature to exceed one's understanding, such that, again, God must utterly transcend one's conception of God.

Marion insists, therefore, that in order to avoid idolatry, theology must avoid applying concepts to God. He thus proposes, first, a "de-nominative" or non-predicative understanding of God-talk; that is, he proposes "the substitution of praise for predication," since praise, on his view, involves a "suspension of all predication."[36] When one uses language to praise God, on this account, one does not predicate concepts of God; on the contrary, one directs one's praise to the unknowable Giver of the gift in view of which one lifts one's voice. One praises God (whom Marion, following Pseudo-Dionysius, here refers to as "the Requisite") by directing one's speech toward the unknown Whence of that for which one gives praise; on this account, then, "each *x*/requestant aims at the Requisite in a relationship where the latter remains inherent in the former (*interior*

---

[35] Marion, "In the Name: How to Avoid Speaking of 'Negative Theology,'" in *God, The Gift, and Postmodernism*, John D. Caputo and Michael J. Scanlon (eds.) (Bloomington, IN: Indiana University Press, 1999), pp. 36–7.

[36] Marion, *L'Idole et la Distance*, p. 197, and "In the Name," p. 32.

intimo meo), yet without pretending that this aim predicates categorically of that at which one aims. That is to say that, for each requestant *x*, there exists at least one determination *y* in accordance with which the Requisite may be praised. This means that *y* aims at the Requisite, but describes the requestant *x*; yet *y* itself is related to the Requisite in that it is this relationship that constitutes the sole stake of the utterance."[37] Marion's argument here is fairly dense, but its point seems clear: when one praises God as wise, for instance, the meaning of "wise" is determined by its usual, predicative use, which entails that its content has reference to creatures; to praise God as wise is not to predicate this concept of God, however, but to point beyond the concept to the One upon whose giving all things – including creaturely wisdom – depend. In this way, "a relationship manifests itself between the speaker (requestant) and the utterance (request), where the 'as' indicates that the request (for example, 'I praise you, Lord, as beauty') aims for a third point on the straight line that is determined by the first two, a point situated infinitely beyond the segment that they suffice to determine."[38] When one praises God as wise, accordingly, one aims at the incomprehensible Giver by seeing this One *as* the Giver of all good things; in this way, "one returns to the Requisite the gifts and the names that the Requisite ensures in distance."[39]

This brings us to the second aspect of Marion's proposal, namely, his insistence on the absolute ontological and theological priority of Charity. Because God is the One who gives-to-be all that is (*es gibt*), it follows that an act of giving, charity, or donation is prior to being/s; this means, on the one hand, that the radical distance of God from being/s *must* be acknowledged, and, on the other, that this distance *can* be acknowledged. All that is – and the fact *that*

---

[37] Marion, *L'Idole et la Distance*, p. 235.

[38] Marion, *L'Idole et la Distance*, p. 236. On this point, see also David Burrell's brilliant *Analogy and Philosophical Language* (New Haven, CT: Yale University Press, 1973).

[39] Marion, *L'Idole et la Distance*, p. 243.

anything is – depends upon a prior act of charity, an act that is necessarily misunderstood if conceived of as if it stood within the realm of that which it gives to be; hence the distance of the Gift must be acknowledged. And yet, because all that is depends upon this prior giving-to-be, it follows that the Giver's distance can be acknowledged precisely by recognizing the Giver's absolute precedence over being/s.[40] The recognition that being/s depend upon a prior Gift thus provides one with a sense of God's "depth," and "this 'depth' offers the inconceivable knowledge of the very one who provides it: the depth which appears only from the point of view of charity, makes charity alone appear (beyond all knowledge)."[41] Marion concludes, then, that Charity is the only name suitable for God, since this name alone signifies that which is infinitely qualitatively different from all being/s.[42] This brings us back to Marion's first point, since to speak this name is both to praise God and to see why praise is the only sort of talk proper to God: "if God gives," Marion argues, then "to say 'God' requires one to receive the gift and – since the gift happens only in distance – to return it. To return the gift, to play in redundancy the imponderable donation, this is not said, but done," and that which is "done" is a life of praise.[43]

On Marion's account, then, to predicate a concept of God would be to contain God within the horizon of being/s, but since God gives-to-be all that is, such containment would be an act of idolatry. Marion thus renounces predicative discourse in favor of a discourse of praise: by praising God as wise, as just, as beautiful,

[40] Similar proposals are offered by Calvin O. Schrag, *God as Otherwise than Being: Toward a Semantics of the Gift* (Evanston, IL: Northwestern University Press, 2002); and Merold Westphal, *Overcoming Onto-Theology: Toward a Postmodern Christian Faith* (New York: Fordham University Press, 2001).

[41] Marion, *L'Idole et la Distance*, p. 310.

[42] Hence Marion: "What name, what concept, and what sign is still useable? Only one, no doubt, love, or as one would say, following St. John – 'God [est] *agape*' (1 John 4:8)" (*Dieu sans l'être*, p. 73).

[43] Marion, *Dieu sans l'être*, p. 154. (I added quotes to the word "God" for the sake of clarity.)

and so on, one aims at the incomprehensible Whence of all good gifts. In this way, Marion's project exemplifies what I am calling apophatic anti-metaphysics: whereas metaphysical theism fits God within the horizon of realities to which human thought corresponds, Marion insists that God is absolutely prior to any and all such realities, since all realities depend wholly upon God's originary act of giving-to-be.

2

Marion's is not the only variety of apophatic anti-metaphysics, however; its main competitor is an equally influential, "deconstructive" anti-metaphysics. We can conveniently summarize the latter approach by considering the work of John Caputo, since he frequently sets his views in critical conversation with Marion, though numerous others have pursued a similar strategy.[44]

Like Marion, Caputo takes it that there is something violent about language, and, indeed, that "violence belongs structurally to, indeed constitutes, language itself."[45] Language is violent, according to Caputo, inasmuch as it seeks to fit objects within its horizon, to

---

[44] A relevantly similar approach is taken by Gordon Kaufman, *The Theological Imagination: Constructing the Concept of God* (Philadelphia: Westminster Press, 1981), *In Face of Mystery: A Constructive Theology* (Cambridge, MA: Harvard University Press, 1993), *Essay on Theological Method* (Atlanta, GA: Scholars Press, 1995), and *In the Beginning … Creativity* (Minneapolis: Fortress Press, 2004); Elizabeth A. Johnson, *She Who Is: The Mystery of God in Feminist Theological Discourse* (New York: Crossroad Publishing, 1992, 2002); Sallie McFague, *Metaphorical Theology: Models of God in Religious Language* (Fortress Press, 1982) and *Models of God: Theology for an Ecological, Nuclear Age* (Fortress Press, 1987); Graham Ward, *Barth, Derrida, and the Language of Theology* (Cambridge University Press, 1995); John Hick, *An Interpretation of Religion* (New Haven, CT: Yale University Press, 1989, 2004); and Kevin Hart, *The Trespass of the Sign: Deconstruction, Theology, and Philosophy* (New York: Fordham University Press, 2000).

[45] John D. Caputo, "How to Avoid Speaking of God: The Violence of Natural Theology," in *Prospects for Natural Theology*, Eugene Thomas Long (ed.) (Washington, DC: Catholic University of America Press, 1992), p. 142.

pin them down, and to hold them within its grasp. This being the case, Caputo reasons that "there really is nothing we can say about God that is not violent in the sense that it does not cast God in certain terms, that it does not subject God to a certain horizontality, and so set up something *anterior* to God, with a kind of ontological violence."[46] Caputo would agree with Marion, therefore, that the application of concepts to God is an attempt to bring God within the horizon of the thinkable, and is as such an act of idolatry. Caputo differs from Marion, however, in maintaining that there is something far more worrisome than this conceptual violence, namely, the blood-spilling violence which inevitably results when one forgets the inescapability of conceptual violence and instead sees concepts as in perfect harmony with reality. His foremost concern, then, is "the system of exclusions that is put in place when a language claims to be the language of reality itself, when a language is taken to be what being itself would say if it were given a tongue."[47] That is to say, if one forgets that one's concepts fit objects into a certain framework, one will be tempted to see that framework as itself natural, in consequence of which objects and persons who disagree with one come to be seen as unnatural, as opponents of the Truth, and so on. Forgetfulness of conceptual violence thus paves the way for physical violence.

Caputo advocates a deconstructive approach, therefore, as a means by which to make explicit the inescapability of conceptual violence, thereby to remind us that our language should not be thought to correspond to objects themselves. He grants that "the primordial yes we say to language is a human necessity, is always already violent," but contends that we should nevertheless "say yes to this archi-violence, which is nothing more than the constraint imposed upon us by our human condition, in order to avoid the violence that

---

[46] Caputo, "How to Avoid," p. 143.
[47] Caputo, *The Prayers and Tears of Jacques Derrida: Religion Without Religion* (Bloomington: Indiana University Press, 1997), p. 17.

excludes, excommunicates, silences."[48] The deconstructive strategy, then, is to demonstrate the extent to which one's talk of any object depends upon, and is caught in the swirl of, historically contingent mediations. Deconstruction thus "insists that there is no reference without difference, no reference outside of a textual chain. It argues that the range of reference of a term is set by its place within a systemic code," in the hope that, once this becomes apparent, one will no longer be tempted to think of one's particular language as corresponding to an object's ownmost reality.[49] By insisting upon the mediatedness of one's access to reality, accordingly, Caputo aims to free us from thinking that objects – God or otherwise[50] – can be pinned down; their otherness is thus protected, and "the thing itself slips away leaving nothing behind, save the name."[51]

This approach is best illustrated by Caputo's "deconstruction" of Marion, which can be summarized in terms of two objections. Caputo claims, first, that there is no non-predicative means by which to refer one's words – even words of praise – to God, since intentionality is an irreducibly conceptual affair. I will say more about the argument underlying this claim in Chapter 4, but for now, it suffices to point out that from Caputo's point of view, one can direct one's words to God only if one has some conceptually specified object in mind; as evidence, he points to the fact that one's praise must be addressed to God (explicitly or not), and however one does so – whether one addresses God as "you," "the God of Israel," or "The Unknown" – one necessarily employs concepts, for apart from such

---

[48] Caputo, "How to Avoid," p. 150.

[49] Caputo, *Prayers and Tears*, p. 17.

[50] Caputo remarks that "like negative theology, deconstruction turns on its desire for the *tout autre* … The difference is that in negative theology the *tout autre* always goes by the name of God, and that which calls forth speech is called 'God,' whereas for [deconstruction] every other is wholly other" (*Prayers and Tears*, pp. 3–4).

[51] Caputo, *Prayers and Tears*, p. 43. Caputo defends a similar argument in "For Love of the Things Themselves: Derrida's Hyper-Realism," *Journal for Cultural and Religious Theory* 1:3 (August 2000).

concept use, one's praise would remain undirected. Caputo thus insists that "we can never eliminate the conditioning to which we subject God without knocking out the conditions in terms of which it is possible to think or speak about God."[52] This objection is related to a second: Marion claims that God must not be subjected to any anterior conditions, such as those proper to being/s, yet by naming God in terms of "love" and its variants ("charity," "donation," "gift," etc.), Caputo argues that Marion has merely substituted one set of conditions for another; contrary to what Marion may think, he has by no means escaped from such conditions. Caputo thus maintains that "when you speak of God without Being, or beyond Being, you have not extricated God from all anterior conditionality. You have not gotten something unconditioned but something better conditioned to a religious sensibility. Such a God is nothing unmediated or unconditioned, and we cannot rightly claim that this is God's point of view." Caputo insists, therefore, that Marion "has not found a world beyond human mediation that speaks God's own language – for God does not have a language – but he simply shows us why we ought to prefer the biblical vocabulary. He has managed to occupy not God's point of view but that of a certain human religious experience that is from one end to the other expressed in the thoroughly human terms of loving, giving, and earthly glory."[53] While it may seem as if "love" does not subject God to human conditions, since love emphasizes God's grasp of us rather than the reverse, this does not entail that the concept escapes either from the flux of mediation or from the violence of subjecting an object to its conditions. The attempt to use "love" as a means by which to avoid conceptual violence is therefore futile, according to Caputo, and it is also dangerous, since it perpetuates the illusion that God corresponds to one's own language for God. That is, if one claims that certain concepts somehow transcend the anterior conditioning which characterizes other concepts, one necessarily "invests one's own finite, mediated

---

[52] Caputo, "How to Avoid," p. 144.   [53] Caputo, "How to Avoid," p. 142.

views with a pretended absolute authority, lends support to absolute violence. The attempt to eliminate ontological violence, to extricate God from any anterior conditions of possibility, is both misguided and hell-bent on producing a worse violence, ethico-ontical violence, violence of the meanest sort."[54] As evidence of this, Caputo points to Marion's seeming willingness to submit all God-talk to the authority of an ecclesial hierarchy.[55]

On Caputo's account, then, the violence of language is inescapable, yet this violence provides one with the resources to avoid something worse, namely, the objectification of otherness and the authorization of a system of exclusions. Because one's grasp of objects is always mediated by concepts, one never grasps the thing itself; the violence of concepts thus fails to hit its target, such that things themselves slip out of one's hands. So long as one keeps this in mind, one is freed from the temptation to see objects as corresponding perfectly to one's language for them, which can free one, in turn, from the temptation to *force* objects to fit one's idea of them.

3

We have before us two apparently contrary means by which to resist the violence of metaphysics: on one account, conceptual idolatry is resisted by means of a non-predicative discourse of praise in which God's originary Charity is affirmed as absolutely prior to all words and being/s; on the other, one resists correspondentism's totalizing effects by demonstrating that one's grasp of objects is always mediated through historically conditioned language, such that objects themselves elude one's grasp. There is no need to try to adjudicate between these proposals here, since, for our purposes, what they have in common is far more important than their differences. So Marion and Caputo agree, for instance, that it would be idolatrous to think that one could conceptualize a "wholly other" God, since

---

[54] Caputo, "How to Avoid," p. 148.   [55] Caputo, "How to Avoid," pp. 146–7.

they see concepts as fitting that to which they are applied into a pre-determined framework. Each rejects the essentialist-correspondentist picture, in other words, according to which one's thoughts and words stand in a one-to-one relationship to the fundamental reality of objects, in order to keep God from being included in this picture. As we have seen, there is good reason to reject this picture, but – and now we are moving into the argument which follows – it would be a mistake to suppose that one's rejection of correspondentism collaterally commits one to some variety of apophaticism. That is to say, one's rejection of correspondentism *would* entail apophaticism only if language and concepts were inherently correspondentistic, which brings us to something else Marion and Caputo have in common, namely, an assumption to the effect that language – at least in its predicative varieties – is essentially correspondentistic. Thus, to take one example among many, Marion claims that "language, when it predicates categorically, produces objects and, whatever they may be, eliminates distance by that very appropriation."[56] For his part, Caputo claims, again, that "violence belongs structurally to, indeed constitutes, language itself," from which he infers that "the only way to keep God's alterity safe is to save him from the cutting tips and incisions of the accusing *kategoriai* of kataphatic theology, from ensnarement by some name."[57] Each seems to think, therefore, that language, and especially concept use, is inherently correspondentistic and so violent, in consequence of which each assumes that one can resist such violence only by maintaining distance between language and its objects (particularly God). From the point of view of the present proposal, however, it would appear that this assumption rests upon, and so implicitly takes for granted, precisely that which Caputo and Marion aim to resist, namely, essentialist-correspondentist metaphysics. (Turnabout is fair play, of course: I have little doubt that the present proposal will appear correspondentistic from their vantage point, though I try to dispel this appearance throughout the

---

[56] Marion, *L'Idole et la Distance*, p. 231.   [57] Caputo, *Prayers and Tears*, p. 44.

following chapters.) Correspondentism projects a certain picture of language according to which, among other things, concepts hook up with objects "in themselves." It is not hard to see why one would want to reject this picture, but it raises a rather obvious question: why would one accept this picture at face value? Why would one assume, in other words, that the essentialist-correspondentist picture of language itself corresponds to language's essential reality? We will return to this question in a moment.

One other assumption deserves note: it would appear that both Marion and Caputo equate transcendence with distance, such that the the otherness of God (or objects) requires that there be a gap between God and that which human persons can know or experience. Caputo thus asserts, for instance, that "the transcendence of the other positively demands that the *Erlebnisse* of the other be inaccessible to my perception, otherwise the other's experience would be mine and her otherness undermined."[58] God must stand apart from one's experience, on this account, for otherwise, God's transcendence would be compromised. For his part, Marion seems to think that a putative experience of God necessarily involves certain preconditions – the conditions of the possibility of any human experience, including a person's historical and physical location – such that God cannot be identified with that which one experiences. Because Marion understands idolatry, recall, as "the subjection of God to human conditions for experience of the divine," he insists that it is precisely God's "distance" from experience "that identifies and authenticates the divine as such."[59] Both authors claim, then, that God must remain distant from one's putative experience of God, for otherwise, God's transcendence would be violated. Moreover, neither seems to think that there is anything controversial about this way of picturing divine transcendence; they seem to think, rather, that this picture is self-evident, and offer no arguments on its behalf. This is not to suggest

---

[58] Caputo, *Prayers and Tears*, p. 22.   [59] Marion, *L'Idole et la Distance*, p. 25.

that they are unwarranted in holding such a view, nor that there are no arguments to be offered for it – I will canvass one such argument in the following section – but it does raise an important question: Why would one assume that God must stand at a remove from that which one experiences (or could experience)? We will return to this question in a moment; for now, it suffices simply to raise it.

***

Apophatic anti-metaphysicians resist correspondentism by insisting that God cannot be set within the horizon of human conceptuality, since concepts are thought to subject that to which they are applied to a set of prior conditions. Marion thus resists what he calls "conceptual idolatry" by proposing a non-predicative discourse of praise, founded upon the recognition that all being/s depend wholly upon an originary act of Charity; Caputo, on the other hand, opposes correspondentism by insisting that one's access to objects is always mediated by historically contingent concepts, such that one cannot grasp objects themselves. Each thus provides a means by which to avoid essentialist-correspondentist metaphysics. These are not the only ways of doing without metaphysics, however, as the next section makes clear.

Therapeutic anti-metaphysics

The previous section considered an apophatic explanation of why it would be difficult to avoid metaphysics: on that view, the difficulty is written into language itself, such that one could avoid metaphysics only by maintaining an appropriate distance between language and God. This section proposes an alternative explanation: metaphysics seems difficult to avoid, on this account, precisely because a metaphysical way of seeing things has become so familiar that we no longer recognize it *as* a way of seeing things; the metaphysical framework has become common sense, in other words, to such an extent that we operate within its bounds without realizing it. From this vantage point, then, in order to do without metaphysics, one would first need to render these commitments visible *as* commitments. There are two canonical means by which to do so: on one approach, one traces the history of certain ideas and practices in order to demonstrate that they are products of cultural developments and interests, thereby stripping away their seeming naturalness; this is the genealogical method practiced by Nietzsche and Foucault. Alternatively, one can render the common-sense metaphysical picture visible simply by setting another plausible picture alongside it; this is the therapeutic strategy made famous by Wittgenstein. This book develops a version of the latter approach.

1

As just noted, a therapeutic approach explains metaphysics' seeming irresistibleness in terms of one's being held captive by a picture; the therapeutic solution, accordingly, is to free one from this picture by setting another alongside it. Not just any picture will do, however; in order to be freed from metaphysics' grip, it is crucial that the alternative picture treat the homesickness one may feel for that which has been left behind; otherwise, the therapy may not take. Such homesickness comes in many forms, each of which is characterized by a sense of alienation: someone long in the grip of metaphysics may feel as if the loss of correspondentism means that he or she is out of touch with the world, or as if a loss of essences entails that he or she experiences "only" appearances. Such feelings indicate that one is still in the grip of a metaphysical framework, since it is that framework's inflationary claims about reality and about being in touch with objects that make one feel as if something is *missing* once one rejects it. Indeed, from a therapeutic point of view, the "distance" which features so prominently in apophatic anti-metaphysics (and several other varieties of postmodernism) could be regarded as exemplifying precisely this sort of homesickness: there, the rejection of correspondentism is thought to leave one out of touch with

God and other objects, whereas the very idea that one could be *out* of touch seems to depend upon a rather inflated notion of what it means to be *in* touch. Certain reductionisms are likewise a sign that one is still in the grip of metaphysical assumptions, as when Rorty insists that in order to see oneself as answerable to one's peers, one must see oneself as *un*answerable to God and other objects. Rorty assumes that answerability to one's peers is incompatible with answerability to objects, yet this assumption seems to depend upon his taking for granted a correspondentist picture of the latter sort of answerability.[60] To shake oneself free from metaphysics, accordingly, it will not do simply to reject it (though this is indeed a start); one must also free oneself from the sense of loss one may feel insofar as metaphysical assumptions continue to inflate one's sense of reality, of "being in touch," of language, and so on; for otherwise, one will remain bound by the metaphysical framework even in rejecting it. Hence, an account is "therapeutic," in the current sense, if it deals with theoretical problems not by trying to solve them as they stand, but by identifying and contesting the presuppositions which made them seem like problems in the first place.[61]

A simple example from Wittgenstein should illustrate the point. Wittgenstein notes that we seem to take for granted "a certain

[60] It is ironic that Rorty is in other respects the very epitome of a therapeutic philosopher; see, for instance, the other essays in *Objectivity, Relativism, and Truth*. For an attempt to disentangle these strands of Rorty's thought, see Stout, "On Our Interest in Getting Things Right."

[61] As I am using the term, then, an approach counts as therapeutic not because it is marked by theoretical quietism – marked, that is, solely by the offering of reminders that ordinary language is in order as it stands and that one is simply confused if one thinks it faces problems that require theoretical solutions – but because it does without one of the key ingredients in one's feeling the need for such solutions, namely, essentialist-correspondentist metaphysics. On my approach, accordingly, theoretical quietism of a certain sort is one of the *consequences* of a therapeutic strategy, rather than the strategy itself. (I have little interest in fighting over the term "therapy," however, so those who insist that it just is theoretical quietism should feel free to affix some other label to my approach – call it "recognition-theoretic pragmatism," for instance.)

picture of the essence of human language. Namely this: the words of language name objects – sentences are combinations of such namings. In this picture of language we find the root of the idea: each word has a meaning. This meaning is coordinated with the word. It is the object for which the word stands."[62] We take for granted a picture of language, in other words, according to which words correspond with meanings and meanings are the fundamental reality of language – which is to say that we think of language in essentialist-correspondentist terms. Wittgenstein then observes a peculiar phenomenon: on the one hand, "a picture has been conjured up which seems to determine the sense *unambiguously*"; on the other hand, "actual use, in contrast with the picture just sketched, seems like something muddied."[63] The essentialist-correspondentist picture portrays a word's meaning as something which, in crystalline purity, transcends ordinary language use, in consequence of which the latter comes to be appear "muddied." It appears muddied, however, only because and to the extent that "a *picture* holds us captive," such that if we were no longer captivated by this picture, we might no longer think that there is anything "muddy" about ordinary language.[64] Wittgenstein aims to free us from this captivity, then, by demonstrating that one can make perfect sense of the workings of ordinary language without appeal to essences, correspondence, and the like, though one cannot understand the latter without appeal to the former – as he summarizes the strategy, "the *preconception* of crystalline purity can be eradicated only if we turn our whole examination around."[65] By explaining the meaningfulness of language in terms of language use itself, accordingly, Wittgenstein aims

[62] Wittgenstein, *Philosophische Untersuchungen = Philosophical Investigations*,
  G. E. M. Anscombe (ed.) (Oxford: Basil Blackwell, 2001), §1.
[63] Wittgenstein, *Philosophische Untersuchungen*, §426.
[64] Wittgenstein, *Philosophische Untersuchungen*, §115. Nietzsche makes precisely this
  point in his famous remarks about the "History of an Error" in *Twilight of the Idols*
  (Cambridge University Press, 2005), p. 171.
[65] Wittgenstein, *Philosophische Untersuchungen*, §108.

to disabuse us of the sense that ordinary language may be out of touch with its fundamental reality. This is what leads him to focus on "language games," for instance, a category which "should accentuate the fact that the *speaking* of language is part of an activity or a life-form"; it likewise leads to his famous dictum that, for a large class of cases, "the meaning of a word is its use in the language."[66] I will discuss these claims at some length in the chapters that follow, but for now, the important point is that Wittgenstein endeavors to free us from an essentialist-correspondentist framework by laying another alongside it, and he frees us from thinking we have thereby lost anything by demonstrating that the former framework's explananda can be explained in terms of ordinary practices.

This brief sketch of Wittgenstein points us to a key feature of what I am calling therapeutic anti-metaphysics, namely, its strategy of reversing metaphysics' usual order of explanation by giving priority to that which lies near to hand, particularly ordinary practices and experience. The strategy, simply stated, is to explain that which metaphysics purports to explain – what reality is like and what it means to be in touch with reality – by means of something non-metaphysical, thereby deflating these notions and demonstrating that one need not appeal to metaphysics in order to do them justice. By deflating metaphysical notions of reality, correspondence, and so on, and explaining how one might begin with ordinary experience in order to arrive at suitably uninflated versions of these same notions, one can exorcize the metaphysical ghosts by which we have been haunted. That is the hope, at any rate.

2

The present proposal is therapeutic in precisely this sense: it aims to make the metaphysical framework visible – and so render it

---

[66] Wittgenstein, *Philosophische Untersuchungen*, §§23 and 43.

optional – by setting another account alongside it, and to do so in such a way that one can shake free from the sense of loss which leaves one feeling alienated from, or nostalgic for, that which metaphysics has habituated one into taking for granted. The first step in the requisite therapy, then, is to contest the assumption that God must stand at a remove from the realm of creaturely experience, such that God's putative appearance in the latter would be, at best, *merely* an appearance – the assumption, in other words, that there must be a gap between God and God-with-us. This step is necessary, since the assumption that God stands at a remove from creaturely experience makes it seem as if one must choose between correspondentism – the establishment of a bridge between oneself and that which transcends experience – and apophaticism of the sort defended by Marion and Caputo.

To understand this assumption, consider the following argument of Gordon Kaufman: Kaufman conceives of "God" as the ultimate point of reference for all experience, and thus claims that "God cannot be conceived as simply one more of the many items of ordinary experience or knowledge, in some way side by side with the others: God must be thought of as 'beyond' all the others, not restricted or limited by any of them but relativizing them all," since, "without such unique logical status, God would be conceived as of the same order as the many things which need to be grounded beyond themselves, rather than as the ground or source of them all."[67] God cannot enter into the realm of creaturely experience as Godself, according to Kaufman, for to do so would mean that God was no longer the ultimate point of reference in terms of which to understand all else – for in that case, God, too, would need to be understood in terms of an ultimate point of reference, such that God would no longer be a good candidate for "God." Kaufman maintains, therefore, that God must stand at a distance from creaturely experience – he thinks the

---

[67] Gordon Kaufman, *The Theological Imagination: Constructing the Concept of God* (Philadelphia: Westminster Press, 1981), p. 81. See also "The Problem of God," *God the Problem* (Cambridge, MA: Harvard University Press, 1972).

very idea of "experience of God" is "a category mistake"[68] – because, according to his definition, something *within* creaturely experience could not be God. On such a view, then, there must be an ontological and epistemological gap between God and one's (putative) experience of God. This view encourages us to think that we are out of touch with God's fundamental reality, or else that we could be *in* touch with God's reality only in virtue of our minds' or words' capacity to transcend experience and so enjoy correspondence-like access to that reality, in which case the loss of such correspondence would once again leave us out of touch with God. In order to achieve the aims of this project, accordingly, this view will have to be subjected to a bit of therapy.

As luck would have it, the doctrine of God is one of the areas in which contemporary theologians have pursued a decidedly therapeutic, anti-essentialist tack – a tack, that is, whose goal is to free us from the assumption that God must stand at a remove from creaturely experience.[69] We might think here, for instance, of Karl Rahner's famous axiom, that "the 'economic' Trinity is the 'immanent' Trinity and vice versa," and his consequent insistence that the God who savingly acts in history is one and the same as God "in Godself."[70] Or again, we might think of Karl Barth's insistence that

---

[68] Gordon Kaufman, *In the Beginning ... Creativity* (Minneapolis: Fortress, 2004), p. 110.

[69] In addition to Rahner and Barth, see, for instance, Catherine Mowry Lacugna, *God For Us: The Trinity and Christian Life* (San Francisco: HarperCollins, 1991); Hans Urs von Balthasar, *Theo-Drama: Theological Dramatic Theory*, vol. III, *Dramatis Personae: Persons in Christ*, trans. Graham Harrison (San Francisco: Ignatius Press, 1992); Robert W. Jenson, *The Triune Identity: God According to the Gospel*, and *Systematic Theology*, vol. I, *The Triune Life* (New York: Oxford University Press, 1996); Eberhard Jüngel, *God's Being Is in Becoming: The Trinitarian Being of God in the Theology of Karl Barth*, trans. John Webster (Grand Rapids, MI: Eerdmans, 2001); and Bruce L. McCormack, "Grace and Being: The Role of God's Gracious Election in Karl Barth's Theological Ontology," in *The Cambridge Companion to Karl Barth*, John Webster (ed.) (Cambridge University Press, 2000), pp. 92–110.

[70] Karl Rahner, "Der Dreifaltige Gott als transzendenter Urgrund der Heilsgeschichte," in *Mysterium Salutis: Grundriss heilsgeschichtlicher Dogmatik*, vol. II, *Die*

"statements about the actuality of divine ways-of-being 'antecedently in Godself' cannot be different, content-wise, from those made about their actuality in revelation," such that God's being-with-us is understood as the repetition *ad extra* of God's being-in-Godself, and God's being-in-Godself as the eternal prototype of this being-with.[71] The point of such approaches, simply stated, is so to think of God that God's appearance in the realm of creaturely experience is not seen as a *mere* appearance, as if God stood at a remove from such appearances. Hence, whether by denying the idea of a being of God "in Godself," or insisting that God's ownmost essence cannot be contrary to that which is experienced of God, or claiming that God's being-in-Godself just is God's being-with-us, several contemporary theologians have sought to free us from the assumption that there need be an ontological and epistemological gap between God and God-with-us. (At the risk of repeating myself, it is crucial here to bear in mind the difference between claiming that God need not be thought to stand at a remove from that which is publicly experienceable of God, and claiming that God's being-in-Godself must correspond to one's preconceived ideas of God.)

Any one of these approaches would suffice for present purposes, but with a view to the argument which follows, it will be worthwhile to consider one such approach in greater detail. I have defended a version of this approach at length elsewhere, so I can afford here simply to outline its key steps.[72] The first is a deployment of the Barthian strategy mentioned in the previous paragraph, namely,

Heilsgeschichte vor Christus, Johannes Feiner and Magnus Löhrer (eds.) (Einsiedeln: Benziger, 1967), p. 328.

[71] Karl Barth, *Die Kirchliche Dogmatik*, vol. I, *Die Lehre vom Wort Gottes*, part 1 (Zollikon-Zürich: Evangelischer Verlag A. G., 1932), p. 503.

[72] For further elaboration and defense of these claims, see my "God's Triunity and Self-Determination: A Conversation with Karl Barth, Bruce McCormack, and Paul Molnar," *International Journal of Systematic Theology* 7:3 (2005), pp. 246–61, and "Immutability, Necessity, and the Limits of Inference: Toward a Resolution of the Trinity and Election Controversy," *Scottish Journal of Theology* (forthcoming); see, too, Barth, *Die Kirchliche Dogmatik* I/1, and Jüngel, *God's Being Is in Becoming*.

to explaining God's being-in-Godself as the eternal prototype, as it were, of God's being-with-us, and explaining the latter as the repetition *ad extra* of God's being-in-Godself. The idea, briefly stated, is to understand God's eternal being as the ongoing activity of triune communion, and God's acts *ad extra* as a continuation of (and persistence in) this activity: so God is thought to create by repeating *ad extra* God's eternal "othering" of Godself (traditionally described in terms of the Father's begetting of a Son) and maintaining communion with this creation; to redeem creation by repeating *ad extra* God's eternal devotion to (and so reflection of) Godself, thereby drawing creation into the communion in which God subsists (traditionally described as the reconciling work of the incarnate Son); and to actualize this inclusion by repeating *ad extra* God's eternal glorification of (and so conformity to) Godself (traditionally, the Spirit's work of conforming creatures to God, thereby effecting their adoption into God's family). The first move, then, is to understand God's being-with-us as the repetition *ad extra* of God's being-in-Godself.

The second move is to understand God as wholeheartedly identified with these acts, such that there is no height or depth in which God is indifferent or opposed to them. Here we find a useful clue in Hegel: "it is solely the risking of life," Hegel asserts, "by which freedom is proved, through which it is proved that the essence of self-consciousness is not *being* (as facticity), not the *immediate* manner in which it emerges, nor its submergence in the dissemination of life, but rather that that which is merely present in it is nothing for it but a vanishing moment, that it is only pure *being-for-self*."[73] Hegel's point is that by risking one's factical existence for the sake of one's being-as-self-constituted, one becomes and thereby essentially *is* that which is so constituted; to use Hegel's idiom, what one is *in* oneself becomes identical with what one

[73] G. W. F. Hegel, *Phänomenologie des Geistes* (Hamburg: Felix Meiner Verlag, 1988), pp. 130–1.

is *for* oneself. To be sure, Hegel's argument must be modified to be applied to God, but for present purposes, the point is simply that if God were to sacrifice that which is factically essential to God for the sake of being with us, it would demonstrate that God had identified wholeheartedly with this being-with; stated in traditional idiom, the fact that God gives God's Son for our sake reveals God's wholehearted love for us, in view of which it is unimaginable that there is any height or depth in which God is indifferent to the act of being-with-us. Hence, whereas the first step was to sketch a picture according to which God's being-in-Godself need not stand at a distance from God's being-with-us, the second step is to understand God as volitionally determined for (and so identified with) that being-with.

So far, then, so good: if God's being-in-Godself is ontologically fit for being-with-us, and if God is wholly devoted to this being-with, it seems to follow that God's appearance in the realm of creaturely experience need not be construed as *mere* appearance. We have yet to address one further problem, however, namely, the fact that the alleged distance between God and God-with-us can be underwritten not only by a particular understanding of God, but by an understanding of creation, too. That is to say, even if God's being-in-Godself is fit for being-with-us, it does not necessarily follow that God *can* be with us as Godself, since it could well be that there is something about creaturely reality that renders it unfit for God to act in it as Godself. This brings us to a final step: if God is wholly committed to us, and if creation is in some respect due to God and so subject to this commitment, it follows that creation, too, can be understood as fit for God's being-with-us. That is to say, if the one who creates and governs the world is one and the same as the one who has determined to be God-with-us, it follows that creaturely reality need not be thought to pose an obstacle to this being-with. This move opens up the possibility of understanding God's entrance into creaturely experience in terms of

Schleiermacher's axiom, namely, that "the supernatural becomes natural."[74]

3

It is at just this point, though, that an earlier problem re-emerges: if language is inherently metaphysical, then even if God need not be thought to stand at a distance from creaturely experience, God *would* have to stand at a distance from talk of God, for otherwise, God would become "God" – that is, an idol. It should be obvious, then, that certain assumptions about language, too, must be subjected to therapy, which brings us to the argument of the following chapters. In order to do without the essentialist-correspondentist picture of language – without thereby cultivating a sense of distance from or nostalgia for what one loses in doing so – the following chapters elaborate and defend an account of language which begins with ordinary social practices and then explains how one could use these practices to arrive at (suitably deflated versions of) that which the metaphysical picture purports to provide. Then, in order to show that the loss of correspondentism does not entail that God is necessarily distant from language, I supply an account according to which God-talk, too, can be an example of "the supernatural becoming natural" – an account, that is, which explains how God could make use of human language, and how language could be fit for this use. Here, several strategic commitments are crucial: there is a commitment, first, to explaining semantical notions such as meaning, truth, and reference in terms of pragmatics – in terms, that is, of the norms implicit in what we do with language – and to explaining pragmatics, in turn, in terms of intersubjective recognition. On

---

[74] See here Schleiermacher's *Der Christliche Glaube nach den Grundsätzen der evangelischen Kirche im Zusammenhange dargestellt*, second edn. (Berlin: Walter de Gruyter, 1960), §88.4.

the basis of these commitments, I propose a non-essentialist, non-correspondentist account of language, according to which (a) to use a concept is to intend one's usage as going on in the same way as certain precedents and to claim this same precedent-status for one's own usage; (b) the meaning of a concept is a product of the normative trajectory implicit in a series of such precedents, which entails that a concept's meaning changes, if only slightly, each time a candidate use is recognized; (c) to refer to an object is to link up with a chain of precedents that carries on the normative commitment implicit in an initial picking-out, in such a way that one inherits (and renders further inheritable) that commitment; and (d) to judge some proposition to be true is to see it as going on in the same way as one's other commitments and to use it to judge still other propositions. One can thus arrive at an account of concepts that do not "contain," of meaning without "meanings," of reference without "presence," and of truth without "correspondentism."[75] We arrive, in other words, at an account according to which language might be fit for God-talk.

With this account on board, we can then explain how language could be used to speak of God (without thereby turning God into "God"). The key to this explanation is a novel understanding of the Holy Spirit's work, according to which the normative Spirit of Christ is carried on from person to person by means of intersubjective recognition. The proposal, briefly stated, is to understand the Spirit's work in the following terms: after Jesus Christ had taught his disciples how to follow him, he recognized them as competent to recognize other persons and performances as doing so; the disciples, in turn, recognized still others as competent recognizers, and so on; in this way, the Spirit implicit in Christ's own normative assessments

---

[75] I hope to avoid misunderstandings by distinguishing "correspondence" from "correspondentism," since the former is ambiguous between what I have been calling "correspondentism" and the common sense notion that a belief counts as true just in case it gets its subject matter right. On this point, see Chapter 5.

was passed along from person to person. When this account of the Spirit is brought together with the account of language discussed in the previous paragraph, a theology of God-talk emerges: (a) to use a concept is, again, to intend one's usage as going on in the same way as a trajectory of precedents; the Spirit of Christ enters into, and so appropriates, these trajectories, thereby bringing them into conformity with Christ; (b) the meaning of a concept is the product of a normative trajectory of precedent uses; when the Spirit appropriates a concept, its trajectory is both judged (insofar as precedent and subsequent applications fall short of the concept's meaning as applied to God) and fulfilled (since its meaning as applied to God is retrospectively recognizable as the trajectory's culmination); (c) because the Spirit carries on the norms implicit in Christ's own commitments, the Spirit renders his reference to God inheritable: by linking one's God-talk to a chain of precedents which defers to Christ's own reference-commitment, one can inherit (and so carry on) that commitment; and (d) one takes a theological proposition to be true if it coheres with one's other commitments, and to take it to be true is to use it to judge still other propositions; in this way, the normative standard by which a candidate belief's truth is assessed is carried on from person to person, and through this process the Spirit conforms one's beliefs to Christ and maintains the standard by which they are to be assessed. The "supernatural," namely, one's ability to speak of God, thus becomes "natural": the Spirit of Christ enters into ordinary discursive practices in order to appropriate human concepts, to judge and fulfill their meaning, to enable one to refer to God, and to provide the possibility of speaking truly of God. The present proposal thus provides a non-essentialist, non-correspondentist account of theological language which enables one to do without metaphysics – and, importantly, without the sense of alienation which characterizes some rejections of metaphysics.

4

Apart from doing without metaphysics, there are several other reasons to pursue a strategy of this sort. One of its virtues is that it questions the assumption – made explicit by Rorty – that one's answerability to God (and objects) is incompatible with answerability to one's peers, and that espousal of the former sort of answerability therefore insulates God-talk (and the agendas it underwrites) from criticism. On the present proposal, one answers to God *by* answering to one's peers, such that one's invocation of God need not be thought to lift one's claims above the fray of reason-giving, critique, and so on. Second, because it sees novelty as the rule in language use rather than the exception, this proposal underwrites a kind of expressive freedom according to which one can use language to say things that have never been said before (which are nevertheless meaningful to others), and can see such language as one's own. Indeed, because one's use of language and recognition of other uses contributes to the standard by which such use is judged, it follows that one can see one's God-talk as self-legislated, since one contributes to, administers, and authorizes the norms by means of which such talk circulates and is judged. And finally, since it takes recognition-theoretic pragmatism as its explanatory primitive, this proposal traces out several pathways by which certain boundaries might be traversed: it provides a path between analytic and Continental philosophy, for example, as well as some paths between theology, philosophy, and social theory.[76]

---

[76] On the one hand, consider some examples of the range of philosophers and social theorists whose thought can be linked up with by means of "recognition," pragmatism, or both: Fichte, Hegel, W. V. O. Quine, Ludwig Wittgenstein, Wilfrid Sellars, Donald Davidson, Hilary Putnam, Richard Rorty, Robert Brandom, Mark Johnston, Bjørn Ramberg, Dagfinn Follesdal, Jürgen Habermas, Axel Honneth, Stephen Darwall, Nancy Fraser, Cheryl Misak, Pierre Bourdieu, Michel Foucault, Judith Butler, Terry Pinkard, Robert Pippin, Hubert Dreyfus, Cornel West, Arthur Fine, Bas van Fraassen, and Danielle Macbeth. On the other hand, consider the extent to which a recognition-theoretic pneumatology enables one to move from the

It is important to note, however, that even if my argument were wholly successful, it would not entail that competing approaches are unwarranted. We need to distinguish here between a strong and a weak version of the argument I am proposing. A strong version would argue for an account that is both necessary and sufficient, which would in turn render incompatible views (including both metaphysical and apophatic approaches) unwarranted. A weak version, on the other hand, argues for a merely sufficient account, one which is entitled to its own view and so entitled *not* to hold alternative views. The argument that follows is a species of the latter, which means, among other things, that if it is successful, it will demonstrate that one *need* not accept the metaphysical or apophatic picture of God and language, not that one *cannot* accept these pictures. These pictures, in other words, are simply to be rendered optional. The fact that I am trying only to render them optional, in turn, imposes certain explanatory burdens on my proposal: in order to persuade readers to exercise this option, I need to demonstrate not only that my account is plausible, but that it does justice to the concerns which might attract someone to one of its competitors. Implicit in the therapeutic strategy itself is a commitment to explaining how one would arrive at a deflated version of that which metaphysics purports to explain, but I still need to show how the present account would do justice to the concerns which animate apophatic anti-metaphysicians. Three such concerns stand out: concern to uphold God's transcendence, concern about the violence of concepts, and concern with the oppressive uses to which concepts are put. I deal with the first concern (in Chapter 3) by distinguishing divine transcendence from "distance" and explaining the former in terms of grace; with the second (in Chapters 2 and 3) by elaborating an account according to which concepts should not be thought

insights of these figures to an account of the inspiration and illumination of Scripture, regeneration, sanctification, and so on. This book traces one such path between these disciplines.

to contain that to which they are applied; and with the third (in Chapter 6) by identifying the critical resources implicit in normative trajectories of recognition, particularly as these resources are made explicit in experiences of disrespect.

5

These remarks about the nature of the present argument lead to some others. First, this book is offered primarily as a contribution to Christian theology, and is, as such, an exercise in "faith seeking understanding" – an exercise, that is, in trying to explain, as far as possible, that which Christians believe.[77] It should be obvious that as such an exercise, the project is free to borrow from philosophy and social theory insofar as these shed light on Christian belief. Indeed, since I am here elaborating an account of God-talk, I not only *can* engage with philosophy, there is a sense in which I *must*, since any such account will involve claims about the way language works, and these claims ought to be independently defensible. It is worth pointing out, however, that because it is faith-seeking-under-standing, theology does not become something else when it makes use of insights from other disciplines. That is to say, insofar as such insights are put into the service of understanding the faith, they thereby become *theological* insights.[78] Hence, even though philosophy does a good bit of work in the chapters which follow, the project remains a decidedly theological enterprise.

A second remark has to do with the decision to focus here on language. There are at least two reasons to focus primarily on language

---

[77] To be clear, "the faith" should be understood as pluriform and as the ongoing product of recognitive practices, as I explain below. I should not be thought guilty, in other words, of holding naïve assumptions about a monolithic, fact-of-the-matter set of beliefs which could simply be identified with "the faith."

[78] For a nice defense of this view, see Victor Preller, "Water into Wine," in *Grammar and Grace: Reformulations of Aquinas and Wittgenstein*, Jeffrey Stout and Robert MacSwain (eds.) (London: SCM Press, 2004), pp. 253–67.

rather than, say, thoughts or the mind. The first is relatively straightforward: given the contemporary landscape, one has little choice but to deal with language, since language has become the principal target of anti-metaphysical critique. One simply could not contribute to the current discussion without considering language. A second reason is related to the first: our best understanding of thoughts, representations, beliefs, and so on depends upon language, not only in the (non-trivial) sense that any explanation will be given in language, but in the sense that concepts and beliefs appear to bear some relationship to the words and sentences which express them. It seems clear, for instance, that one's initial learning of concepts depends upon the use of language, which suggests that there must be some relationship between the two. There is good reason, accordingly, to focus on language. It is important to note, though, that the account which follows focusses almost exclusively on just one stretch of language about God, namely, assertions, statements, propositions, claims, and so forth. Naturally, there is a good deal more than assertion involved in God-talk; there are questions, commands, laments, and so on. To be perfectly clear, the fact that I focus on assertions should not be taken to imply that this is the only variety of God-talk, nor that it is more important than the others. There is good reason to focus on assertions, however, since the most widely accepted accounts of the meaning of questions, commands, and other speech acts understand them in terms of their relation to assertional content: so the meaning of a question is understood in terms of the range of assertions that would count as an answer, the meaning of a command in terms of what assertible state of affairs one would have to bring about in order to count as obeying it, and so on.[79] There is reason to think, then, that if we can get an explanatory grip on the

---

[79] The classic treatment of questions is elaborated in Lauri Karttunen's "Syntax and Semantics of Questions," *Linguistics and Philosophy* 1 (1977), pp. 3–44; for a comparable account of some other speech acts, see Donald Davidson, "The Emergence of Thought," *Subjective, Intersubjective, Objective* (New York: Oxford University Press, 2001), pp. 123–34.

assertional varieties of God-talk, we can use it to get a grip on the others. In what follows, accordingly, I focus almost exclusively on the former.

One last remark: the argument defended here is necessarily characterized by a kind of circularity, in consequence of the fact that one can neither compare theological beliefs with something strictly belief-free, nor ground such beliefs on an indubitable foundation.[80] I will say more about this point in Chapters 4 and 5, but for now, it is important to realize one of its implications for theological construction, namely, that such construction cannot proceed by testing beliefs all at once, as it were, since there is no belief-free foundation on the basis of which one might do so. This does not entail that these beliefs are exempt from criticism, however; it entails only that we cannot criticize all of them simultaneously. To invoke Otto Neurath's famous image, "we are like sailors who must rebuild their ship on the open sea, without ever being able to disassemble it in dry-dock and build it anew out of the best materials."[81] So long as we leave a sufficient number of other beliefs in place, we are free to test the correctness of any one of them. This is the procedure adopted here: I have already discussed an account of God, for instance, according to which there need be no distance between God and creaturely experience of God; this account contributes to subsequent claims about language, but the very possibility of such an account obviously presupposes some ability to talk about God. The procedure, then, is (a) to suspend questions about God-talk in order to develop an understanding of God, (b) to use this understanding of God in

---

[80] For arguments on this point, see e.g. W. V. O. Quine, "Two Dogmas of Empiricism," in *From a Logical Point of View: Nine Logico-Philosophical Essays*, second edn., revised (Cambridge, MA: Harvard University Press, 1953, 1961, 1980), pp. 20–46; and Wilfrid Sellars, *Empiricism and the Philosophy of Mind* (Cambridge, MA: Harvard University Press, 1956, 1997).

[81] Otto Neurath, "Protokollsätze," *Erkenntnis* 3 (1932), p. 206. For an elaboration on this view, see Donald Davidson, "A Coherence Theory of Truth and Knowledge," *Subjective, Intersubjective, Objective*.

order to help make sense of God-talk, and then (c) to use the result-ing account of God-talk to support the already-established under-standing of God. Like Neurath's sailors, however, I can repair only one board at a time, and I have here focussed my repair work almost exclusively on the problem of theological language. Naturally, that does not mean that other boards are not in need of repair, only that their repair falls outside the scope of the present project. This means, in particular, that while I have tried to render an independently defensible account of theological language, my account presupposes accounts of certain other subjects, especially God, which may also be independently defensible – so I would argue – but are not here explicitly defended.

***

The present approach is thus therapeutic in that it aims to free us from the metaphysical picture by setting an alternative picture alongside it. By taking ordinary practices and experience as its explanatory primitive, the latter picture frees us from the grip of metaphysics not only by rendering metaphysics optional, but by helping us see that nothing of value is lost when we exercise this option. If we understand God on the basis of God's being-with-us, the semantics of ordinary language on the basis of recognitive practices, and the Spirit of Christ as entering into, and mediated through, these same practices, we can arrive at an account according to which one's dis-avowal of metaphysics does not entail that God stands at a distance from one's language about God.

Conclusion

Metaphysics, as the term is being used here, is characterized by two features: *essentialism*, the supposition that that which is fundamen-tally real about an object is an idea-like "essence" (which stands at a remove from that which one experiences); and *correspondentism*, the claim that human minds or words are in touch with this reality in virtue of their enjoying a kind of privileged access to it. No wonder, then, that generations of theologians have rebelled against such metaphysics, since metaphysics seems to alienate us from experience, to do violence to objects, and to reduce God to an idol. Many today who reject metaphysics do so by means of an apophatic approach, but this is not the only available option; in what follows, I elaborate and defend what I am calling by contrast a therapeutic approach, the aim of which is not only to do without metaphysics, but so to free us from its grip that we feel no sense of loss upon leaving it behind. We turn, then, to an account of language which aims to free us from the assumption that to talk of God is necessarily to inscribe God within a metaphysical framework.

2 | Concepts, rules, and the Spirit of recognition

The present project aims to render optional a particular picture of God and language – namely, one framed by essentialist-correspondentist metaphysics – by setting alongside it a picture which takes ordinary practices and experience as its explanatory basis, and which thus frees one from the nostalgia one might otherwise feel for such metaphysics. As noted in the first chapter, metaphysics encourages one to hold inflationary notions of fundamental reality and of what it means to be in touch with reality, such that to be freed from its grip, one must be freed from the continuing influence of these notions; otherwise, the rejection of metaphysics will feel like a limitation, as if one were alienated from reality. The previous chapter already discussed an account according to which there need be no distance between God and God-with-us, but this claim faces an obvious problem: even if that account were wholly persuasive, it would not follow that metaphysics had been rendered optional, for the simple reason that the very use of language may betray even the best of anti-metaphysical intentions. According to one highly influential view, at least, metaphysics is written into language itself, from which it would follow that an anti-metaphysical discourse about God is necessarily self-defeating. On this view, language, particularly in its predicative varieties, is thought to be inescapably violent, since it forces objects to fit into predetermined categories.

I agree that such violence must be avoided, but, from a therapeutic point of view, it would appear that the problem is overstated, and that this overstatement seems plausible only on the assumption of a residually metaphysical picture of language. This and the following three chapters aim to free us from this assumption by elaborating an alternative account of language and its relationship to God. The overall strategy is (a) to explain semantical notions such as meaning, truth, and so forth in terms of the norms implicit in recognitive practices, in order to construct a non-metaphysical account according to which language is fit for God's use of it, and then (b) to argue that the normative Spirit of Christ enables language to be meaningful and true of God by entering into, and so circulating through, these same practices. The present chapter begins, therefore, by explaining the norms implicit in ordinary concept use by appeal to social practices in which performers and performances are recognized as "going on in the same way" as certain precedents. On the strength of this explanation, it will become clear that concepts need not be thought of as "containers," nor as necessarily violent. I then argue that the normative Spirit of Christ is mediated through these same recognitive practices, and use this account to explain theological concept use: one's use of a concept counts as following Christ, on this view, only if it goes on in the same way as precedent uses which have been recognized as doing so, in a chain of mutual recognition that stretches back to those recognized by Christ himself.[1] This account thus provides some crucial resources with which to free us from the metaphysical picture of concepts, according to which one's use of a concept corresponds to an essence-like idea or "meaning," and so free us from the sense that concept use fits objects into predetermined categories.

Before turning to this account, however, something further needs to be said about the relationship between language and concept use. The relationship should become clearer in the argument that follows, but for now, the most economical way of explaining it is to consider the following points: (a) if a concept is a predicate of a possible

---

[1] "Theological concept use" is shorthand for the use of concepts to think and talk about God, just as "theological reference" is shorthand for reference to God, "theological truth" is shorthand for the truth of statements about God, and so on.

judgment (so Kant), then to use a concept is to make such a judgment, that is, canonically, to predicate a concept (say "red") of some object (say "that hydrant"); (b) such judgments are (explanatorily) basic to language use, since there are well-known ways of explaining non-predicative uses of language in terms of predicative uses; (c) the content of such predications can be explained, in turn, in terms of the normative trajectory that precipitates out of their actual use (so a series of utterances of "red" exerts normative constraint upon would-be "red"-sayers, and it is in virtue of this constraint that "red"-saying counts as the undertaking of a normative commitment, or, in Kant's idiom, as making a judgment *by* predicating a concept); (d) this explains, finally, why the use of a word can count (both philosophically and in everyday discourse) as the application of a concept, since predicates-of-possible-judgments just are the product of our ongoing use of certain words and assessment of those uses. Again, this should all become clearer in the sections that follow.

The violence of concepts

We begin with a claim discussed in the previous chapter, to the effect that language – especially in its predicative varieties – does violence to objects. This is the case, it is suggested, because the very application of concepts to objects is totalizing: to apply a concept to an object is to assimilate that object to an antecedently defined, essence-like category, from which it follows that concepts do violence to that to which they are applied. This is doubly the case, it would seem, when concepts are applied to God, since God is infinite, boundless, measureless, and so on, which means that concepts cannot possibly be applied to God without cutting God down to their size – without turning God into "God," in other words.[2] To

---

[2] In addition to the "apophatic" figures cited in Chapter 1, see Paul Tillich, "The Nature of Religious Symbols," *Theology of Culture*, Robert C. Kimball (ed.) (New York: Oxford

see why this would be the case, consider that, on one influential account, the meaning of a concept is established by comparing that which a series of objects have in common; thus the concept "red" means something like, "whatever this stop sign, that fire truck, and those cherries have in common."[3] On this view, the meaning of a concept is established once and for all by its application to a series of (creaturely) objects, and it then correctly applies to whatever bears the characteristic picked out by this series. Hence, if (a) the meaning of a concept is fixed by its application to creaturely objects, and (b) the concept applies only to objects that stand in a uniform series with these objects, then (c) to apply such concepts to God would be to set God in a uniform series with creatures – to cut God down to creaturely size, as it were. Karl Barth draws precisely this conclusion, insisting that since God is "infinitely qualitatively different from human persons and all human objects," it follows that God "is never and nowhere identical with that which we name God, nor with that which we experience, apprehend, and worship as God."[4] It would appear, then, that if God is unlike everything we know, and if concept application depends upon setting objects in a uniform series with other objects, then our concepts cannot apply to God.

University Press, 1959), pp. 59–60, and *Dynamics of Faith* (New York: HarperCollins, 1957, 2001), pp. 59–60; Gordon Kaufman, *God the Problem* (Cambridge, MA: Harvard University Press, 1972), p. 82, *The Theological Imagination: Constructing the Concept of God* (Philadelphia: Westminster Press, 1981), pp. 269–70, and *In the Beginning ... Creativity* (Minneapolis: Fortress Press, 2004), p. 23.

³ For a characteristic statement along these lines, see, for instance, J. S. Mill, *A System of Logic*, vol. II (London: John W. Parker, 1843), Book IV, Ch. 2, pp. 455–6.

⁴ Barth, *Der Römerbrief*, second edn. (Zürich: Theologischer Verlag Zürich, 1922, 2005), p. 344. Cf. Elizabeth A. Johnson, *She Who Is: The Mystery of God in Feminist Theological Discourse* (New York: Crossroad, 1992, 2002), pp. 105–9; Kaufman, *The Theological Imagination*, pp. 86, 268, and *In Face of Mystery: A Constructive Theology* (Cambridge, MA: Harvard University Press, 1993), p. 303; Victor Preller, *Divine Science and the Science of God: A Reformulation of Thomas Aquinas* (Princeton, NJ: Princeton University Press, 1967), pp. 10–15; and Tillich, "The Nature of Religious Symbols," p. 59.

The point can also be formulated in terms of a necessary unlikeness of meaning between concepts as applied to God and to creatures; at the very least, it has been thought that concepts cannot mean the same thing when applied to God.[5] With a view to the argument that follows, it is important to clarify the "sameness of meaning" at issue here. The sameness to be avoided, it would appear, is that which has traditionally gone by the name of univocity.[6] In order to understand what is meant by this sort of sameness, it will be helpful to think of concepts (for the moment) as a kind of rule: as Kant argues, a concept is "something universal that serves as a rule," where a "rule" is "the representation of a universal condition according to which a certain manifold can be posited in uniform manner."[7] If one thinks of concepts in this sense, it is not hard to imagine what "sameness of meaning" might imply: just as one carries on a series such as "1, 2, 3, 4 ... " by following the same rule (say, "$x + 1$") over and over again, so, on this picture, one uses a concept by following the same rule over and over again. On this view, when one says "this tomato sauce is red, that barn is red, and these poppies are red," one would be applying the concept "redness" over and over again in the same way one might apply the rule "$x + 1$." Sameness of meaning, in this "univocal" sense, would thus imply uniformity and predictability; indeed, just as one can apparently project into infinity what the rule "$x + 1$" entails (" ... 1,000,001, 1,000,002 ... "), so, on this view, one can project into infinity what the concept "red" will mean, precisely insofar as it means the same thing. It would follow, then, that

---

[5] For which see Preller, *Divine Science and the Science of God*, pp. 90–1; Kaufman, *Essay on Theological Method* (Atlanta: Scholars Press, 1995), p. 16; Tillich, *Systematic Theology*, vol. I, (Chicago: University of Chicago Press, 1951), p. 235, and *Dynamics of Faith*, pp. 59–60; and Kai Nielsen, "Talk of God and the Doctrine of Analogy," *The Thomist* 40 (1976), p. 33.

[6] The classic definition of "univocity" derives from the first chapter of Aristotle's *Categories*, *The Complete Works of Aristotle*, (ed.) Jonathan Barnes (Princeton University Press, 1984), 1a6–12.

[7] Immanuel Kant, *Kritik der reinen Vernunft, Kants Werke: Akademie Textausgabe* (Berlin: Walter de Gruyter, 1968), pp. A106, A113.

unless God can be fit neatly into a series with the rest of our concept applications – "1, 2, 3, God, 5, 6 … " – a concept cannot mean the same thing when applied to God.[8]

It might thus appear that essentialist-correspondentist metaphysics – and so violence – is written into the very heart of predicative language use, since (a) one's use of a concept supposedly corresponds to a fixed, essence-like idea or meaning, (b) that to which a concept is applied is thus fit neatly within an antecedently established category, and, therefore, (c) concepts do violence to an object's particularity or otherness. That is to say, if concepts contain the objects to which they apply – if they set such objects in a uniform series with other objects – then such violence appears inescapable. There is reason to think, however, that concepts do not work this way, and that the very idea that they could so work is itself a kind of metaphysical fantasy. This and the following chapter aim to free us from the influence of such fantastic pretensions by sketching an alternative picture of concepts.

The normative pragmatics of ordinary concept use

We turn, then, to an account of ordinary concept use, one that frees us from the idea that concepts contain that to which they are applied, that their meaning is fixed in advance by application to creaturely

---

[8] For an argument along these lines, see Tillich, *Systematic Theology*, vol. I, p. 131. As is well known, the vast majority of Christian theologians have tried to escape this dilemma by appeal to some version of analogy or "similarity in difference"; on this point, see, for instance, E. L. Mascall, *Existence and Analogy* (New York: Longmans, Green and Company, 1949) and *Words and Images: A Study in Theological Discourse* (New York: The Ronald Press, 1957); James F. Ross, "Analogy as a Rule of Meaning for Religious Language," *International Philosophical Quarterly* 1:3 (1961), pp. 468–502, "The Logic of Analogy," *International Philosophical Quarterly* 2 (1962), pp. 633–42 and 658–62, "Analogy and the Resolution of Some Cognitivity Problems," *The Journal of Philosophy* 67:20 (1970), pp. 725–46, and *Portraying Analogy* (New York: Cambridge University Press, 1981); and Richard Swinburne, *Revelation: From Metaphor to Analogy* (Oxford University Press, 1992, 2007). I discuss these matters in the following chapter.

objects, and that they set objects in a uniform series with other objects. Here as elsewhere, the key move is to understand semantics on the basis of pragmatics: this section explains concept use in terms of the norms implicit in our social practices, and the next section explains *theological* semantics – here, the application of concepts to God – in terms of *pneumatological* pragmatics, that is, the way Christ's normative Spirit is mediated through these same practices. On the basis of this account, we can render optional the essentialist-correspondentist picture of concept use and can, accordingly, do without the idea that language is necessarily metaphysical and so unfit for use with respect to God – we can, in other words, inoculate ourselves against the sense that the loss of metaphysics leaves one out of touch with God.

1

We begin with a fairly standard account of concepts, namely, Immanuel Kant's just-cited claim that a concept is "something universal that serves as a rule," where a "rule" is "the representation of a universal condition according to which a certain manifold can be posited in uniform manner."[9] On this account, a concept is a rule that one applies to the manifold of one's experience, thereby ordering it and setting it in relation to that which has already been so ordered. The explanatory key here is the connection Kant draws between applying a *rule* and positing a *uniformity*: to apply a rule, on this view, is to judge some aspect of one's experience to be relevantly similar to something else.[10] This definition might sound a

---

[9] Kant, *Kritik der reinen Vernunft*, pp. A106, A113. Note that throughout this chapter, I follow the more or less standard philosophical procedure of equating concept use with making a judgment, holding a belief, and their cognates. Given that we are focussing specifically on assertional sorts of God-talk, this move should be relatively uncontroversial.

[10] As Wittgenstein later remarked, "The use of the word 'rule' is interwoven with the use of the word 'same'" (*Bemerkungen über die Grundlagen der Mathematik*, Schriften, vol. VI, G. E. M. Anscombe, Rush Rhees, and G. H. von Wright [eds.] [Frankfurt am Main: Suhrkamp Verlag, 1974], VII.59, p. 421).

bit abstract, but it refers to something familiar enough. As I look at my desk, for instance, I see books, papers, pens, and several other items all at once – a "manifold," in other words. In order to describe my desk in the terms just used, I had to judge certain aspects of my experience to be relevantly similar to other experiences; on the view under consideration, I judged some of my sense-impressions to be similar to other sense-impressions I have categorized as books, papers, and so on. A concept, then, is here thought of as a rule by which one orders the manifold of one's experience, and one does this by judging certain aspects of that experience to be relevantly similar to other aspects.

In what follows, I depart from this account in certain key respects. It is important to note, however, just how much of this account I can take on board: I accept the claim that to apply a concept is to judge an object to be relevantly similar to something else, for instance, and that there is something "rulish" about these judgments. As we have seen, these are two of the very suppositions that have led some theorists to see concept use as inherently metaphysical, which means that if I am going to explain concepts along these lines, I will have to demonstrate that they need not be understood as containers, as setting objects in a uniform series, nor as having their meaning fixed in advance by application to creaturely reality. On the one hand, then, I will presuppose that to apply a concept is to judge some object to be relevantly similar to other objects, and that the making of such judgments is akin to following a rule; on the other hand, I will have to revise, somewhat drastically, what is usually understood by similarity and rule-following. The rest of this chapter provides a revised account of the latter: to use a concept, on this account, is to undertake a commitment which is susceptible to normative assessment, and to use it correctly is to contribute to the norm by which other uses may be assessed. There is a sense, then, in which a concept just is a norm, since one's use of a concept is a matter of one's being normed by precedent uses, and, in turn, of norming subsequent uses. To arrive at an understanding of concepts as fit for application to God, accordingly, it will be necessary to reconstruct an account of such normativity; doing so is the aim of the present chapter. This account is then rounded out, in the following chapter, with a reconstruction of the similarity claim implicit in such norms.

2

We can begin elaborating this account by considering how one would distinguish behavior that counts as concept use from that which does not. So, to begin with, the mere use of certain word-like sounds does not necessarily count as concept use, since one could make such sounds accidentally: children who are a few months old, for instance, might make the sound "mama," but this does not entail that they are using the *concept* "mama"; they just happen to be making noises that sound like a familiar word. Suppose, though, that they made this sound always and only when their mothers were around (and "red" when red things were around, "dog" when dogs were nearby, etc.). Would their sounds then count as their use of the concepts "mama," "red," "dog," and so forth? Their sounds may be correlated with objects, but again, they would not necessarily count as using concepts, since all sorts of non-concept users respond reliably and differentially to particular aspects of their environment: ice responds to the presence of heat by melting, for instance, but does not thereby count as applying the concept "heat" – not even if it were rigged to a sound-making device that said "lo, heat!" whenever the ice melted. Using the concept "heat" (or "red," or "mama") thus involves something more than merely making certain noises in certain circumstances.[11]

---

[11] An argument along these lines is defended in Brandom, *Making it Explicit: Reasoning, Representing, and Discursive Commitment* (Cambridge, MA: Harvard University Press, 1994), pp. 32–4, and Donald Davidson, "The Problem of Objectivity," *Problems of Rationality* (New York: Oxford University Press, 2004), pp. 3–9.

So when does a particular behavior count as concept use? On the account to be defended here, a behavior counts as such when we recognize it as intending to go on in the same way as precedent uses. This condition can be analyzed into two components: *intending* to go on in the same way, and intending to go on *in the same way*. Consider the latter requirement first: unless someone's "red"-sounding noises go on in the same way as other uses of the concept "red," we will not take these noises to be uses of the concept. That is, unless a creature's noises match up with certain other behaviors that we take to be uses of a concept, we have no reason to count the creature as using that concept. It would appear, then, that "going on in the same way" is a necessary condition for someone to count as a concept user.[12] Necessary, but not sufficient, since, again, this condition could be met by an ice patch that was hooked up to a sound-making device. A further condition, to which we will turn momentarily, is that one must *intend* one's use as going on in the same way as others, which is just to render oneself *responsible* for doing so.

3

Before turning to this condition, we need to take a closer look at what it would mean for one to go on in the same way as others. We can clarify the issue by eliminating two apparent dead ends: the idea that such sameness is determined by a rule, and that it is determined by the regularity implicit in a series of behaviors. Consider, first, the idea that sameness is determined by a rule. On this view, one would count as "going on in the same way" if and only if one's performance followed a rule, such that a series like "20,004, 20,006, 20,008" would

---

[12] On this point, see Wittgenstein, *Bemerkungen über die Grundlagen der Mathematik*, I.149–50, VI.21; Kripke, *Wittgenstein on Rules and Private Language* (Cambridge, MA: Harvard University Press, 1982), pp. 92–6; and Donald Davidson, "On the Very Idea of a Conceptual Scheme," *Inquiries into Truth and Interpretation* (New York: Oxford University Press, 1984, 2001), pp. 183–98.

be thought to go on in the same way as "0, 2, 4, 6 … " because it followed the rule "$x + 2$." This construal faces a serious objection: if rules are supposed to determine what it means to go on in the same way, and if such determination depends upon the rule itself being applied in the same way to case after case, then we need another rule to tell us how the rule should be applied, a rule to tell us how to apply the application rule, and so on; we are thus locked into an infinite regress of rule applications.[13] On the other hand, suppose one tried to avoid this problem by claiming that the series of numbers itself, or the regularity implicit therein, determines what counts as going on in the same way. This solution faces a serious problem of its own, since the series itself underdetermines what would count as carrying it on. Consider again the series "0, 2, 4, 6 … " and consider the following candidates for continuing it: "8," "4," "0," and "12." One might imagine that the series "0, 2, 4, 6 … " must continue like this: "0, 2, 4, 6, 8, 10 … " but *the series itself* tells one no such thing; it could equally well go like this: "0, 2, 4, 6, 4, 2, 0 … " or "0, 2, 4, 6, 0, 2, 4, 6 … " or any number of other possible combinations. The series of numbers could determine how one is supposed to go on only if it exhibited just one regularity, but there are innumerable ways of specifying the regularity implicit in such a series, from which it follows that the series itself does not tell one how it should be carried on. Hence, if we claim that the regularity implicit in the series is supposed to determine what counts as going on in the same way, we run into what Robert Brandom calls a "gerrymandering problem."[14]

One might think that these problems could be avoided by appealing to communal dispositions, since most of us are indeed disposed to carry on the series "0, 2, 4, 6 … " with the numbers "8, 10, 12 … "[15]

---

[13] On this point, see Wittgenstein, *Philosophische Untersuchungen = Philosophical Investigations*, (Oxford: Blackwell, 1953, 2001), §§29 and 84, as well as Kant, *Kritik der reinen Vernunft*, pp. A133, B172.

[14] For Brandom's characterization of this problem, see *Making It Explicit*, pp. 28–9.

[15] Leaving aside the possible appeal to *individual* dispositions as determining the right way to carry on the series, since it seems obvious that such an appeal cannot

On this view, the right way to go on would be determined neither by a rule nor by a regularity implicit in the series, but by our disposition to go on in a certain way: since we are disposed to carry on the series with the numbers "8, 10, 12 … " it would follow that this is what it means to go on in the same way. There is something right about this solution, but in its present formulation, it faces two serious problems. First, it is not clear what should count as *the* communal disposition. Who counts as a member of the community? And within this community, whose dispositions are supposed to establish how one should go on? To see the problems here, suppose we are trying to distinguish between diamonds and high-quality cubic zirconia, and that our dispositions are supposed to determine how to do so correctly. Now consider three different candidates for the "us" whose dispositions are supposed to supply this determination: (a) all of the licensed gemologists in the United States; (b) every person within a 100-mile radius of one's present location; and (c) every competent speaker of English. Which community's dispositions are supposed to determine what counts as a correct application of the concept "diamond"? If we already know what counts as a diamond, it is easy to decide whose dispositions should count – but if dispositions are themselves supposed to supply the right answer, it would beg the question to appeal to this answer as a way of determining whose dispositions to count. Hence, given that there are innumerable ways of specifying the community in question, and given further that it would beg the question if we selected from among these candidates

---

do any normative work – whatever *seems* right to me would, on this view, *be* right. On this point, see Wittgenstein, *Philosophische Untersuchungen*, §258. Things get interesting only when one's dispositions diverge from someone else's – which is why we focus here on the idea of *communal* dispositions. For a clear statement of the latter sort of view, see Crispin Wright, *Wittgenstein on the Foundations of Mathematics* (Cambridge, MA: Harvard University Press, 1980), p. 19 – though Wright later recants this view; Kripke's *Wittgenstein on Rules and Private Language* has customarily been read in this way, though there is reason to think that Kripke could as well be interpreted along the lines defended here.

on the basis of a prior determination about the *right* disposition, it is hard to see how communal dispositions could solve the problem at hand. (Note the parallel here between the regularities displayed in a series of numbers and the regularity that is supposed to count as *the* communal disposition.) This approach faces a second problem as well: even if one could specify the relevant disposition in a non-question-begging way, it is still not clear whether it would pick out the right regularity. Consider again the classification of diamonds and cubic zirconia. Suppose every one of us were disposed to classify both sets of objects as diamonds; if so, it would follow (on the view under consideration) that the classification "diamond" includes both diamonds and cubic zirconia.[16] This is an obvious case of *mis*-classification, but the present view provides us with no resources by which to recognize it as such; it cannot account for cases, that is, in which an entire community is wrong. As a result, it appears that the communal-disposition view, like the rule-following and regularity views, provides an inadequate account of how to determine what should count as going on in the same way.

So how should we explain what it means to go on in the same way? How does one know how to follow a rule, apply a concept, and so forth? We have canvassed some candidate answers and found each wanting, but if we pay attention to what they have in common, we find an important clue about how to proceed. Each of the foregoing answers attempted to derive normativity (in this case, how one should go on) from a supposedly un-normed fact ("what the rule says," "the pattern in the numbers," "our dispositions," etc.). Each thus faces a version of the same problem: one is supposed to draw normative conclusions from some ostensibly un-normed set of data, but in each case, several different conclusions could be drawn, and the data cannot do normative work until one knows which conclusion is right. Hence, in order for these data to tell one how to apply norms,

---

[16] For a relevantly similar argument, see Paul A. Boghossian, "The Rule Following Considerations," *Mind* 98:392 (October 1989), pp. 507–49.

one needs to apply norms to them – but since they are supposed to supply the norm by which such applications are judged, one cannot do so without begging the question. We can learn something from this failure: if it is to avoid a similar fate, our account must not try to derive norms from some (supposedly) un-normed "given"; that is, it cannot try to bring norms into the picture as explanatory latecomers.[17] To meet this requirement, I will elaborate an account according to which norms are implicit in, and the creatures of, everyday social practices. In order to count as an adequate account of *norms*, however, an additional requirement must be met, namely, it must explain how such practices supply an objective standard according to which we could all be wrong by their lights.[18] The account that follows aims to meet both requirements.

4

So how can we explain what it means to go on in the same way? I mentioned earlier that we count someone as using concepts only when we recognize his or her behavior as intending to go on in the same way as a certain set of precedents (usually how *we* use the concept), and I promised that I would eventually provide an account of such intending. We now turn to this account, which will provide further resources, in turn, with which to explain what it means to go on in the same way. What does it mean, then, for one to count as *intending* to use a concept? To get some grip on this question, consider again a simple example. Suppose I am trying to teach my son the concept "heat": I say "heat" when and only when heat is sensibly present, and he eventually starts saying "heat" in those circumstances, too. Now suppose I have also rigged a patch of ice with

---

[17] On this point, see John Dewey, "The Need for a Recovery of Philosophy," *The Middle Works of John Dewey, vol. x, 1899–1924: Essays on Philosophy and Education, 1916–1917*, Jo Ann Boydston (ed.) (Carbondale, IL: Southern Illinois University Press, 1985).

[18] For an important defense of this requirement, see Davidson, "Truth Rehabilitated," *Truth, Language, and History* (New York: Oxford University Press, 2005), pp. 3–17.

a moisture sensor and a sound-making device, such that whenever it starts to melt, it emits the sound, "heat!" On what grounds would I take it that my son is trying to use the concept "heat," whereas the ice patch is not? Well, if he were to make judgments, for instance, about the correctness of his "heat"-saying, or if such judgments were implicit in his behavior, I would certainly take it that he was trying to use the concept. Consider a relevant example: he hears air blowing from a vent and says "heat," but then, as he gets closer, his behavior indicates the realization that it is *not* heat. (Perhaps it is summer's first blast of air conditioning.) He may explicitly say, "I thought it was heat, but it's not" (or the child-speak equivalent), or his face may register surprise. If his behavior indicates that he is judging whether his "heat"-saying was correct, then I would take it that he is trying to use the concept. Other behaviors would likewise suffice: if he corrected me, for instance, when I said "heat" in heat-less circumstances, or if I had already counted him as using other concepts, I would count it as evidence that he was trying to use the concept in this case, too. That which distinguishes his behavior (as concept use) from the noise-making ice patch, it seems, is that he recognizes that his behavior is something that can be done correctly or incorrectly. To recognize this is to recognize not only that one's behavior is subject to normative assessment, but that by undertaking this behavior, one is in some respect *inviting* such assessment.[19]

The fact that it renders one liable to normative assessment provides one of the keys to our understanding of concept use, namely, that such use can be understood in terms of the broadly Hegelian notion of recognition. (The next section elaborates this notion further and exhibits its theological genealogy.) To use a concept, on this view, is to recognize others and seek their recognition, to confer authority on others and seek authority for oneself, to demarcate an

---

[19] For further elaboration and defense of this point, see Donald Davidson, *Subjective, Intersubjective, Objective* (New York: Oxford University Press, 2001), and *Truth, Language, and History.*

"us" and seek inclusion in it. "Recognition," in this Hegelian sense, has to do with acknowledging another as having a certain status, namely, the status of concept user or, more broadly, of "subject."[20] The idea, briefly stated, is that to use a concept is to recognize the concept use of others as having a certain normative authority over one, and to claim this same status for one's own use. To count as using a particular concept, in other words, one's usage must be recognizable as using the same concept as others, which is to say that it must go on in the same way as uses that are recognized as precedential – that is, as uses of the concept in question. One thus recognizes certain uses as correct and confers upon them normative authority over one's own usage. At the same time, in the normal (assertional) case, one intends one's use to be recognized, too, which means that one implicitly offers it as a precedent for still further uses. In trying to use a concept, then, one not only confers normative authority upon certain precedent uses, one simultaneously claims authority for one's own use. One thus intends to use a concept by trying to go on in the same way as precedent uses that one recognizes as correct, which means, on the one hand, that one confers authority upon those uses, and, on the other, that one seeks this status for one's own use.

Again, we will say more about this model in the following section, but for now, it will help to illustrate it by drawing an analogy

---

[20] On this point, see Hegel's *Phenomenology of Spirit* (Oxford University Press, 1977); illuminating interpretations of this material can be found in Robert B. Pippin, "What is the Question for which Hegel's Theory of Recognition is the Answer?" *European Journal of Philosophy* 8:2 (August 2000), pp. 155–72; Axel Honneth, *The Struggle for Recognition: The Moral Grammar of Social Conflicts* (Cambridge, MA: MIT Press, 1995); Judith Butler, *Subjects of Desire: Hegelian Reflections in Twentieth-Century France* (New York: Columbia University Press, 1987); Robert R. Williams, *Hegel's Ethics of Recognition* (Berkeley and Los Angeles, CA: University of California Press, 1997); and John O'Neill (ed.), *Hegel's Dialectic of Desire and Recognition: Texts and Commentary* (Albany, NY: State University of New York Press, 1996). Note well that the subjectivity in question is of the Hegelian-Foucauldian, rather than so-called "Cartesian," variety; this is spelled out in Chapter 6.

with common-law jurisprudence.[21] In the common-law tradition, a judge decides a novel case by considering prior cases which he or she takes to establish the precedents relevant to this one; the judge's recognition of these cases thus constitutes a precedential tradition out of them and, in turn, grants them a kind of authority, since he or she will justify his or her decision in terms of its carrying on their normative trajectory. If his or her decision is recognized as such by other judges, on the other hand, then it, too, becomes part of the authoritative tradition. Likewise when one uses a concept: in using a concept, one intends one's usage to be recognizable as such by those whom one recognizes as users of the concept, and one intends this by trying to use it in the same way as certain precedents. In this way, one's recognition of certain performances confers authority upon them, to which one's performances are then answerable – but since one intends that one's performances would be recognized, too, it follows that one's use of a concept implicitly seeks this same authority for oneself.

This being the case, it is not hard to see why philosophers customarily claim that to use a concept is to undertake a certain responsibility.[22] The view elaborated here explains why this would be the case, as well as the nature of the responsibility thus undertaken: since one's use of a concept is an implicit claim to normative authority over other users, one undertakes a certain responsibility *to* those users, from which it follows that one undertakes responsibility *for* one's usage. When one uses a concept, that is, one offers it as a precedent according to which others can determine what counts as a correct use; if they use the concept incorrectly as a result, it follows that one bears some responsibility for their doing so. If I use the

---

[21] I borrow the analogy from Brandom; see his "Some Pragmatist Themes in Hegel's Idealism," *Tales of the Mighty Dead: Historical Essays in the Metaphysics of Intentionality* (Cambridge, MA: Harvard University Press, 2002).

[22] See, for instance, Kant's account of concept use as spontaneous judgments in *Kritik der reinen Vernunft*, pp. A84–130, B116–69; cf. the section *De Imputatione* in his *Lectures on Ethics* (Cambridge University Press, 1997), 27:288–90.

concept "chicken" incorrectly, for instance, by applying it indiscriminately to chickens, ducks, pheasants, and other birds, and if my daughter learns the concept by following my example, then I bear some responsibility for her erroneous use of it. Because one's use of a concept counts as a claim to the effect that others should recognize it as going on in the same way as authoritative precedents, it follows that one's use implicitly authorizes further uses. One thus bears some responsibility for the further uses that are authorized by one's usage, which is why we treat concept users as (implicitly) committed to using concepts correctly, as susceptible to correction, and as possibly obligated to justify their usage.[23]

On the model defended here, then, to use a concept is to intend for one's use to be recognizable as such by those whom one recognizes as users of the concept, and one intends this by trying to go on in the same way as precedent uses which one recognizes as correct. One's recognitions thus pick out a set of authoritative precedents to which one's performances are answerable, and one seeks this same recognition for one's own performance.

5

Three features of this account require further elaboration, beginning with the just-mentioned obligation to justify one's use of a concept. The preceding paragraphs have occasionally noted that the relevant recognitions are *implicit* in our use of concepts: in everyday discourse, we seldom say explicitly which precedents we are recognizing as correct; rather, we implicitly recognize certain uses by

---

[23] This explanatory order differs from that advocated by, say, Immanuel Kant (the Kant of *Kritik der praktischen Vernunft*, [Berlin: Walter de Gruyter, 1968] 5:29–31), Donald Davidson (the Davidson of "The Emergence of Thought," *Subjective, Intersubjective, Objective*, and "Truth Rehabilitated," *Truth, Language, and History*), and Robert Brandom (the Brandom of *Making It Explicit*, Chapter 3). Akeel Bilgrami, on the other hand, pursues an approach relevantly similar to the one defended here; for this, see his *Self-Knowledge and Resentment* (Cambridge, MA: Harvard University Press, 2006), pp. 50–68.

the way we treat them – indeed, we commonly treat a concept use as correct by *not* making explicit our recognitive attitude toward it. Like Heidegger's hammers, we tend not to notice concept use *as such* until something breaks – when a candidate usage appears to diverge from uses we take to be precedential, for instance – at which point its use becomes explicit. And, like those hammers, our coming to "see" a would-be concept use involves making explicit the relationships in which it stands, particularly its relationship to certain precedents. One of the paradigmatic ways a concept becomes explicit, accordingly, is by considering what would entitle one to use it, since the canonical way of entitling oneself to such usage is by exhibiting it as the conclusion of a series of recognized precedents. We can thus see what is implicit in the ordinary use of concepts, namely, the recognition of certain precedents and of their authority over one's own usage, as well as one's implicit claim to this same recognition.

The fact that we can make our concept use explicit is important, since, by doing so, we can make judgments about the norms implicit in our everyday use of them. It is critical that we be able to make such judgments, since, if (a) the use of a concept involves submission to the authority of precedent uses, and (b) we were unable to make judgments about whether these uses were themselves correct, it would follow (c) that the present model would simply underwrite the conceptual status quo. I will deal with this problem at considerable length in Chapter 6, but for now, it is important to note that on the present account, what counts as an authoritative precedent is answerable to our judgments, and that our so counting them is itself something that can be done correctly or incorrectly (in view of other precedents whose propriety we recognize). The fact that our use of concepts is answerable to precedent usage, therefore, does not entail that these precedents are immune from criticism. Quite the contrary.

One last feature requires clarification: so far I have moved back and forth between two kinds of recognition – the recognition of performances (i.e., uses of a concept) and the recognition of performers

65

(i.e., concept users) – and while there is some warrant for this procedure, this needs to be spelled out. Consider, first, the recognition of performances. On the account defended here, a candidate performance counts as correct only if it goes on in the same way as precedent performances which are recognized as such, and if the performance is itself recognized, then it contributes to the precedential trajectory in view of which still other performances can be recognized. Now consider the recognition of performers: a person should be recognized as competent in a particular practice only if he or she can purposely and appropriately carry it on, and he or she is recognizable as such only if his or her judgments about what would carry it on themselves go on in the same way as those whose judgment has been recognized. ("Judgment" is used here in the loose sense of "normative assessment," whether such assessment is implicit in what one does or explicit in self-conscious deliberation.) The process goes something like this: a person recognizes certain persons as knowing how to engage in a particular practice, and he or she learns the practice by submitting his or her performances (including his or her judgments about those performances) to their judgment. When those whom he or she recognizes as competent in turn recognize his or her performances as going on in the same way as theirs, they (should) recognize him or her as one of them – that is, as someone who knows how to engage in the practice. Once he or she has attained this status, his or her know-how becomes the basis for still others to learn the practice. Moreover, his or her know-how now contributes to the normative conception of "knowing how to engage in this practice," such that his or her judgments are authoritative not only for newcomers, but for those from whom he or she learned the practice, too.[24] We can, then, explain the authority of performances

---

[24] All this talk of "knowing how" appears liable to some challenges leveled in recent philosophical literature, for which see Jason Stanley and Timothy Williamson, "Knowing How," *Journal of Philosophy* 98:8 (August 2001), pp. 411–44; and Paul Snowdon, "Knowing How and Knowing That: A Distinction Reconsidered," *Proceedings of the Aristotelian Society* 104:1 (September 2003), pp. 1–29. For relevant

and performers in terms of one and the same reciprocal-recognition model, which explains why the preceding exposition could move back and forth between the two.

This account thus provides us with a way of explaining the discursive communities to which philosophers and theologians commonly appeal (and which will play an important role in the following proposal). On the view defended here, such a community is constituted every time one recognizes certain others' performances and judgments as authoritative over one's own performances and judgments, and when these others in turn recognize the recognizer as one of them. That is to say, recognition demarcates the "us" relevant to assessing one's performances, which means that community is the ongoingly constructed product of our normative attitudes rather than an extra-normative "given."[25] We can, accordingly, avoid one of the problems facing the community disposition account outlined above. That account, recall, faced two sorts of problems, one of which had to do with identifying who counted as a member of the community and which dispositions were supposed to be normative. (The other problem – that of finding a sufficiently *objective* account of norms, according to which we might all be wrong – is addressed below.) The view defended here provides a fairly straightforward answer to this problem: the communities in question are instituted through an ongoing process of mutual recognition, and the dispositions that count are the judgments which the community recognizes as going on in the same way as precedent judgments that it recognizes. We can avoid this problem, in other words, precisely

---

responses to these challenges, see John Koethe, "Stanley and Williamson on Knowing How," *Journal of Philosophy* (2002), pp. 325–8; Ian Rumfitt, "Savoir Faire," *Journal of Philosophy* 100 (2003), pp. 158–66; Alva Noe, "Against Intellectualism," *Analysis* 65 (2005), pp. 278–90; and Tobias Rosefeldt, "Is Knowing-How Simply a Case of Knowing-That?" *Philosophical Investigations* 27 (2004), pp. 370–90.

[25] There is an important point of contact here between this account of "community" and that offered (somewhat more skeptically) by Ernesto Laclau in *On Populist Reason* (New York: Verso, 2005).

because "we," in the normative sense, are constituted by an ongoing process of mutual recognition.

6

We can thus explain the communities involved in our use of norms, but we still need to spell out how this account would explain "sameness." What does it mean, on this account, for a performance to "go on in the same way" or (what comes to the same thing, according to Wittgenstein) to follow a rule? By this point, our answer should be evident: a candidate performance counts as going on in the same way as precedent performances if and only if it is recognizable as such by those who know how to undertake such performances. A candidate use of the concept "red," for instance, counts as going on in the same way as precedent uses only if it is recognizable as such by those who know how to use the concept, where both "precedent uses" and "those who know how to use the concept" are products of our recognition. And if the candidate use is recognized as going on in the same way, it contributes to the precedential trajectory in view of which still further uses can be recognized as such. The norm by which a candidate use is to be assessed, accordingly, is a product of precedent uses, and the candidate use itself, if recognized as correct, contributes to the norm by which further uses may be assessed.

This entails that there is an important perspectival component in what it means to go on in the same way. Consider a case in which someone suggests "5" as a candidate for carrying on the series "1, 2, 3, 4 … " From a retrospective point of view – looking back, that is, over the series "1, 2, 3, 4, 5" – it looks as if it were self-evident and predictable that this is the way the series would be carried on. From a prospective point of view, however, things look different: as we have seen, the series itself does not decide which way it should be carried on; prospectively speaking, therefore, the series' continuation is unpredictable (though not, for that reason, indeterminate). Other candidates would likewise have been recognizable as carrying on the series: "1, 2, 3, 4, 3, 2, 1 ... " or "1, 2, 3, 4, 1, 2, 3, 4 ... " for instance. Hence, when a candidate is recognized as going on in the same way, it affects what it *means* to do so. And since the recognition of (future) candidates will further determine what it means to go on in the same way, it follows that this "same way" cannot be determined in advance.[26] We can thus explain sameness as the product of an ongoing process of recognition, which means that going on in the same way is neither uniform nor predictable. As we shall see, the significance of this point can hardly be overstated.

7

This account is liable to some serious objections, one of which I will address here. (A second objection, with respect to the objectivity of norms thus explained, will be taken up in the following section and again in Chapter 5.) The objection, simply stated, is that the present account fails to explain where norms come from; far from explaining anything, according to this objection, we have merely shifted the explanatory burden from the source of one performer's norms to the source of another's norms. We were wondering about the standard by which one's performances might be assessed, and we answered that this standard is supplied by previous performances which have been recognized as precedential. But whence the normative standard by which *these* performances are to be assessed? If one answers, "from the performances of those from whom he or she learned the practice," it would appear that one is locked into an infinite explanatory regress. One way to avoid the apparent regress would be to explain how norms might be instituted "out of nothing." Consider, for example, the moment when parents name their children. In general,

---

[26] On this point, see Brandom, "Vocabularies of Pragmatism: Synthesizing Naturalism and Historicism," in *Rorty and His Critics*, Robert B. Brandom (ed.) (Oxford: Blackwell, 2000), pp. 156–83; "Some Pragmatist Themes in Hegel's Idealism," *Tales of the Mighty Dead*; and *Reason in Philosophy: Animating Ideas* (Cambridge, MA: Harvard University Press, 2009).

we recognize parents' authority to name their children, such that if we want to know the proper way to refer to a child by name, we submit our performances to the authority of the norm instituted by the parents. But by what norm is their performance assessed? There is a sense in which the initial naming is unnormed, since (in our culture) it makes little sense to object that parents misnamed their child (apart from a few exceptions, such as naming one's child "God"). The parents cannot, in other words, make a mistake according to anyone else's norms. Once they have named the child, of course, they can make mistakes; they may, for instance, accidentally refer to him or her by their dog's name. In any event, the naming itself institutes a norm out of nothing, yet this institution suffices to establish a norm according to which others' performances might be assessed. We can think of all sorts of conceptual norms being instituted in roughly the same way, since everything from sneakers to the color red to justice was given a name at some point.[27] The point is that we can make sense of norms being instituted out of nothing, which seems to entail that we are not locked into an explanatory regress.

One could further object, however, that while we may be able to account for the institution of particular norms out of nothing, these institutions themselves depend upon a background of normative practices: though the naming of a child is sufficient to institute a normative standard according to which further performances might be assessed, this institution is itself possible only against the background of other normative practices which are already up and running. So then: can the present account explain how norms could be instituted out of nothing *without* relying upon already-instituted norms?[28] One way of addressing this question

---

[27] I elaborate an account of naming in Chapter 5; in the meantime, refer to Saul A. Kripke, *Naming and Necessity* (Cambridge, MA: Harvard University Press, 1972, 1980), pp. 91–5.

[28] For a nice treatment of this objection from a Brahmanical point of view, see Dan Arnold, "On Semantics and *Saṃketa*: Thoughts on a Neglected Problem with Buddhist *Apoha* Doctrine," *Journal of Indian Philosophy* 34 (2006), pp. 415–78; an

would be to think of norms as emerging through roughly the following process, beginning with the differential responsiveness characteristic of both organic and inorganic objects; such responsiveness includes an ice cube's melting in the heat, a sunflower's leaning toward the sun, and capillaries dilating in response to a rise in body temperature.[29] To such responsiveness, we can then introduce the possibility of erroneous responses by considering responses that aim to satisfy a *desire*, as when, for instance, an animal responds differentially to certain objects as *food* (paradigmatically by eating them). At this point, the animal can respond not only to its environment, but also to its responses, since it can treat certain of those responses as incorrect (as when it stops eating something that turns out not to satisfy its desire for food). A third step is taken when a creature responds differentially not only to its own responses, but to others' responses, too, as when an animal responds not only to certain parts of its environment (as food, danger, etc.), but responds, in addition, to other animals' responses – so a flock of birds sees another bird eating something and swoops down to join it. Crucially for our purposes, the latter responses, too, can be treated as incorrect, as when a group of monkeys ignores an oft-mistaken fellow's signal that the coast is clear.[30] At this point, a creature can respond differentially not only to its environment, to its responses to its environment, and to others' responses, but also to those others themselves (and not just to their individual responses) by treating them as either reliable or unreliable responders. This brings us to a final step, which

argument along these lines is also raised in Herder's *Essay on the Origin of Language* (Chicago: University of Chicago Press, 1966).

[29] Here I am drawing on Donald Davidson, "The Emergence of Thought," *Subjective, Intersubjective, Objective*, pp. 128–30; and Robert B. Brandom, "The Structure of Desire and Recognition: Self-Consciousness and Self-Constitution," *Philosophy and Social Criticism* 33:1 (2007), pp. 127–50.

[30] The example, but not the point, is borrowed from Daniel Dennett, *The Intentional Stance* (Cambridge, MA: MIT Press, 1987), pp. 272ff.

is taken when one responds differentially to others' treatment of certain responders as reliable or unreliable – that is, responds to such treatment as itself reliable or unreliable – and, in turn, one is oneself treated as reliable or unreliable by those whom one treats as reliable recognizers of reliability. So then: breathless as it has been, this account indicates how a primitive practice of norm institution and assessment might have emerged from mere differential responsiveness – from "nothing," normatively speaking – and how a practice of recognition might have emerged, in turn, from these practices of institution and assessment. Given that the emergence of each of these steps can be seen in nature, it seems plausible to think that norms could indeed have emerged from nothing, so to speak, and that we need not be overly concerned with the threatened regress.

***

Thus far, an account of concept use: a concept, on the view under consideration, is a norm by which one orders the manifold of one's experience, and one does so by treating certain aspects of that experience as the same as other aspects. To count as a concept user, I have argued, one must intend one's use as going on in the same way as precedent uses, from which it follows (a) that in using a concept, one recognizes the authority of certain precedents and seeks such authority for oneself; (b) that "the same way," and its cognate, "correctness," is the product of an ongoing process of mutual recognition; such that (c) if concepts are norms, it follows that they are continually being rewritten, since every time a novel use is recognized, it changes the norm by which still other uses are constrained. It makes little sense, accordingly, to think of concepts as fixed in advance or as setting objects in a uniform series. Each of these points deserves further elaboration – and I have not yet said anything about conceptual *content* – but it should already be clear that this model of concepts provides us with some important clues about their fitness for application to God. To this we now turn.

Theological concept use and the normative Spirit of Christ

The previous section argued that concept use depends upon one's going on in the same way as precedent uses, and explained this going-on in terms of an ongoing process of recognition: to use a concept, on this view, is to recognize certain performers and performances as precedential (thereby conferring authority upon them), and to seek such recognition for one's own performances (thereby claiming authority for oneself). There is reason to think that such an account could be used to explain theological concept use, not least because this account can be seen as the product of a trajectory internal to Christian (especially Protestant) thought – indeed, looking back from the perspective afforded by this section, the previous section can now be seen as having sketched an independently defensible account of some specifically theological insights.

1

The rest of this chapter, in combination with the next, pursues an explanatory strategy according to which the Spirit of Christ enters into normative (specifically discursive) social practices, thereby taking up ordinary concepts and enabling them to apply to God. The best way of explaining how this would work, I think, is to begin with two decisive insights of Friedrich Schleiermacher, namely, his explanation of how norms circulate through social practices, and of how the Holy Spirit enters into such circulation. The best way to explain his account of the circulation of norms, in turn, is to exhibit it as the culmination of some crucial developments in the prevailing understanding of normativity. By doing so, we can (a) shed further light on the previous section's claims about normativity, (b) provide a theological anchor for those claims, and (c) identify some of this proposal's own precedents.

So then: as a point of departure, consider, first, a series of shifts precipitated by the Protestant Reformation. As is well known, the Reformation was driven, at least in part, by certain material concerns, particularly with respect to justification, indulgences, and so on. Yet, for obvious reasons, these concerns were coupled with formal concerns about the Roman Catholic Church's model of authority, since that model seemed unable to fund an objective standard by which to judge prevailing teachings about justification and the like. The latter concerns led, in turn, to two of the Reformation's key commitments: the commitment, on the one hand, to judging for oneself whether a particular teaching is correct (rather than simply taking it on the authority of tradition), and, on the other, to the authority of Scripture as the standard by which to judge such judgments. Polemics for and against these commitments eventually brought about a shift in the epistemic landscape. First, the mere contestation of tradition's authority sufficed to set it on a different epistemic footing, since, in a context in which its authority is at issue, it would beg the question to appeal to tradition as a means by which to justify one's claims *about* tradition. The authority of tradition was further undermined by the emergence of modern scientific inquiry, the divergence of its results at certain points from traditional teachings, the Church's dogmatic opposition to these results, and so on.[31] For these and other reasons, there was a shift in the prevailing conditions of belief, away from the authority of tradition and toward "thinking for oneself," the aim of which is to avoid believing anything simply because it is what one has been taught, what one has always believed, etc. The mere fact of Protestantism, in other words, tilted the epistemic balance in a recognizably Protestant direction.

Protestantism faced problems of its own, however, in the form of devastating Counter-Reformation polemics against its appeal to

---

[31] For a helpful account of these developments, see, for instance, Jeffrey Stout's *Flight from Authority: Religion, Morality, and the Quest for Autonomy* (Notre Dame, IN: University of Notre Dame Press, 1981).

Scripture.[32] As Roman Catholic apologists were quick to point out, it is not clear whether Scripture can play the adjudicatory role that Protestants asked it to, since, in order to appeal to the authority of Scripture, one must know the answers to several questions – one must know what texts to count as Scripture, how to interpret Scripture, how to draw inferences from Scripture, and so on – but since Scripture itself is here at issue, Scripture cannot be called upon to support a particularly Protestant answer to these questions.[33] It appeared, then, that Protestants were no better off than Catholics, since their account of authority ran into the same sort of question-begging problems as the views they criticized. Moreover, Protestants themselves soon provided an all too apt illustration of these criticisms: within a generation of Luther posting his theses, Protestants had become irresolvably split over the nature of the Lord's Supper, an outcome which seemed to give the lie to Protestantism's supposition that Scripture is sufficiently perspicuous to adjudicate among competing interpretations without appeal to tradition. Equally well-intentioned, intelligent persons could not agree about what Scripture says about the Supper; as a result, the Protestant Reformation splintered, just as the Protestant understanding of authority looked to be discredited.

The moral usually drawn from this story was that one must think for oneself about one's commitments, and that Scripture alone could not supply the standard by which to judge such thinking. Several generations of philosophers and theologians thus developed ambitious justificatory programs which might meet the resulting need, the most famous of which were based upon an appeal to experience or an appeal to reason – we usually refer to the former as empiricism,

---

[32] On these developments, see Richard Popkin's classic *History of Skepticism from Erasmus to Spinoza* (Berkeley, CA: University of California Press, 1979).

[33] The most famous of these polemicists, apparently, was François Veron, whose arguments were famously reproduced in Paul Feyerabend's polemics against empiricism (for which see "Classical Empiricism," in *The Methodological Heritage of Newton*, Robert E. Butts and John W. Davis [eds.] [Toronto: University of Toronto Press, 1970], especially pp. 152–3).

exemplified by Locke, and to the latter as rationalism, exemplified by Spinoza and Leibniz. We need not linger over the details of these programs, since each was called fundamentally into question by Kant and his successors. One of Kant's basic claims is that it is a mistake to think that what one *ought* to infer, judge, believe, or do can be read directly off the face of some "given," that is, some fact of the matter conceived as strictly external to any norms we apply to it. His paradigmatic argument to this effect is the Transcendental Deduction, where Kant claims that sense-experience is meaningless apart from the application of concepts (which, for Kant, are a species of norm), yet that sense-experience itself does not determine which concept should be applied. The appropriate concepts, that is to say, "are not borrowed from experience, but rather they supply appearances with their lawlikeness and so make experience possible." From this, Kant draws the remarkable conclusion that "the understanding is not merely a faculty of making rules through comparison of appearances; *it is itself the lawgiver of nature*."[34] Kant takes the point to be suitably general: it is a mistake, he insists, to think that any datum (including sense-experience, Scripture, the contents of one's own mind, and the laws of nature), can dictate what one ought to do or think apart from the application of norms to that datum.[35] In order for some fact to exert normative authority over one's beliefs and actions, one needs to know why it is a fact to which one ought to hold oneself accountable, how it is to be interpreted, what would count as evidence that one's beliefs or actions had lived up to this standard, and so on, but the fact in question cannot provide answers to these questions, upon pain of circularity. Kant's critique thus marks a potential watershed, since instead of trying to shore up the problems facing one account's "given" by appeal to yet another, he insists that our judgments must be involved from the

[34] Kant, *Kritik der reinen Vernunft*, p. A126; emphasis added.
[35] On this point, see *Grundlegung zur Metaphysik der Sitten*, (Berlin: Walter de Gruyter, 1968), especially pp. 4:408–9.

very beginning – he insists, that is, that ultimately we must answer to the norms implicit in our own judgments.

This spells the theoretical end of empiricism of a certain sort, but at the same time, it raises a rather obvious question: if our judgments are involved from the very beginning, how are *they* to be judged? Kant's answer seems to be that a judgment is correct insofar as one can give appropriate reasons for it, yet this just moves the bump in the rug, since these reasons can be judged appropriate only insofar as appropriate reasons can be offered for them, and so on. Kant's appeal to universalizability notwithstanding,[36] it would appear that the commitment to reason-giving threatens to set off an infinite regress, which is precisely what emerged in the so-called *Grundsatzkritik* of the 1790s. It appeared, to borrow the language of the day, that one had to choose between positivism, on the one hand, and an incipient nihilism, on the other.[37]

The pressure exerted by this dilemma, in turn, provoked a period of astonishing creativity. Of the many novel proposals advanced during this time, I want to focus on just one, that of Friedrich Schleiermacher. Schleiermacher's proposal turns upon his notion of *Gefühl*, usually translated as "feeling," which refers to "the immediate presence of whole, undivided existence (sensible as well as spiritual), the unity of a person and his or her sensible or spiritual world," an immediate presence where "the subject–object opposition is entirely excluded as inapplicable."[38] "*Gefühl*" refers, that is, to a pre-reflective harmony

---

[36] For which see his essay, "Was heißt: Sich im Denken orientiren?" (Berlin: Walter de Gruyter, 1968), p. 8:146n, as well as *Grundlegung zur Metaphysik der Sitten*, pp. 4:434–40.

[37] Robert B. Pippin's *Modernism as a Philosophical Problem: On the Dissatisfactions of European High Culture*, (Oxford: Blackwell, 1991, 1999) offers a penetrating analysis of this dialectic.

[38] The first quotation is from Henrich Steffens, *Von der falschen Theologie und dem Wahren Glauben* (Breslau, 1823), p. 99, which Schleiermacher cites approvingly at §3.2 of the *Glaubenslehre* (the full text of which is supplied in Martin Redeker's editorial notes, *Der Christliche Glaube*, second edn. [Berlin: Walter de Gruyter, 1960], p. 17n – hereafter "CG"); the second is from Schleiermacher's *Dialektik*, Rudolf Odebrecht (ed.) (Frankfurt: Suhrkamp, 2001), p. 287.

or at-oneness between oneself and one's environing circumstances, though it is important to note that this harmony includes a kind of comportment to or disposition toward those circumstances – important, because Schleiermacher understands *Gefühl* as prior to knowing and doing, yet providing direction to each.[39] It is also important to note that this at-oneness, because pre- (or non-) reflective, does not involve conscious deliberation; it is, rather, simply how one finds oneself in certain circumstances.[40] "*Gefühl*" thus has to do with the innumerable ways in which one is affected by, and copes with, various circumstances prior to and apart from conscious reflection and judgment – the ways, in other words, that one is always already disposed toward oneself and one's environment. For example: one hears a Christmas carol and is overcome with nostalgia (or revulsion); a teacher says "3 × 4" and the number "12" springs automatically to mind; one spies a misspelled word and it just looks wrong; a child runs in front of one's car and one hits the brakes before one has realized what is happening. Innumerable examples could be adduced, but the pattern should be familiar enough: one has an immediate, non-inferential feel for oneself and one's circumstances, and it is by means of this feel that one is always already attuned to these circumstances.[41]

For Schleiermacher, then, *Gefühl* refers to one's pre-reflective attunement to one's circumstances. To elaborate this notion

---

[39] For which claims, see *Schleiermachers Sendschreiben über seine* Glaubenslehre *an Lücke*, Hermann Mulert (ed.) (Gießen: Töpelmann, 1908), pp. 14–15; *Friedrich Schleiermachers Ästhetik*, Odebrecht (ed.) (Berlin: Walter de Gruyter, 1931), pp. 46–51, 71; *Brouillon zur Ethik* 1805/06, Hans-Joachim Birkner (ed.) (Hamburg: Felix Meiner Verlag, 1981), 60th and 86th instructional Hours, pp. 103 and 147, respectively.

[40] Schleiermacher describes the feeling of absolute dependence, for instance, as an "immediate self-consciousness of finding-oneself-absolutely-dependent" (CG §32 Leitsatz; cf. §32.2). Schleiermacher thus claims that *Gefühl* is distinguished from *Wissen* by virtue of the fact that *Gefühl* is not brought about by a person but rather "comes about" within him or her and thus "belongs wholly to the realm of receptivity" (CG §3.3).

[41] I defend this account in greater detail in my "Attunement and Explicitation: A Pragmatist Reading of Schleiermacher's 'Theology of Feeling,'" in *Schleiermacher, the Study of Religion, and the Future of Theology*, Brent Sockness and Wilhelm Gräb (eds.) (Berlin: Walter de Gruyter, 2010), pp. 215–42.

further – and to see how it could be the culmination of the historical trajectory just sketched – it will help to consider a much-remarked problem facing Schleiermacher's proposal.[42] The problem can be stated in the form of a dilemma: on the one hand, in order to avoid the regress-of-reasons problem, it is crucial that *Gefühl* be construed as an *immediate* (i.e., non-reflective, non-deliberative) conscious-ness of and attunement to oneself and one's circumstances; yet in order to avoid Kant's critique of givenness, on the other hand – his critique, that is, of the idea that some datum could exert norma-tive constraint upon our beliefs and judgments prior to and apart from any norms we might apply to it – it would appear that one's attunement to circumstances must be mediated by the application of concepts. Schleiermacher solves this problem, on the present reconstruction, by arguing that attunement is simultaneously non-inferential *and* norm-laden, and he lends plausibility to this claim by explaining attunement in terms of the circulation and internaliza-tion of custom. On Schleiermacher's account, a person expresses his or her attunement through a variety of gestures, while at the same time his or her attunement is an imitation (and internalization) of others' expressions. His model can be summarized in terms of the following steps. (1) A person responds non-inferentially to some (internal or external) circumstance, and his or her gestures simul-taneously express this response to others with whom he or she iden-tifies.[43] (2) Insofar as others identify with this person – and identify

---

[42] A version of this problem is central to the interpretation of Schleiermacher on offer in what are arguably still the two most influential treatments of him in the English-speaking world, namely, Wayne Proudfoot's *Religious Experience* (Berkeley, CA: University of California Press, 1985) and George Lindbeck's *The Nature of Doctrine: Religion and Theology in a Postliberal Age* (Louisville, KY: Westminster John Knox, 1984).

[43] Schleiermacher thus claims that "attunement, as a self-contained determination of the disposition … will also, simply in virtue of the kind-consciousness (*Gattungsbewußtseins*), not be exclusively for itself, but rather primordially and without determinate aim or connection become something outward through countenance, gesture, tone, and indirectly through words, and thus become to others a revelation of the inner" (CG §6.2, p. 42).

his or her expression as "how one responds" – they may imitate that response in similar circumstances.[44] (3) If the latter becomes reliably disposed to respond non-inferentially in this way, the response becomes his or her own attunement to these circumstances; still others may then identify his or her response as how one responds and imitate it, and so on; "a multifarious community of attunement" thus emerges in which each person is "both expresser and perceiver," both imitator and imitated.[45] (4) By means of this process, the we-consciousness definitively shapes one's self-consciousness (and vice versa): Schleiermacher claims that, as a result of this process of circulation, an individual's attunement is modeled after that of others to such an extent that the we-consciousness is included within his or her self-consciousness.[46] This explains why a person's gestures can be perceived by others as an expression of that person's attunement (as in [2] above), and provides the background in terms of which Schleiermacher will explain how Jesus' attunement is mediated through the community he founded (as discussed below).[47] (5) The we-consciousness is not only the condition of *Gefühl*'s circulation, it

---

[44] As Schleiermacher claims, "this bare expression of feeling ... arouses in others to begin with only a representation of the expressed disposition-state; simply by virtue of kind-consciousness, however, this passes over into lively imitation, and the more the perceiver is able to pass over into this state (due in part to greater livingness of expression and because of nearer affinity), the easier will this state be brought forth by means of imitation" (CG §6.2, p. 43).

[45] CG §6.2, p. 43. Schleiermacher elsewhere writes of "the individual's participation in the circulation and dissemination of excitations" through "his or her excitableness through and effectiveness on that community" (CG, §6 Zusatz, p. 45). It is important to note that not every expression is either imitated or offered for imitation, such that some expressions have no connection with the kind-consciousness; for Schleiermacher's discussion of this point, see CG §60.2, p. 323.

[46] CG §60.2, p. 323.

[47] With respect to the former, Schleiermacher claims that the "inner union of kind-consciousness with the personal self-consciousness ... is alone the precondition of the fact that the inner is known and perceived along with and by means of expressions" (CG §60.2, p. 323); with respect to the latter, Schleiermacher insists that this is a necessary condition for the Redeemer's God-consciousness to be communicated to and through the redeemed (CG §60.3, p. 324).

is also continually produced *by* that circulation: as Schleiermacher claims, it is "the inner union of kind-consciousness with the personal self-consciousness which procures all recognition (*Anerkennung*) of others as of similar essence," or again, that it is precisely in virtue of this "ever-renewing circulation of self-consciousness" that one can come to "some determinate recognition of which individuals belong to a community and which do not."[48] It is only because one recognizes another's expressions as similar to one's own that one can recognize him or her as "one of us," in other words, or "of the same kind" – and because such regularity of expression is a product of this process of circulation, it follows that the we-consciousness is likewise to be explained in terms of it.

On Schleiermacher's account, then, a person's outward expression manifests his or her disposition toward some circumstance; this expression is perceived by another as how "we" respond to such circumstances; the latter thus imitates that expression in similar circumstances until he or she has become reliably disposed to respond in this way, at which point the response is an expression of his or her own disposition; others may then perceive his or her outward expression as how "we" respond, and so on. Particular ways of being attuned thus circulate through a community and become one's own attunement, in consequence of which one finds oneself with an immediate, non-inferential feel for oneself and one's circumstances.

Such attunement provides one with a kind of primordial directedness toward, or immediate take on, oneself and one's circumstances, and it is in terms of this inclination that Schleiermacher is able to avoid Kant's critique of givenness. Kant's critique, recall, applies to the supposition that what one *ought* to believe, do, and so on can be read directly off the face of some fact of the matter conceived as strictly external to any norms one applies to it. Schleiermacher accepts this critique, yet he responds to it – on the present reconstruction – by claiming that it is a mistake to construe all norm application on the

---

[48] CG §60.2, p. 323; §6.4, p. 45.

model of an explicit judgment. To understand Schleiermacher's point, consider an example: suppose one hears someone say, "Would you mind holding the door for me?" One understands the corresponding noise as a series of words only if one breaks it up into distinct, word-like units, but assuming that the noise itself does not supply these breaks, it follows that they must be supplied by the listener. Yet, in the vast majority of cases, a competent English user will not have to decide where the breaks belong; without thinking about it, he or she simply hears the noise *as* words. One's response is thus non-inferential, but nevertheless norm-laden.[49] If one then tries to explain how one understood these noises as words, one may do so in terms of one's application of particular norms to particular objects, but this step must be an explanatory latecomer relative to the normativity implicit in one's non-inferential responsive disposition – it must be an explanatory latecomer, for otherwise, a regress would follow: if (a) all norm application were construed in terms of explicit judgments about how to apply a particular norm to particular circumstances, and (b) these judgments are themselves susceptible to normative assessment, then (c) the norm application by which the latter judgment was judged would itself be susceptible to judgment, and so on, from which it follows (d) that if all norm application were construed in terms of explicit judgments, an infinite regress of judgments would be required in order to apply any norm. The moral of this story, to paraphrase Wilfrid Sellars, is that the game of explicit norm application, unlike that of implicit normative responsiveness,

---

[49] As this example should make clear, this model accommodates – but by no means requires – the possibility that one may initially become attuned to certain circumstances through explicit instruction and judgment, though these ways of being attuned count as such, in the present sense, only after they become part of one's immediate "take" on oneself and one's circumstances. This does not mean, however, that one's internalization of custom *always* depends upon explicit training or instruction, since, on the one hand, evolution seems to have played a role in attuning us in certain ways, and on the other, one finds oneself imitating all sorts of attunements without even realizing it.

is not a game that one could play though one played no other, which entails that the former cannot be explanatorily prior to the latter.

Schleiermacher thus defends an account according to which (a) *Gefühl* is one's non-inferential attunement to one's circumstances, and (b) this attunement circulates through custom. Schleiermacher then aims to shed light on how such circulation works – and how it can be judged – by attending to a particular candidate for circulation, namely, the claims of theology. Theology's task, according to Schleiermacher, is to make the prevailing attunement (in this case, piety) explicit, but since theological claims are likewise candidates for circulation, and yet circulate more explicitly than other expressions, they afford a means by which to gain insight into the general nature of such circulation. So then: Schleiermacher understands theology as "the discipline which systematizes the doctrine prevalent (*geltenden Lehre*) in a Christian Church at a given time," and he understands such doctrines, in turn, as "accounts of the Christian pious disposition-states portrayed in speech" – as accounts, that is, of "that which, in the public proceedings of the Church ... can be heard as a portrayal of its common piety."[50] Doctrines are thus offered both as an expression of current piety and as themselves candidates for currency, as is evident in the authority conferred upon the community's acceptance of these expressions. At its most basic, the acceptance in view involves the community's recognition of a particular expression *as* an expression of its piety, which entails that, to gain currency, the expression must be recognizable as such. Schleiermacher's explanation of the nature of "currency" can be seen as an elaboration on the conditions of meeting this requirement. Two conditions are particularly relevant. First, for a theological claim to circulate as an expression of the community's piety, it must be recognizable as going on in the same way as precedents which have circulated as such. It is for this reason that Schleiermacher claims that "we could not at all grant the name of Dogmatics to a presentation composed

---

[50] CG §19 Leitsatz, p. 119; §15 Leitsatz, p. 105; §19.3, p. 121.

of nothing but idiosyncratic doctrines," and that, indeed, "even the earliest presentations of the evangelical faith could bear that name only insofar as they linked up with what went before and had most of their system in common with what was ecclesially given."[51] In order to be recognizable as an expression of the community's piety, accordingly, an expression must be recognizable as going on in the same way as previous expressions which the community recognizes as such. Being recogniz*able* as an expression of the community's piety is obviously distinct from being recogniz*ed* as such, however, which leads to a second condition, namely, that a community treat this expression as normative for subsequent expressions. To recognize a candidate expression is to treat it as going on in the same way as precedent expressions of the community's piety, which means that subsequent expressions can then be recognized as such if they go on in the same way as a series of precedents which now includes the expression in question. Hence, as Schleiermacher puts it, a doctrine counts as an expression of Christian piety only if a community "finds its norm" in that doctrine – only if, that is, it takes that expression as normative for future expressions of piety.[52] Taken together, these conditions indicate that, in order to make an expression explicit in its circulation, one must exhibit it as "a product of the past and a kernel of the future" – that is, as carrying on the normative trajectory implicit in a series of recognized precedents and as exerting normative constraint on future candidates for currency.[53] On this account, then, the norm by which a novel expression is assessed is provided

---

[51] CG §25.1, p. 142.

[52] As Schleiermacher comments, "an edifice [of doctrine], even if entirely coherent, of nothing but wholly peculiar opinions and views, which, even if really Christian, did not link themselves at all to the expressions used in the churchly communication of piety, would always be taken only as a private confession and not as a dogmatic presentation, until there came to be attached to it a likeminded society, and there thus emerged a public preaching and communication which found in that doctrine its norm" (CG §19.3, p. 121).

[53] *Kurze Darstellung des theologischen Studiums* (1811), *Kritische Gesamtausgabe*, vol. VI, Dirk Schmid (ed.) (Berlin: Walter de Gruyter, 1998), I§33.

by prior expressions which have been recognized as expressions of a community's attunement, and if the novel expression is recognized as going on in the same way, it contributes to the norm according to which still other expressions might be recognized.

Two important consequences follow from this account. It follows, first, that the normative criterion by which candidate expressions are to be judged is itself the product of a trajectory implicit in expressions recognized as precedential, since one judges a candidate expression of the prevailing piety by determining whether it goes on in the same way as other expressions one recognizes as such. It also follows that the criterion changes, if only slightly, each time a new expression is recognized, since, on the one hand, the relevant norm is itself a product of the normative trajectory implicit in a series of precedents, and on the other, the recognition of a further precedent contributes to the shape of that trajectory.[54]

Schleiermacher thus provides an account according to which norms are implicit in attunement, attunement is an internalization of that which circulates in custom, and this circulation is explained in terms of an ongoing process of recognition. With this account on board, we can now turn to Schleiermacher's explanation of how the Spirit of Christ enters into circulation, but before doing so, I should at least mention a problem to which we shall return in Chapter 6, namely, that because these norms circulate non-inferentially, they come to seem natural, and can accordingly serve to reinforce certain social arrangements without anyone noticing that they are doing

---

[54] Thus Schleiermacher: "Consider ... how much there is which was originally decried as heterodox in our Church, which afterwards came to count as orthodox but always through an earlier orthodoxy becoming obsolete" (CG §25 Zusatz, p. 145). Or again, "if heterodox matter comes to be counted as being better attuned to the spirit of the Evangelical Church than is the letter of the Confessions, then the latter become antiquated and the former becomes orthodox" (CG, §25 Zusatz, p. 145). This prospective/retrospective distinction is crucial to understanding how "changes nevertheless do not compromise the unity of [the Church's] essence," since it explains how novel expressions can be seen as both carrying on and contributing to that essence (*Kurze Darstellung* [1830] §47).

so – and without anyone having to engage in explicitly coercive acts in order to enforce these arrangements. This is a real problem for an account such as Schleiermacher's, and we will consider it at length in Chapter 6.

2

With this account up and running, Schleiermacher then explains how the Spirit of Christ enters into normative circulation. According to Christian tradition, the Holy Spirit is the one who, among other things, indwells one, writes God's law on one's heart, transforms one into God's child, bears witness to Christ, and leads one into all truth.[55] Scripture and tradition ascribe more to the Spirit than these works, of course, but these appear to be central. Hence, if we suppose that theology is faith seeking understanding, it follows that a theology of the Holy Spirit might reasonably include some explanation of how the Spirit does that which is here ascribed to it. What I am calling Schleiermacher's "pneumatological pragmatics" is just such an explanation: he explains the Holy Spirit as the Spirit of Christ – more specifically, as the Spirit who enables one to go on in the same way as Christ – explains this going-on in terms of Christ's norms being carried on through a process of mutual recognition, and thus explains how the "supernatural" Spirit could enter into the "natural" circulation of norms.

To understand this account, we can begin by focussing on the Spirit's work of transforming one into God's child. Since, according to Christian belief, Jesus Christ is the only begotten child of God, it would appear that one is transformed into God's child precisely

---

[55] For an excellent overview of the tradition, see Hans Urs von Balthasar, *Theo-Logic*, vol. III, *The Spirit of Truth*, trans. Graham Harrison (San Francisco: Ignatius Press, 2005); and Yves Congar, *I Believe in the Holy Spirit*, 3 vols., trans. David Smith (New York: Seabury, 1983).

through being conformed to Christ.[56] Following a long line of Christian theologians, we can say that one is conformed to Jesus just insofar as his covenant faithfulness has become one's own: Jesus' childship is a matter of his wholehearted devotion to God's will, and one becomes God's child by repeating his devotion as one's own.[57] This last clause is crucial: in order for Christ's devotion to count as one's *own*, one's repetition of it must be more than *mere* repetition. That is to say, insofar as one's conformity to Christ is a matter of sheer imitation or of simply doing what one is told, it does not yet count as one's own conformity; to count as such, it is necessary that one be able to produce Christ-conforming performances *as* one's own, which turns out to mean that one must be able to produce them *on* one's own.[58] A repeated performance can indeed count as one's own, of course, yet it would appear that we can distinguish spontaneous repetition from *mere* repetition only insofar as there is reason to believe that

[56] So Thomas Aquinas, for instance, writes that we are "made the adoptive sons of God by assimilation to the natural Son of God," and it is the Holy Spirit who accomplishes this assimilation, "precisely because he is the Spirit of the Son of God" (*Summa Contra Gentiles*, IV.24.2, trans. Charles J. O'Neil [Notre Dame, IN: University of Notre Dame Press, 1957], p. 134).

[57] So Thomas: "The free man is the one who belongs to himself; the slave, however, belongs to his master. Whoever acts spontaneously therefore acts freely, but whoever receives his impulse from another does not act freely." Thomas claims that the Spirit frees one in precisely this sense, by "inwardly perfecting our spirit by communicating to it a new dynamism, and this functions so well that man refrains from evil through love, as though divine law were ordering him to do this. He is therefore free not because he is not subject to divine law, but because his inner dynamism leads him to do what divine law prescribes" (*In 2 Corinthians*, chapter 3, lecture 3, quoted in Yves Congar, *I Believe in the Holy Spirit*, vol. II, p. 125). Cf. Hans Urs von Balthasar's claim that God has adopted human persons as God's children and fulfilled the new covenant in that "the Holy Spirit has freed us from the external law and replaced it with the 'law' of inward freedom, which is identical with the obedience unto death that Christ rendered to the Father" (Hans Urs von Balthasar, *Theologik*, vol. III, *Der Geist der Wahrheit* [Einsiedeln: Johannes Verlag, 1987], p. 80).

[58] For arguments to this effect, see Basil of Caesarea, *De Spiritu Sancto* (Crestwood: St Vladimir's Seminary Press, 1980), 21.52; Barth, *Die Kirchliche Dogmatik*, vol. I, *Die Lehre vom Wort Gottes*, part 2 (Zollikon-Zürich: Evangelischer Verlag A.G., 1938) §16; as well as Schleiermacher, CG §122.

one could produce at least some such performances *without* having to imitate others or be told what to do.[59] (If I can produce an appropriate Italian sentence only when an Italian speaker tells me what to say, I do not count as knowing how to speak the language.) As Schleiermacher argues, in the case of "mere repetition," "the impulse to such modification of action comes only from without and remains effective only for so long as the moment's stimulation endures; it is not in a position to reproduce itself from within, as one commonly finds when, under external compulsion, one does something that seems foreign to oneself. Such actions belong not to the life of the actor him- or herself, but to an external life manifesting its power in him or her."[60] It turns out, then, that in order to count as one's own, one must be able to produce *spontaneous* performances that conform to Christ – and given that one's judgment about what conforms to Christ is itself an activity that must be conformed to Christ, one must be able to produce these judgments for oneself, too. Indeed, there is a sense in which one's Christ-conformed performances count as one's own only if one can judge for oneself that they do so, if only implicitly, for in order to *intend* one's performance as conforming to Christ (and so be able to recognize it as one's own), one must have some idea of what would *count* as doing so.[61] (I can so much as try to whistle "Amazing Grace" only if I have some idea of how the tune goes.)

---

[59] Brandom makes a parallel point with respect to language acquisition: "Learning the language is not just learning to use a set of stock sentences which everybody else uses too. One has not learned the language, has not acquired the capacity to engage in the social practices which are the use of the language, until one can produce *novel* sentences which the community will deem appropriate, and understand the appropriate novel utterances of other members of the community (where the criterion for this capacity is the ability to make inferences deemed appropriate by the community)" ("Freedom and Constraint by Norms," in *Hermeneutics and Praxis*, Robert Hollinger [ed.] [Notre Dame, IN: University of Notre Dame Press, 1985], p. 185).

[60] CG §110.2, p. 184.

[61] This is a fairly common point in the literature on intentional action; see, for instance, the first part of Donald Davidson's *Essays on Actions and Events* (New York: Oxford University Press, 1980, 2001); Schleiermacher makes a similar point at §122 of *Der Christliche Glaube*.

To be conformed to Christ, therefore, one must learn to distinguish whether a performance or judgment counts as following him.

So how does one know whether a performance or judgment conforms to Christ? Looking at his immediate followers, we might be tempted to answer that one knows one's performances conform to Christ if and only if Christ recognizes them as such, but there are two problems facing such an answer: first, if a performance's conformity to Christ depends upon Christ's own recognition of it as such, it would be hard to see how anyone other than the original disciples could undertake such performances. Second, this answer fails even as an account of the original disciples' conformity, since their performances, too, would count as "theirs" in the relevant sense only insofar as they could judge for themselves that they were following Christ – only insofar, that is, as they could recognize these performances as such apart from Christ's judgments. The latter problem provides us with an important clue, however, about how to proceed: the critical moment in the original disciples' transformation, on Schleiermacher's account, occurred when Christ not only recognized certain of their performances as following him, but also recognized them as fellow recognizers, that is, as themselves competent judges of what counts as such. Prior to that, Jesus had taught the disciples how to follow him by telling them what to say and do, correcting their missteps, and so on, but at some point he recognized them as reliably able to judge what would count as following him, at which point their so following became fully their *own*.

Schleiermacher explains this process as proceeding through roughly the following steps: first, "in spending time together with Christ, the disciples' receptivity developed, and by perceiving what he held before them, a foundation was laid for their future effectiveness for the Kingdom of God." Christ's activity had not yet become the disciples' own, however, for "at this point, what Christ expected of them was only practice in the sense of training-through-repetitive-exercise (*übende*), not practice in the sense of skillful practitioning (*ausübende*), in consequence of which it was not yet their own free activity, because each expression still needed a particular prompting." The crucial step in the disciples' development thus occurred when Jesus recognized their authority to bind and loose sin, since "the right binding and loosing of sin is essentially just an expression of a fully cultivated receptivity for what pertains to the Kingdom of God."[62] On the basis of such recognition, accordingly, "there is more in the individual than receptivity, and his or her own activity is not merely the activity of Christ simply passing through him or her."[63] To be sure, the disciples could not have recognized themselves as such, since Christ alone was competent to judge when others' judgments went on in the same way as his. But once they had become reliably disposed to reproduce Christ's normative assessments as their own, he recognized them as fellow recognizers, and their Christ-following performances could now count as fully their own, since they could judge for themselves whether a performance followed him and could therefore intend a performance as such.

This account thus provides us with a way of addressing the second problem mentioned above – and if we take it a few steps further, it will help us address the first problem as well, namely, the fact that those who came after the disciples could not submit their performances directly to Christ's authority. Given that Christ recognized some of his disciples as fellow recognizers of what counts as conforming to him, it follows that after Christ had departed, those who wanted to conform to him could learn how to do so by submitting their performances to the authority of those whom Christ recognized. One could learn to follow Christ, in other words, by recognizing the authority of those whom Christ recognized, in much the same way that they learned to follow Christ by recognizing Christ's own authority. And once the latter would-be followers were recognized

---

[62] CG §122.1, p. 255. Note well that Schleiermacher is here alluding to the so-called Johannine Pentecost (for which see John 20:22–3), especially the connection there made between the sending of the Spirit and the binding and loosing of sins, rather than to the binding-and-loosing passages in the Synoptic Gospels.

[63] CG §122.3, p. 257.

as fellow recognizers, others could learn how to follow Christ from them, too, and so on. A "multifarious community of attunement" thus emerges: those who have been attuned to Christ express that attunement through their gestures, words, actions, and recognition-laden responses *to* such expressions (whether their own or others'); if others recognize such expressions as following Christ, they may imitate them in similar circumstances until they have become reliably disposed to do so, at which point these expressions become part of their own attunement; still others may then recognize the latter's expressions as attuned to Christ, imitate those expressions, become reliably disposed to repeat them, and so on. In this way, the Spirit of Christ's own recognition is carried forward through a chain of mutual recognition, and the practice of following him is passed along to those who never encountered him directly. Schleiermacher thus concludes that "this effect of the community in bringing forth faith is simultaneously the effect of the personal perfection of Jesus himself."[64]

In broad outline, then, we can see how Schleiermacher explains the Spirit's work: the Spirit transforms one into God's child, he claims, by conforming one to Christ, and he explains the process through which one becomes so conformed in terms of a chain of recognition that stretches back to Christ himself. This chain of recognition, in turn, is understood as the Spirit's work, since what is carried forward through this chain just is the normative Spirit of Christ: the Spirit, on this account, is first of all the Spirit of Christ's recognition of what counts as following him, a Spirit that he conveyed to those whose practices he recognized, and that they conveyed to still others. In this way, the norms according to which Christ assessed whether one was following him were passed along to others, and, since these norms are the means by which one is conformed to Christ, it follows that this account provides some explanation of one of the central works traditionally ascribed to the Holy Spirit. (To be clear, the

---

[64] CG §88.2, p. 21.

intent is not to *reduce* the Spirit's work to the content of this account; if anything, it provides a means by which to discern other, more "extraordinary" works ascribed to the Spirit.) Hence, given (a) that, according to traditional Christian belief, the Holy Spirit is the one who is sent by Christ to guide his followers into all truth, to transform them into God's children, to write God's law on their hearts, and so forth, and (b) that neither Scripture nor tradition has offered any canonical explanation of how the Spirit does these things, it follows (c) that there is no reason, in principle, not to think of the Spirit as accomplishing that which is ascribed to it by circulating through a process of intersubjective recognition in which one links up with (and carries on) a chain of recognition that stretches back to Christ's own recognition of the disciples.[65]

On this account, then, when one undertakes a commitment to follow Christ, one implicitly undertakes certain further commitments: in order to learn how to go on in the same way as Christ, one must submit one's performances to Christ's authority; hence, if Christ recognized his disciples' authority to judge what counts as following him, then one's recognition of Christ's authority commits one to recognizing theirs, too. And since they, in turn, recognized others as knowing how to follow Jesus, and so on, it follows that in order to follow Jesus, one must try to go on in the same way as those who have been recognized as knowing how do so; one must recognize the judgments, that is, of those who have been recognized by (those who have been recognized by …) Christ. Moreover, in trying to follow Christ, one not only recognizes the authority of certain precedents, one implicitly seeks this same status for oneself – and because one's performance is being offered as a precedent for

---

[65] To be sure, something more needs to be said here, since knowing how to do something is obviously distinct from actually doing it. It is not hard to imagine a child who works countless hours to become a proficient cellist, then decides that she hates the cello and refuses to play it ever again. Nor is it hard to imagine someone who knows how to follow Jesus but who, for whatever reason, does not do so. I return to these matters in Chapter 5.

further performances, it follows that one undertakes responsibility for getting this performance right, thus rendering one's performance liable to – and, indeed, inviting – the assessments of those whom one recognizes. The normative practice of going on in the same way as Christ is thus mediated through an ongoing process of mutual recognition, a process which, made explicit, could go by the name of "apostolic succession" (with a small "a," as it were).

At this point, though, one might wonder whether Schleiermacher's account depends upon a rather far-fetched claim to the effect that a homogeneous community stretches from Jesus' first disciples to those who would follow him today. In response to this concern, it is important to note, first, that this community need not (and, on the present account, cannot) be "homogeneous," since the community in question is ongoingly constituted by a process of mutual recognition: as argued above, a community is constituted by one's recognition of certain performers and performances as normative and by their recognition of one, which means that the community in question (in this case, "the Church") is continually *re*constituted, and so changed, through the ongoing process in which one demarcates a "we" and seeks inclusion in it. What the present account requires, then, is not a homogeneous community, but the possibility that a set of normative commitments could be carried on through historical, human social practices over a span of several hundred years – and this, it turns out, is not so far-fetched after all: we can recognize certain linguistic communities, for instance, as having been in recognizably continuous existence for at least as long, just as we can recognize the briefer, but no less relevant, continuity of various game-playing and skill-employing communities. It would appear, then, that the present proposal does not require an unrealistic degree of continuity or homogeneity between Jesus' disciples and those who follow him today.

On Schleiermacher's account, then, to follow Christ is to intend one's performances to be recognizable as such by those who are recognized as following him, and one intends this by trying to go on in the same way as precedent performances which are recognized as doing so; one's recognitions thus pick out a set of authoritative precedents to which one's performances are answerable, and one seeks this same recognition for one's own performance. In this way, Christ's normative Spirit can be carried on by a chain of recognition that stretches back to Christ's own recognition of the disciples.

3

We have thus sketched an account, following Schleiermacher, according to which the norms by which one's beliefs and actions are assessed are supplied by Christ and mediated by his Spirit. We can now begin making some headway into explaining theological concept use, though the account to be defended here cannot emerge clearly into view until further resources are brought on board in the following chapter. At this point, that is to say, we can account for the "rulishness" or normativity of theological concept use, as well as for God's role in this normativity, but because we have yet to account for the content of such concepts, we are not yet in position to claim that concepts can be applied non-violently to God. This much, at any rate, should already be clear: if Jesus Christ is the "final revelation" of God (to borrow Tillich's term for the traditional Christian belief), then theological concept use must be normed by him. With respect to concept use, then, the picture looks something like this. In the previous section, I argued that concepts are a species of norm, since to use a concept is to try to answer to the normative trajectory implicit in a series of precedent uses, and one's use is itself offered as precedent for further uses. We can now use this model to understand theological concept use: one's concepts are applied correctly to God, on this view, if they are faithful to God's revelation in Christ, and they count as such if they go on in the same way as precedent applications which carry on a normative trajectory that stretches back to Christ. Jesus recognized certain claims about God as correct and eventually recognized certain persons as competent judges of such correctness; these persons recognized certain claims as correct and eventually recognized certain persons, and so on. To count as using (Christian) theological concepts, then, one's use must be recognizable as trying to carry on the normative trajectory implicit in this chain, which means subjecting one's concept use to precedent uses that are recognized as doing so, and seeking this same precedential status for one's own use; one's use of theological concepts thus simultaneously answers to, and carries on, Christ's normative Spirit. We can, accordingly, understand Christ as supplying the norm according to which theological concept use is to be assessed, and as supplying the Spirit by which this norm is carried on. On this account, therefore, theological concept use depends upon one's being answerable to Christ by the power of his Spirit.

So then: suppose my son says "God is wise." On the present view, in order to apply the concept "wisdom" to God, he must intend his usage as going on in the same way as certain precedents. In this case, he must intend to use the word in the same way his parents and other teachers do: they may have applied the concept in response to a strange turn of events, for instance, or in looking back over the course of their lives, and he may apply it in response to the wondrous fact that ice floats. In turn, if his use of "wisdom" is recognized as correct, others (his younger sister, for instance) can try to use the concept by going on in the same way as his usage. In this way, his use of the concept "wisdom" depends upon, and carries on, a normative trajectory that is itself carried on by a series of precedent uses. And if this trajectory carries on a chain of recognition which stretches back to persons and performances which were themselves recognized by Christ, it follows that his concept use both depends upon, and mediates, Christ's normative Spirit. The fact that he is trying to use these concepts correctly, moreover, implies that the success of his usage depends in some respect upon its actually getting its subject matter right. This means that according to his own normative commitments, his theological concept use must not only go on in the same way as precedent uses that *he* recognizes as correct; it must be conformable to uses that *Christ* recognized as such. We cannot do justice to the latter claim here, since it brings us into the deep waters of theological *truth*, a promissory note not to be redeemed until Chapter 5. The point, for now, is that his use of theological concepts depends upon the work of the Spirit (who norms one's usage through a process of mutual recognition) and of Christ (as the one who sent the Spirit and who is the standard by which to determine whether one's performances conform to God).

On the present account, then, theological concept use turns out to be a trinitarian affair, which leads to a decisive implication: the norms according to which one assesses one's concept use are not external to God – and neither are the concepts themselves. On the present account, one learns how to use theological concepts by submitting one's performances to Christ, and one is able to submit them to Christ through the power of the Spirit. If it is the case that concepts are a species of norm, and if it is further the case that theological concept use is normed by the Spirit of Christ, then it follows that theological concepts are themselves the work of the triune God. One conceptualizes God through God, which is to say that one conceptualizes God by grace alone.[66]

We have thus assembled some of the key resources with which to argue that concepts do not contain that to which they are applied, that they do not set objects in a uniform series, and so on. Some of the requisite resources are not yet on board, but it should already be clear that, on the present proposal, concept use is neither predictable nor fixed in advance. To use a concept, on our account, is to intend one's usage to be recognizable as such by those who are recognized as using it, and one intends this by trying to carry on the normative trajectory of uses that one recognizes as correct. If one's use is recognized as going on in the same way, it contributes to the normative trajectory

---

[66] In light of this understanding of theological concept use, we could see ordinary concept use, too, as dependent upon (and so fit for) God's triune activity, since ordinary concept use is governed by and for the sake of that same activity.

that further uses will try to carry on; hence, when a candidate use is recognized as going on in the same way, it affects what it means to do so. That is to say, if a concept is the product of a series of precedent uses, and if this series changes every time a new use is recognized as carrying it on, it follows that concepts are continually being reconstituted. This means, as we will see in the following chapter, that it makes no sense to talk about the meaning of a concept being fixed by its application to creaturely reality, since it makes little sense to talk about "the meaning" of a concept, nor about such a meaning ever being fixed. Moreover, it makes little sense to talk about concepts as "containers," since we have done without the characteristics necessary to thinking that they could contain something: either that concepts are literally thing-like containers, or that every possible extension of a concept is contained in it in advance. Finally, since our account explains the sameness of a concept's applications in terms of an ongoing process of intersubjective recognition, and since this process both allows for and depends upon novelty and unpredictability, it follows that we need not think that concepts work by setting items alongside one another in a uniform series.[67] We will return to each of these points in the following chapter; for now, it is important to note that if concepts are not necessarily metaphysical (in the sense that one's use of them corresponds to an essence-like idea or predetermined category), then it

---

[67] This sort of unpredictability is dramatically illustrated by the process through which Christians arrived at "the Christian doctrine of God": prospectively speaking, it was by no means self-evident that the trajectory stretching from the Apostolic Fathers through Justin Martyr and Origen would eventuate in the claims of Athanasius and Gregory of Nazianzus (nor that the latter would be recognized as correct). In view of the fact that the latter were recognized as going on in the same way as their precedents, on the other hand, it looked as if this was precisely what it *meant* for this trajectory to "go on," and it meant further that in order to go on in the same way as this earlier trajectory, one now had to go on in the same way as Athanasius and Gregory. For an account along these lines, see R. P. C. Hanson's *The Search for the Christian Doctrine of God: The Arian Controversy 318–81* (Edinburgh: T&T Clark, 1988).

is at least possible that they could be applied to God *without* thereby cutting God down to creaturely size.

The previous section claimed that concepts are a species of norm: to use a concept, I argued, is to undertake a commitment which is normed by precedent uses and which aims to provide the norm for subsequent use. I then argued for an account according to which the Spirit of Christ is itself carried on through a series of precedents, such that the norm by which theological concept use is assessed – and which theological concepts in fact are – can itself be understood as a work of the Spirit. As we shall see, these moves have decisive implications for an understanding of language's relationship to God.

4

This account may appear liable to a serious objection, namely, that it collapses (God's) objectivity into (human) subjectivity. According to this objection, if we understand the Spirit as working through, and therefore in some sense immanent in, human activity, there will be nothing objective about that work – the Spirit's work, in other words, will become identical with whatever one takes it to be, from which it apparently follows that Christ will become identical with whatever one takes him to be, God will become identical with whatever one takes God be, and so forth.[68] This is a serious objection. Fortunately,

---

[68] One might wonder here, too, whether the Spirit's *personhood* has been adequately affirmed. In response to this concern, it should suffice to note that the tradition understands the being of God as pure activity, from which it follows that each of the triune hypostases is pure activity, too. The tradition further understands the Holy Spirit's activity as the activity of perfecting the love between Father and Son; this being the case, for the Spirit to act as itself – that is, "personally" – in the economy of grace is for the Spirit to continue this activity. Hence, when I propose that the Spirit works by mediating Christ's normativity to us, we can understand this as the Spirit repeating *ad extra* the activity which is proper to the Spirit's triune personhood. (Recall here the discussion of the previous chapter.) Given that this activity *is* the Spirit's personhood, it would appear that my proposal is not liable to an objection along these lines.One might also worry that the present proposal identifies the Spirit's

there is good reason for thinking that it does not hold against the account proposed here, since (a) "these norms are socially mediated" does not entail (b) "these norms mean whatever one takes them to mean." It does not follow because, in order to count as correct, one's beliefs, actions, judgments, and so forth must go on in the same way as precedent judgments which have been recognized as correct, which means that one's performance is constrained by those precedents. Not just anything will count as a correct use of the concept "God," for instance, since, to count as using the concept, one's use must be recognizable as going on in the same way as precedent uses. If one deviates too far from these uses – if one's mistakes are too large – then one's performances will not be recognizable as uses of the concept. (We return to this point in Chapter 4.) Moreover, if the correctness of one's concept use depends upon its answerability to Christ, then, again, not just anything will count as doing so – especially if the Spirit constrains that answerability through a process of mutual recognition. We can, of course, imagine the possibility that a particular trajectory of judgments is, in fact, wrong, though we can make sense of this possibility only against a background of other trajectories which we continue to take as correct. In other words, one can contest any particular judgment or trajectory, just not all at once. As long as one is not massively in error, therefore, one can make sense of particular uses going wrong – objectively so.[69] It should be clear, then, that this account can indeed explain the objective correctness or incorrectness of theological concept use, as Chapter 5 will demonstrate.

✳✳✳

work too closely with human activity. The proper response to this concern, it seems to me, is to insist that divinity and humanity need not be thought to compete with one another, such that an increase in human activity would not entail a decrease in divine activity. I elaborate this point further in Chapter 6.

[69] On this point, see for instance Donald Davidson, "A Coherence Theory of Truth and Knowledge," *Subjective, Intersubjective, Objective*, pp. 137–53; for a theological version of this claim, see Congar, *The Meaning of Tradition* (San Francisco: Ignatius Press, 2004), pp. 51–8.

On the account offered here, theological concept use is conformed to Christ by the power of the Spirit: one's concepts are applied to God by answering to God's revelation in Christ, and they are so answerable if they carry on the Spirit of precedent applications which have been recognized as such. Theological concept use is, accordingly, a trinitarian affair. Moreover, since theological concept use depends upon an ongoing process of intersubjective recognition, and since this process both allows for and depends upon novelty and unpredictability, it follows that we need not think that concepts work by setting items alongside one another in a uniform series, nor that their meaning is fixed in advance, nor that they contain that to which they are applied. We can thus do without several elements of the picture which has led some theologians to think that concepts necessarily do violence to that to which they are applied, which means that we are one step closer to freeing ourselves from the idea that God must stand at a distance from God-talk.

Conclusion

Contemporary theologians frequently claim that concepts cut objects down to the size of predetermined categories, such that one can avoid doing violence to God only by insisting that concepts (in their predicative use) never quite reach God. From a therapeutic standpoint, this claim seems to remain stuck within a metaphysical framework, in two respects: on the one hand, it takes for granted metaphysics' own (essentialist-correspondentist) picture of concepts, and on the other, the idea that language never reaches God seems to presuppose a decidedly correspondentistic picture of what it would mean for language to do so. In order to render this picture optional, this chapter began by sketching an alternative account of the way concepts work. A concept, on this view, is a norm by which one orders the manifold of one's experience, and one does so by judging certain aspects of that experience to be relevantly similar to other aspects. In order to count as using a concept, one must intend to go on in the same way as precedent uses, which means, first, that in using a concept, one recognizes the authority of certain precedents and seeks such authority for oneself, and second, that what it means to go on in the same way is the product of an ongoing process of mutual recognition, from which it follows that concepts are continually being rewritten. This entails, as we will see in the following chapter, that it makes little sense to talk about the meaning of a concept being fixed by its application to creaturely reality, since it makes little sense to talk either about "the meaning" of a concept or about such a meaning ever being fixed. Moreover, it makes little sense to think of concepts as containers, since the present account does without the characteristics necessary to thinking that they could contain something: either that they are literally thing-like containers, or that every possible extension of a concept is contained in it in advance. Finally, since our account understands "sameness" on the basis of an ongoing process of intersubjective recognition, and since this process both allows for and indeed depends upon novelty and unpredictability, it follows that "sameness of meaning" and "using the same concept" need not be understood in terms of univocity, that is, in terms of uniformity and predictability.

Building on this account of ordinary concept use, I sketched a parallel account of theological concept use: to use a theological concept, I claimed, is to try to go on in the same way as precedent uses which are recognized as correct, where "correct" turns out to mean "in the same way as those recognized by Christ." I then claimed that the normative Spirit of Christ is mediated through the practice of mutual recognition: one's use of a concept counts as following Christ just in case it goes on in the same way as precedent uses which have been recognized as doing so, in a chain of mutual recognition that stretches back to Christ's recognition of his disciples. On the basis of these claims, I argued that we can avoid some of the problems facing the very idea of applying concepts to God, and can therefore do without one of the reasons for thinking that God must stand at a distance from language. In order to free ourselves fully from the metaphysical picture of concept use, however, we still need to provide a therapeutic account of conceptual content and to explain how such contents could be applied to God. To this we now turn.

3 | Meaning and meanings

I have been arguing for an account of language and of God that will free us from essentialist-correspondentist metaphysics, as well as from the sense of limitation one may feel so long as one remains in the grip of metaphysical assumptions. Toward that end, the previous chapter advanced two lines of argument: first, that concepts are a species of norm, that their normativity is carried on through a process of intersubjective recognition, and that concepts are therefore continually changing; and, second, that the normative Spirit of Christ enters into, and is carried on by, this same process of recognition, so as to conform such norms to God. On the resulting picture, concepts can be seen as fit for God's appropriation, and God can be seen to appropriate them through the work of Jesus and his Spirit. The previous chapter thus defended an account according to which the *form* of concepts – that is, their "normishness" – is fit for God's use of them, which thereby renders optional one reason for thinking that God must stand at a distance from language. The present chapter rounds out this account by explaining the *content* of concepts, that is, their meaning.

The problem here, recall, is this: if (a) the meaning of a concept use is its correspondence to an essence-like idea or "meaning," and (b) this meaning is fixed once and for all by the concept's application to certain creaturely objects, it follows (c) that to apply a concept to God would be to cut God down to the size of creaturely objects. It might seem, then, that in order to avoid setting God within a metaphysical framework, one must avoid the application of concepts to God, which would entail that God must be thought to stand at a remove from language about God. From a therapeutic point of view, however, this set of inferences can be seen to depend upon residually metaphysical assumptions about the meaning of concepts. The therapeutic strategy is thus to defend an account of meaning which calls into question premises (a) and (b), thereby rendering optional conclusion (c). Toward that end, this chapter argues, first, for an account according to which a concept's meaning is the product of a normative trajectory implicit in a series of recognized precedents, such that its meaning is continually changing, and second, for an account according to which the Spirit of Christ applies certain concepts to God by appropriating these trajectories, thereby judging and fulfilling their meaning. With this account on board, it should be clear that the problems facing essentialist-correspondentist metaphysics need not be thought to entail that concepts cannot apply to God, since the inability of concepts to correspond to God would result in their distance *from* God only on the assumption that concept use depends upon such correspondence.

The meaning of concepts

We begin, then, with an account of conceptual content or meaning.[1] On the view to be defended here, the meaning of a concept is a product of the normative trajectory implicit in a series of precedents, such that its meaning changes, if only slightly, every time a new use is recognized as carrying on that trajectory. With this account on board, we can remove one of the main obstacles to thinking that concepts could be applied to God, namely, the idea that their meaning is fixed once and for all by their application to creaturely objects.

---

[1] I am here using "conceptual content" and "meaning" as rough equivalents, though there are cases where the two diverge: there are accounts of meaning that are not accounts of conceptual content, for instance, though not vice versa. The following chapter deals with another meaning of "meaning," namely, intentionality.

This idea is itself a product of an essentialist-correspondentist picture of language – as Quine observed, "meaning is what essence becomes when it is divorced from the object of reference and wedded to the word"[2] – and it is this picture that the present section aims to render optional.

1

In the previous chapter, I claimed that concepts are norms by which one judges some aspect of one's experience to be relevantly similar to something else, and that their "normishness" should be understood in light of an account of intersubjective recognition: one intends to use a particular concept, on this account, by demarcating a class of precedent uses and offering one's own use as a candidate for inclusion in that class. One's use of a concept thus confers normative authority upon a class of uses whose propriety one recognizes, while at the same time implicitly claiming this authority for one's own use. One intends one's concept-using behavior to be recognizable as "what we do," accordingly, where (a) the relevant "we" consists of those whom one recognizes as users of the concept in question, (b) one is recognized as one of "us" when one's behavior is treated *as* a use of the concept, and (c) one's treatment as such is a matter of one's use being taken to license others to use the concept in the same way. On this account, then, a concept just *is* a norm, in that a particular use is both normed by precedent uses and, in turn, norms subsequent uses.

An account of meaning precipitates out of this understanding of concepts: to use a concept is to (attempt to) carry on the normative trajectory implicit in a series of precedents, from which it follows that one interprets the meaning of a candidate use (one's

---

[2] Quine, "Two Dogmas of Empiricism," *From a Logical Point of View: Nine Logico-Philosophical Essays*, revised second edn. (Cambridge, MA: Harvard University Press, 1953, 1961, 1980), p. 22.

own or another's) by seeing it *as* carrying on such a trajectory.[3] The meaning of a concept use, accordingly, is a product of the relevant normative trajectory as that trajectory eventuates in this particular use, from which it follows that one interprets a use by trying to see it as standing at the end of a series of precedents. Hence, if my wife calls me to say that she painted our bathroom red, I understand her use of "red" by seeing it as going on in the same way as previous uses, thus taking her to be saying that the paint is relevantly similar to other objects to which the concept "red" has been applied (fire hydrants, stop signs, apples, etc.). More generally, one understands statements of the form "*a* is φ" by seeing object *a* as relevantly similar to other objects to which the concept φ has been applied, and understands φ itself in terms of previous φ sayings (φ', φ", φ'", etc.); one thus understands a statement such as "the deregulation of financial markets is unwise" by trying to understand the deregulation in question as relevantly similar to other objects that have been called unwise (non-investment in infrastructure, the scaling back of Head Start programs, building one's house upon the sand, etc.),

---

[3] The philosophical strategy of this section is to embed an inferentialist semantics in a pragmatic account of meaning-as-use, and to explain this pragmatics in terms of intersubjective recognition. The section thus draws together the work of Michael Dummett, *Frege: Philosophy of Language* (Cambridge, MA: Harvard University Press, 1973, 1981); Wilfrid Sellars, "Inference and Meaning," *Pure Pragmatics and Possible Worlds: The Early Essays of Wilfrid Sellars*, Jeffrey F. Sicha (ed.) (Atascadero, CA: Ridgeview Publishing, 1980), pp. 218–37; Ludwig Wittgenstein, *Philosophical Investigations*, trans. G. E. M. Anscombe (Oxford: Blackwell, 1953, 2001) and *Remarks on the Foundations of Mathematics*, G. H. von Wright, R. Rhees, and G. E. M. Anscombe (eds.) (Cambridge, MA: MIT Press, 1978), especially part VI; Quine, "Two Dogmas of Empiricism," *From a Logical Point of View* and *Word and Object* (Cambridge, MA: MIT Press, 1960); Saul Kripke, *Wittgenstein on Rules and Private Language* (Cambridge, MA: Harvard University Press, 1982), pp. 55–113; Donald Davidson, *Subjective, Intersubjective, Objective* (New York: Oxford University Press, 2001) and *Truth, Language, and History* (New York: Oxford University Press, 2005); and Robert Brandom, *Making It Explicit: Reasoning, Representing, and Discursive Commitment* (Cambridge, MA: Harvard University Press, 1994), and *Articulating Reasons: Introducing Inferentialism* (Cambridge, MA: Harvard University Press, 2000).

and understand the concept "unwise" itself in terms of the salient (because similar) features of these objects. On the present account, accordingly, one interprets the meaning of a concept use by seeing it as carrying on the normative trajectory implicit in a series of precedent uses, though it is important to note that, unless something goes wrong, this "seeing as" is usually implicit in one's interpretation of a concept use rather than explicit (as if one interpreted every concept use by actually rehearsing a series of precedents).

Two key elements of meaning thus emerge. First, in view of the examples just considered, it should be evident that one interprets a concept use by seeing it as applied in *circumstances* relevantly similar to those of precedent applications. To interpret a concept use, that is, one must understand it as implicitly asserting a likeness between the object to which it is being applied and others to which it has been applied: so one must understand the paint to which "red" is applied as relevantly similar to other red objects and the deregulation to which "unwise" is applied as relevantly similar to other unwise circumstances. The meaning of a concept-use, accordingly, includes its circumstances of application (as these are seen as similar to the circumstances of precedent uses). And, in some cases, to understand a concept's proper circumstances of application (or "assertibility conditions," as these are sometimes called) is by itself sufficient to understand its meaning, as when my wife tells me she painted the bathroom red; to know what her use of the concept "red" means in this case just is to know the sense in which the paint is relevantly similar to other red objects.[4]

There are many cases, however, where something further must be understood, as when, for instance, one applies the concept "red" to a traffic signal rather than to a bathroom's walls. To understand

---

[4] Philosophers such as Timothy Williamson have thus argued, against inferentialism, that there is a fundamental asymmetry between circumstances and consequences of concept application, for which see his "Reference, Inference, and the Semantics of Pejoratives," in *The Philosophy of David Kaplan*, J. Almog and P. Leonardi (eds.) (Oxford University Press, 2009), pp. 137–58.

what the concept means in these circumstances, one must, again, see the traffic signal as relevantly similar to other objects to which the concept has been applied, but one must also have a sense of the *consequences* of its application, namely, that one should hit the brakes. Likewise, consider the concept "strike" in baseball: to know what its application to a particular pitch means, one must understand the pitch as relevantly similar to precedent pitches to which the concept has been applied (namely, those which flew through a certain area over home plate) and as implying certain consequences (e.g., that three "strikes" in one at-bat entails an "out"). For the sake of theoretical unity, we can understand these consequences themselves in terms of the application circumstances of still other concepts, since a concept's use contributes to circumstances in which (a) one may be *obligated* to apply further concepts (one's application of the concept "excellent" to an essay may establish circumstances in which one is also obligated to apply the grade-concept "A"); (b) one may be *entitled* to apply further concepts though not obligated to do so (one's judgment that a certain object is food entails that one could eat it, but not that one must); and (c) one may be *obligated not* to apply certain further concepts and so not entitled to do so (application of the concept "language user" to a person means that one is obligated not to apply the concept "massively irrational").

So then: if the meaning of a concept use is a product of the normative trajectory implicit in a series of precedent uses as that trajectory eventuates in this use, two elements of meaning emerge: first, a candidate use implicitly asserts some likeness between that to which a concept is being applied and that to which it has been applied, and second, one's use of a concept entails relevantly similar consequences for the application of further concepts. The account of meaning that emerges could accordingly be seen as a variety of conceptual role or inferentialist semantics, though, with a view to certain objections to which such approaches have been thought liable, it is important to note that the present account embeds this semantics within a normative-pragmatic explanation of concept use, and explains this pragmatics, in turn, by appeal to intersubjective recognition.

To see why this embedding is important, and to clarify the account further, consider an obvious question: how does one determine which precedents *count*? This question is related to an objection commonly raised against accounts of this sort, namely, that they are unable to explain the possibility of communication, since, if (a) interpersonal communication depends upon shared meaning, and (b) the meaning of a concept use is supposed to depend upon a claimed likeness to certain precedent uses, then (c) it would appear that interpersonal communication is impossible, since no two persons share precisely the same set of precedents.[5] Moreover, if one knows the meaning of a concept only if one knows the inferential relations in which it stands, it would appear that one must either know *all* of these relations, in which case one would have to be omniscient in order to know the meaning of any given concept, or else one must be able to determine which of these relations are supposed to count. Assuming the absurdity of the former, it would appear that an account of the sort defended here had better be able to offer a non-question-begging explanation of the latter – yet the very attempt to do so has commonly been thought to require a return to the much-maligned analytic–synthetic distinction.[6] So then: how does one determine which precedents are relevant to the meaning

---

[5] As Jerry Fodor and Ernie Lepore put the point, "How can we use the form of words 'It's raining' to communicate to you our belief that it's raining unless the word 'raining' means the same to all of us? And, how can it mean the same to all of us if, on the one hand, its meaning is determined by its inferential role and, on the other hand, no two people could conceivably agree on all the inferences in which 'raining' occurs … ?" (Fodor and Lepore, "Brandom Beleaguered," *Philosophy and Phenomenological Research* 74:3 [2007], pp. 684–5).

[6] Fodor and Lepore, "Brandom Beleaguered," p. 689. For a more extensive response to this charge (from the point of view of conceptual-role semantics), see Ned Block, "Holism, Hyper-analyticity and Hyper-compositionality," *Mind and Language* 8:1 (1993), pp. 1–27, and Michael Devitt, *Coming to Our Senses: A Naturalistic Program for Semantic Localism* (Cambridge University Press, 1995).

of a concept use? Recall that, on the present account, one intends to use a particular concept by trying to go on in the same way as precedent uses whose propriety one recognizes, which seems to suggest that what counts as a precedent is simply a matter of what is recognized as such. However, although it stands to reason that the series of precedents picked out by two persons may differ significantly, this does not entail that they are entirely unconstrained in their determination of what counts as such, for the simple reason that, insofar as they intend their use of concepts to be recognizable as "what we do," and recognize the other person as one of "us" – insofar as they intend to communicate with someone, in other words – they must be able to establish substantial overlap between what each would count as a correct use. Hence, as Wittgenstein remarks, "it is of the greatest importance that all of us, or the vast majority, agree in certain things … It is of the greatest importance that a conflict hardly ever arises between persons about whether the color of this object is the same as the color of that; the length of this stick the same as the length of that, etc."[7] Theoretically, then, someone could specify the relevant precedents however he or she chooses, irrespective of their convergence with the set of precedents recognized by others, though only at the cost of being unable to communicate with them and rendering him- or herself unrecognizable as a user of the particular concept.[8]

---

[7] Wittgenstein, *Bemerkungen über die Grundlagen der Mathematik*, Schriften, vol. VI, G. E. M. Anscombe, Rush Rhees, and G. H. von Wright (eds.) (Frankfurt am Main: Suhrkamp Verlag, 1974), VI.39 and 21, pp. 342 and 323. Cf. also Wittgenstein's colorful example of the timber sellers at I.149–50, p. 94, as well as Kripke's important discussion at the culmination of *Wittgenstein on Rules and Private Language*, pp. 91–6.

[8] Thus Kripke: "One who is an incorrigible deviant in enough respects [discursively speaking] simply cannot participate in the life of the [discursive] community and in communication" (*Wittgenstein on Rules and Private Language*, p. 92). It is important to note, however, that this does not entail that one's use of concepts is wholly beholden to, and thus unable to criticize, the discursive status quo: as we will explain at length in Chapter 6, although the dominant class may "misrecognize" concept uses that criticize the power relations implicit in the discursive order, this misrecognition itself depending upon an implicit recognition of those uses – otherwise, there would be no reason to misrecognize them.

The model defended here thus explains the relevant precedents as a matter of ongoing interpersonal negotiation: one interprets another as using a particular concept by taking his or her performance to be carrying on a series of precedent uses of that concept (x, x'', x''', etc.), and one intends to use a particular concept by trying to carry on a series of precedent uses that one recognizes as such (y, y'', y''', etc.). In order to communicate with one another, two persons' lists of precedents need not actually overlap, but they must be able to agree on what would count as carrying on the normative trajectory implicit in each list, which is to say that the normative trajectories themselves must overlap considerably (especially in uncontroversial cases). Two persons could explicitly determine the extent to which this is the case by working out an ad hoc list of precedents that both could agree upon, though it is important to note that, in practice, one almost never has to do so – in practice, we tend to agree, in the vast majority of cases, about what normative trajectory a candidate performance would carry on.

On the present account, then, to use a concept is to try to go on in the same way as precedent uses, such that the meaning of a concept use is a product of the normative trajectory implicit in a series of such precedents as that trajectory eventuates in the candidate use. Several important consequences follow from this. First, since one intends to use a concept by trying to go on in the same way as precedent uses that one recognizes as such, and since a candidate use, if recognized as going on in the same way, contributes to the series of precedents in view of which others might try to use the concept, it follows that the meaning of a concept changes, if only slightly, every time it is used. Hence, if the meaning of a concept use is specified in terms of its being applied in ways that carry on a series of precedents, and if we are constantly negotiating both what counts as a relevant precedent and what counts as carrying on the normative trajectory implicit in a given series, it follows that the meaning of a concept use – one's own or that of others – cannot be fixed in advance, since such meaning is the product of an ongoing practice of recognition.[9] This leads to a second implication: if the meaning of a concept use is a product of an ever-changing series of precedents, it follows that its meaning should not (or at least need not) be thought of as its correspondence to an essence-like "meaning" – and yet, so long as we understand meaning as precipitating out of our *use* of concepts, we need not think that the loss of such meanings entails a loss of meaning. We will return to both of these points in the following subsection.

2

This account can be further clarified (and justified) by considering the meaning of a particular discursive phenomenon, namely metaphor. Metaphor is worthy of further attention for two reasons: first, as we shall see, there is reason to think that something like metaphor is pervasive in everyday language, such that an account of the meaning of metaphor would have implications for an account of meaning per se. And second, metaphor provides an instance in which meaning-making practices step into the light of day, such that its consideration renders possible a kind of phenomenology of meaning. That is to say, by contrast with a statement such as "that barn is red," whose meaning one grasps without having to think about it, one's interpretation of a live metaphor such as "Jesus is a migrant worker" may require one to stop and think, and may, accordingly, provide some insight into the workings of ordinary, unreflective interpretation.

In order to account for the meaning of metaphor, we have to begin with a brief consideration of some relatively inadequate attempts to do so. We begin with the infamous "substitution theory," which understands metaphor as a flowery way of saying something that could just as well be expressed non-metaphorically; on this view, a

---

[9] On this point, see especially Robert B. Brandom, "Vocabularies of Pragmatism: Synthesizing Naturalism and Historicism," in *Rorty and His Critics*, Robert B. Brandom (ed.) (Oxford: Blackwell, 2000).

metaphorical statement such as "Richard is a lion" means, simply, that Richard is courageous. This account, often taken to be the classical view, is unanimously rejected by contemporary theorists of metaphor.[10] Their key objection is that although some tired metaphors may be susceptible to such literal substitution – metaphors such as "it's raining cats and dogs," and "she's a diamond in the rough" – there are a great many others, including almost all of the interesting ones, for which such substitution will not suffice. Suppose someone refers to a presidential candidate as "a haunted tree," or talks about metaphor as "the dreamwork of language"; what one-for-one literal substitute is supposed to be "the meaning" of these metaphors?[11] According to the vast majority of metaphor theorists, the answer is none, particularly since metaphors open up new ways of seeing things. (More on this in a moment.) It would thus appear that the substitution view is inadequate as an explanation of the meaning of metaphors.

The perceived inadequacy of the substitution view has led some philosophers to defend what could be called a "comparison" or "elliptical simile" account of metaphor.[12] According to this view, the

---

[10] This view is commonly attributed to Aristotle on the basis of *Poetics* 1458a, although Janet Martin Soskice provides compelling reason to attribute this view not to Aristotle, but to modern-day empiricists such as Locke; for this, see Soskice, *Metaphor and Religious Language* (New York: Oxford University Press, 1985), pp. 1–14. For the attribution of this view to Aristotle, see Max Black, "More about Metaphor," *Metaphor and Thought*, Andrew Ortony (ed.) (New York: Cambridge University Press, 1979, 1993), p. 22; Mary B. Hesse, *The Construction of Reality* (New York: Cambridge University Press, 1986), pp. 150–61; Eberhard Jüngel, "Metaphorical Truth: Reflections on the Theological Relevance of Metaphor as a Contribution to the Hermeneutics of Narrative Theology," *Theological Essays* I, J. B. Webster (ed.) (Edinburgh: T&T Clark, 1989), pp. 33–48; and Paul Ricoeur, *Interpretation Theory: Discourse and the Surplus of Meaning* (Fort Worth, TX: Texas Christian University Press, 1976), pp. 46–9.

[11] The former is taken from Charlie Brooker, "Dumb Show," *The Guardian*, October 23, 2004; the latter from Donald Davidson, "What Metaphors Mean," *Inquiries into Truth and Interpretation*, second edn. (New York: Oxford University Press, 1984, 2001), p. 245.

[12] For a contemporary example of this approach, see John R. Searle, "Metaphor," in *Expression and Meaning: Studies in the Theory of Speech Acts* (New York: Cambridge University Press, 1979), pp. 76–116.

meaning of a metaphor can be analyzed in roughly the following terms: when someone makes a metaphorical statement of the form "*A is b*," he or she means "*A is like b*."[13] Hence, given a statement such as "private property is theft," the comparison theorist would render the statement's meaning as "private property is *like* theft (in *x*, *y*, and *z* respects)." A metaphor works, on this view, by getting us to see one thing in terms of another, thereby shedding some light on the object of the comparison. In the majority of cases, metaphors could then rather easily be paraphrased in literal, non-metaphorical terms: the metaphor simply says that something is like something else. As with the substitution view, however, the comparison view has come under heavy criticism. One of the obvious criticisms is that whereas most metaphors appear to be literally false, on the comparison view, they all turn out to be trivially true. A second, more serious objection is that the comparison view does not explain anything about how a metaphor works – or that, if it does, it thereby renders metaphor pointless. That is to say, if the comparison view claims that metaphors work by suggesting that something is like something else, this tells us nothing about the meaning of the metaphor, since everything is like everything else in innumerable respects.[14] On the other hand, if, in order to avoid such vacuity, the comparison theorist were to specify the precise respect in which a thing is like something else – "Richard is a lion" means "Richard is like a lion in respect of his courage" – it would appear that he or she has returned to a version of the substitution view, along with its problems.

We turn, then, to a more popular approach to metaphor, namely, the "interactionist" view.[15] This approach understands metaphor as a

---

[13] Janet Martin Soskice is right to point out that metaphors need not, and often do not, come in the form of predicative statements, but for reasons noted in Chapter 1, I will focus here only on such forms.

[14] For such an objection, see Davidson, "What Metaphors Mean," p. 254, and Max Black, "Metaphor," *Models and Metaphors: Studies in Language and Philosophy* (Ithaca, NY: Cornell University Press, 1962), p. 37.

[15] For defenses of this view, see Black, "Metaphor" and "More about Metaphor" as well as Mary Hesse, "The Cognitive Claims of Metaphor," *Metaphor and Religion,*

sort of filter through which one sees an object, and understands this filtering in terms of an "implicative complex."[16] The idea here is that when one says something such as "the mind is a computer," "computer" functions as a lens through which one sees "mind." According to this view, one tends to associate certain ideas with "computer" and with "mind," so that when one is told "the mind is a computer," one uses the ideas associated with the latter to organize or select from the ideas associated with the former. Hence, if one associates the having of hardware and software with a computer, or the idea of going to power-saver mode after a period of inactivity, one might try to understand the mind as having hardware and software, too, or of going to power-saver mode. One does so, on this account, by identifying certain ideas associated with one object as in some respect isomorphic with ideas associated with another, thereby discovering structural correspondences between the two.[17] Moreover, as a result of seeing an object in terms of ideas one associates with something else, one sees the latter object, too, in a new light: one may see structures one had not previously recognized, new ways of relating the object to other things, and so forth. On this account, then, metaphor is irreducible to a paraphrase or even a comparison, for two reasons: first, there is no end to the number of insights that may be opened up by a new way of seeing an object, and second, the use of a metaphor changes the way one sees both the object and whatever lens one sees it through, such that there is no going back to earlier understandings which might then be compared with one another.[18] Proponents of this view thus claim to have provided a more adequate explanation of how metaphor works.

J. P. van Noppen (ed.) (Brussels: Vrije Universiteit Brussel, 1983), pp. 27–45, and *The Construction of Reality*, pp. 156–7; and Sallie McFague, *Metaphorical Theology: Models of God in Religious Language* (Philadelphia: Fortress Press, 1982), pp. 23–4, 37–8.

[16] See Black, "Metaphor," pp. 39–41, and "More about Metaphor," pp. 28–30.

[17] Black, "More about Metaphor," pp. 28–30.

[18] Hesse, "Cognitive Claims," pp. 31–2.

As with the other views, however, this one, too, has been thought liable to some objections, the most important of which has to do with the relationship between a statement's literal and metaphorical meanings. According to a common understanding of the interaction theory, the metaphorical meaning of a statement is distinct from its literal meaning, since a statement such as "the mind is a computer," taken literally, means that the mind is a computer, whereas its metaphorical meaning lies in seeing the mind in light of one's ideas about computers. It would appear, then, that metaphorical statements have not one but two meanings, and it is the latter that counts. This leads to a problem, however: how, one might ask, is the literal meaning related to the metaphorical? The most obvious answer is, roughly, that the literal meaning seems either too absurd or too obvious to be what a speaker really means, which leads one to search for other ways understand the utterance. This raises an obvious question: if this is the way the two meanings are related, why locate the latter meaning in the statement itself? It would appear, on the contrary, that the latter meaning is not in the statement at all, but emerges from one's attempt to deal with the absurd/trivial meaning which *is* in the statement.[19] And if this is the case, it makes little sense to talk of *two* meanings; it makes more sense to talk of one meaning – the literal – and the way one copes with that meaning's apparent absurdity. According to this objection, then, interaction theorists have illicitly tried to explain metaphor by simply reading one's (subjective) response into the (objective) meaning of the words themselves; to say that metaphorical statements work in virtue of having a

[19] This is the argument made by Davidson, "What Metaphors Mean"; Nancy K. Frankenberry, "On the Very Idea of Symbolic Meaning," in *Interpreting Neville*, J. Harley Chapman and Nancy K. Frankenberry (eds.) (New York: State University of New York, 1999), pp. 93–110, and "Religion as a 'Mobile Army of Metaphors,'" *Radical Interpretation in Religion*, Nancy K. Frankenberry (ed.) (New York: Cambridge University Press, 2002), pp. 171–87; and Richard Rorty, "Unfamiliar Noises: Hesse and Davidson on Metaphor," *Objectivity, Relativism, and Truth*, Philosophical Papers, vol. I, (New York: Cambridge University Press, 1991), pp. 162–72.

meaning over and above their literal meaning would thus be akin to saying that sleeping pills work in virtue of their dormitive powers.

It is not clear whether this critique hits its mark – I am inclined to say that it does not[20] – but for present purposes, we can set the critique itself to one side in order to focus on a more fundamental issue raised by it, namely, the extent to which a particular picture of meaning, shared by all three candidate accounts, makes metaphorical meaning seem second-rate, superfluous, and so on. This emerges most clearly into view in the substitution model, where a statement's literal meaning is its *only* meaning, such that metaphor is demoted to the status of decoration. We see something similar, though, in the comparison view, where the meaning of a metaphorical statement is understood, again, as its literal meaning, and even in (the criticized version of) the interaction view, where the metaphorical meaning of a statement is still thought of as something added onto its literal meaning.[21] This raises the suspicion that these theories are held captive by a picture according to which the meaning of a statement is its correspondence to a more or less fixed, literal meaning, such that metaphorical meaning could be, at best, something added onto it, or, at worst, something deviant, second-rate, or decorative. Turning this suspicion into a respectable assertion would require substantially more elaboration than I can offer here, but I can at least lend it some plausibility by considering how matters would appear if one were to explain metaphor in terms of an account that did without such a picture.

---

[20] Mary Hesse, for instance, is clearly innocent of this charge, claiming as she does that "the extensions of meaning that occur by means of similarities and differences in metaphor are only the more striking examples of something that is going on all the time in the changing and holistic network that constitutes language. In this sense metaphoric meaning is normal, not pathological, and some of the mechanism of metaphor is essential to the meaning of any descriptive language at all" ("Cognitive Claims of Metaphor," pp. 28–9).

[21] Max Black and Paul Ricoeur have both been criticized – by Davidson and Frankenberry – for holding such a view.

To see what this would look like, recall two features of our account of concept use: first, that to use a concept is to (try to) go on in the same way as precedent uses, and second, that to understand the meaning of a concept use is to see it as carrying on the normative trajectory implicit in a series of precedent uses, especially with respect to the circumstances and consequences of such uses. This account can be used to shed some light on the meaning of metaphors. To begin with, consider the way one learns a concept: a learner makes a certain noise, say, "shepherd," in certain circumstances, and if this noise matches the noises a teacher would make in those circumstances, he or she will approve of them. In order for such teaching to work, the teacher must know that the learner is responding to the same thing the teacher is. At any given moment, however, there are innumerable environmental features to which each might be responding, so how does the teacher know that the learner is responding to the *right* feature? How, in other words, do certain features count as *salient*? There may be several ways to account for the relevant similarity, but each depends upon the learner identifying a pattern in the responses that he or she shares with the teacher: so the learner may first associate "shepherd" with the shepherd and everything else in a set of circumstances, but then notice that the teacher uses the same word in different shepherd-involving circumstances (and that the teacher corrects the learner if he or she utters "shepherd" in shepherd-less circumstances), such that the learner narrows the relevant circumstance down to the shepherd him- or herself; or perhaps the learner has been initiated into the practice of pointing-and-naming, so that it will do the trick if the teacher simply points to a couple of shepherds while saying "shepherd." The point is that in order to make the *right* association, the learner has to be able to identify the environmental features to which his or her teacher is responding. So then: the learner responds to his or her environment and watches the teacher's responses; the teacher responds to his or her environment and watches how the learner responds.[22] In this way, one learns to identify the circumstances relevant to a particular response: one learns to associate certain words with certain salient features of the environment, and one learns to identify such features through correlating one's responses with a teacher's. One likewise learns what follows from a concept's use: if the object is a shepherd, it follows that it would normally be in charge of a flock of sheep, would try to protect them (from wolves, say), would provide them with food and shelter, etc. One thus learns to associate certain concepts with certain circumstances, and one learns what usually follows when the concept is applied in those circumstances. When one subsequently uses this concept (or interprets others' use of it), one tries to go on in the same way as these precedents, from which it follows that the meaning of such a use is a product of these precedents (as they eventuate in that use).

Before applying this account to metaphor, one further feature needs to be reiterated: while it is certainly true that different persons use concepts differently, and while it is also true that persons sometimes use them incorrectly, in order for one to be able to make any sense of another's utterances, one must take these utterances to be correct in the vast majority of instances – which is to say that one must understand them as going on in the way one would in the vast majority of instances. If one took others to be wildly incorrect, one would have no reason for taking it that one was interpreting their utterances correctly, nor any reason to think that they were in fact speaking *in*correctly. To see why this would be the case, imagine that I am listening to someone and I interpret most of his or her concept uses as mistaken. If so, then I am taking it that his or her concept use does not at all go on in the same way as my usage – but if this is the

[22] Here I am following Donald Davidon's approach to "salience," for which see the essays in *Subjective, Intersubjective, Objective*, especially "The Irreducibility of the Concept of the Self," "The Emergence of Thought," "Epistemology Externalized," "The Myth of the Subjective," "Rational Animals," "The Second Person," and "Three Varieties of Knowledge," as well as "Truth Rehabilitated," in *Truth, Language, and History*.

case, what would entitle me to think that the person is trying to use the concept I have in mind? I can take a person to be using a concept *erroneously* only if I have some reason to take him or her as trying to apply the concept I have in mind, but I can take him or her as so trying only if his or her usage would agree to a considerable extent with mine. I will say more about this in a moment; for now, the point is simply that the very possibility of interpreting another's utterances depends upon one's taking them to be correct in the vast majority of concept applications.[23]

On this account, then, if one hears someone say "Mary is a shepherd," one interprets the application of the concept "shepherd" by seeing it as going on in the same way as precedent applications. If the concept has been applied to persons who watch over flocks of sheep, and if its application has entailed that sheep follow the person to whom the concept has been applied, that this person protects the sheep from dangers (such as wolves), and so on, then one will interpret the statement "Mary is a shepherd" to mean that Mary watches over a flock of sheep, that the sheep follow her, and that she protects them from dangers. Hence, by seeing the speaker's concept use as going on in the same way as precedent uses, one can interpret what he or she is saying. Now consider what happens if one hears a person say "The Lord is my shepherd." Given that interpretation depends upon taking others to be using concepts in the same way as precedent uses, it follows that one must try to see this statement, too, as going on in the same way as the relevant precedents. In this instance, then, in order to interpret "The Lord is my shepherd," one will (try to) see "the Lord" as relevantly similar to others to whom the concept "shepherd" has been applied; one will try, in other words, to understand "the Lord" as one who watches

---

[23] This is Donald Davidson's "Principle of Charity": Davidson argues that "if we cannot find a way to interpret the utterances and other behavior of a creature as revealing a set of beliefs largely consistent and true by our own standards, we have no reason to count that creature as rational, as having beliefs, or as saying anything" ("Radical Interpretation," *Inquiries into Truth and Interpretation*, p. 137).

over a flock of sheep, who protects the sheep from danger, whom the sheep follow, etc., and in order to take it that the speaker is correct, one will likely understand the sheep in question as a person whom the Lord watches over, who is protected by and follows the Lord, and so on. When someone makes such a statement, accordingly, one copes with it in the same way one copes with any other concept application, namely, by seeing it as going on in the same way as precedent applications. Hence, whereas some accounts of metaphor posit a special metaphorical meaning over and above a statement's literal meaning, the present account maintains that one makes sense of metaphor in precisely the same way one makes sense of any statement, which entails that there is no reason to look for an additional meaning. This is not, to be sure, because the statement itself has only a literal meaning, such that the metaphorical meaning lies outside the statement (in one's reaction to it); the point, rather, is that one arrives at the meaning of a statement in the same way whether it is literal or metaphorical, and whatever meaning one arrives at in this way *is* the statement's meaning.[24] On the account offered here, that is, it is not as if one first assigns a literal meaning to a statement, decides that this cannot be what the speaker had in mind, and then casts about for some other way of making sense of it. No: whether someone says "Dolly is a sheep" or "We are God's sheep," one copes

---

[24] This position thus diverges from Davidson *and* Black. Davidson argues that "we must give up the idea that a metaphor carries a message, that it has a content or meaning (except, of course, its literal meaning). The various theories we have been considering mistake their goal. Where they think they provide a method for deciphering an encoded content, they actually tell us (or try to tell us) something about the *effects* metaphors have on us. The common error is to fasten on the contents of the thoughts a metaphor provokes and to read these contents into the metaphor itself" ("What Metaphors Mean," p. 261), whereas Black claims that "Davidson seems fixated on the explanatory power of the standard sense, but when such an explanation is plainly defective, there can be no objection in principle to invoking what the speaker means when speaking metaphorically" ("How Metaphors Work: A Reply to Donald Davidson," *On Metaphor*, Sheldon Sacks [ed.] [Chicago: University of Chicago Press, 1978], p. 191).

with their statements by taking them as going on in the same way as precedent concept uses, which is to say that one sees their concept application as following from features similar to those to which the concept has been applied and as implying consequences similar to those implied by precedent applications. The application will not be exactly the same as precedent applications, and one will not infer all of the application's consequences, but knowing how to deal with such dissimilarities is indispensable to one's interpretation of *any* statement. There is, accordingly, no problem of trying to connect a literal and a metaphorical sense, nor any danger of seeing the latter as second-rate, deviant, etc.

With this account of metaphor in view, we can return to the claims with which this subsection began. First, there is reason to think that something relevantly similar to metaphor is pervasive in ordinary language use, such that this account could be generalized. To see why this would be the case, consider Noam Chomsky's remarkable observation that the majority of sentences uttered in an average day have never before been uttered, from which it follows (a) that novelty is the rule in language use rather than the exception, and (b) that the interpretability of such sentences likely depends upon a set of abilities similar to those employed in the interpretation of metaphor.[25] Mary Hesse's conclusion thus seems reasonable: "The extensions of meaning that occur by means of similarities and differences in metaphor," she argues, "are only the more striking examples of something going on all the time in the changing and holistic semantic network that constitutes language."[26] This being the case, the preceding account of metaphor entails two consequences for a *general* account of meaning,

---

[25] On this point, see Chomsky, *Aspects of the Theory of Syntax* (Cambridge, MA: MIT Press, 1965), as well as Donald Davidson's claim that we each have our own "list of proper names, with their uniquely contextualized references, our private endearments and verbal twists, our own mispronunciations and malapropisms" ("Seeing Through Language," *Truth, Language, and History*, p. 128).

[26] Hesse, *The Construction of Reality*, p. 151.

each of which can be summarized with reference to the work of Donald Davidson. The first, that which Davidson calls "The Principle of Charity," is at every step a necessary ingredient of interpretation. Here it is important to recall that, on the account defended here, one's use of a concept implicitly petitions others to recognize that use as carrying on a trajectory of precedent uses, which means that if an interpreter is committed to interpreting another's utterances as would-be concept uses, he or she must understand them as trying to carry on such a trajectory. This is especially the case because, second, one's interpretation of another's utterances is a matter of reaching a passing convergence rather than of identifying some sort of meaning essence to which those utterances correspond. So, in his groundbreaking essay "A Nice Derangement of Epitaphs," Davidson claims that sharing a set of "meanings" is neither necessary nor sufficient to explain one's ability to interpret the utterances of others, which leads him to argue that one interprets another's marks and noises by continually arriving at, and continually revising, a "passing theory" of the relationship between the latter's utterances and that which one recognizes as precedential.[27] One never arrives at a "final" theory by which to interpret others, accordingly, not least because one's ad hoc or "passing" theories change every time one completes a successful speech transaction: one's ad hoc theory "includes every successful – i.e. correctly interpreted – use of any other word or phrase, no matter how far out of the ordinary," which means that "we must give up the idea of a clearly defined shared structure which language users acquire and then apply to cases."[28] We will return to these claims in the following chapter – where they turn out to have important consequences for the

[27] Thus Davidson: "An interpreter has, at any moment of a speech transaction, what I persist in calling a theory ... As the speaker speaks his piece the interpreter alters his theory, entering hypotheses about new names, altering the interpretation of familiar predicates, and revising past interpretations of particular utterances in the light of new evidence" ("A Nice Derangement of Epitaphs," *Truth, Language, and History*, p. 100).

[28] "Nice Derangement," pp. 102, 107.

very idea of language standing between us and objects – but for now, the relevant consequence is that if (a) the meaning of a candidate concept use is determined by its relationship to certain precedents, (b) the trajectory implicit in a series of precedents changes every time a novel use is recognized as carrying it on, and (c) such novelty is the rule rather than the exception, it follows (d) that the meaning of a concept is continually changing, and (e) that we need not – and probably should not – understand the production and consumption of meaning by appeal to fixed, extra-discursive *tertia* such as "the literal meaning" to which one's words are supposed to correspond.

On the present account, then, the meaning of a concept use is a product of its relationship to a series of precedents, from which it follows that its meaning is not a matter of its correspondence to an essence-like "meaning." This should not be thought to entail, however, that one is out of touch with what a concept really means, nor that one may be systematically mistaken about the meaning of another's concept use – or, better, this account would so much as *appear* to entail such things only to the extent that one is held captive by an essentialist-correspondentist picture of meaning and "being in touch." To be sure, there may be times when one is mistaken about the meaning of a particular concept – I systematically confused the concepts "pink" and "yellow" when I was a child – but if we do without the essentialist-correspondentist picture and understand meaning, instead, in terms of a series of precedents upon which we passingly converge, then such mistakes can be explained in terms of one's divergence from ordinary usage (rather than one's failure to correspond with an extra-discursive *tertium*) and, all things considered, these mistakes must be the rare exception rather than the rule.

***

The picture of meaning that emerges looks something like this: (a) to use a concept is to try to carry on the normative trajectory implicit in a series of precedents, (b) the meaning of a particular use is a product of its relation to precedent uses, particularly the circumstances and consequences of those uses, and (c) the trajectory in a series of precedents changes, if only slightly, every time a new use carries it on, and because such novelty is pervasive, it follows that a concept's meaning, too, is continually changing. Since the meaning of a concept is thus the product of an ongoing negotiation, it follows that it is neither fixed in advance nor to be explained in terms of a "meaning" other than that which arises out of our use of it. As we shall see, these implications play a crucial role in explaining how concepts could be fit for theological use.

The meaning of theological concepts

With this account of conceptual content on board, we can now return to some of the problems raised at the beginning of the previous chapter. Those problems, recall, have to do with the application of ordinary concepts to God: on the one hand, the very nature of concepts is thought to render them unfit for application to God, since, it is argued, they contain whatever they are applied to, whereas God is uncontainable; and on the other, their meaning, too, is thought to render them unfit for theological application, since this meaning is supposedly fixed by their application to creatures. The previous chapter laid the groundwork for dealing with the former problem, though a fully adequate response depends upon a solution to the latter. This section outlines such a solution. And just as the argument of the previous chapter was anchored in a reading of Friedrich Schleiermacher's pneumatology, so the argument of this chapter will be anchored in a reading of Karl Barth's theology of meaning.[29]

---

[29] Barth is hardly alone, of course, in recommending an account of theological meaning in terms of analogy; for relevantly similar approaches (which could likewise be embedded in the present account), see Roger White, "Notes on Analogical Predication and Speaking about God," *Philosophical Frontiers of Christian Theology*, B. Hebblethwaite and S. Sutherland (eds.) (Cambridge University Press, 1982); James F. Ross, *Portraying Analogy* (New York: Cambridge University Press, 1981);

1

As is well known, Barth is absolutely insistent that God should not be thought to conform to our ideas of God, because a "God" so conformed becomes a way of underwriting our projects, of paying ourselves metaphysical compliments, and so on. This insistence leads Barth to worry, in turn, about the application of concepts to God, since such application seems, in the nature of the case, to cut God down to the size of human categories; Barth thus claims, for instance, that "that which is regarded as one in a series of objects would not be God," from which he concludes that "God does not belong among the objects that we can ever subject to the process of our intuition, conception, and expression, and so to our mental oversight and control."[30] Barth's concern, simply stated, is that if our concepts are thought to correspond to God's fundamental reality, then God will be thought to fit within our categories and ideas – God will be thought, in other words, as "God." Barth concludes, therefore, that "the images in which we intuit God, the thoughts with which we think God, the words with which we define God, are in themselves unfit for this object and thus in themselves unsuited to express and to establish this knowledge, because God – the living

Wolfhart Pannenberg, "Analogy and Doxology," *Basic Questions in Theology*, vol. I, trans. George H. Kehm (Philadelphia: Fortress Press, 1970); E. L. Mascall, *Words and Images: A Study in Theological Discourse* (New York: The Ronald Press, 1957); Richard Swinburne, *Revelation: From Metaphor to Analogy* (Oxford University Press, 1992, 2007); and Ralph McInerny, *Aquinas and Analogy* (Washington, DC: Catholic University of America Press, 1996). Current accounts of analogy tend to center on its "ontological" aspects, for which see John Milbank, *Theology and Social Theory: Beyond Secular Reason* (Oxford: Blackwell, 1990, 2006); David Bentley Hart, *The Beauty of the Infinite: The Aesthetics of Christian Truth* (Grand Rapids: Eerdmans, 2003); and John R. Betz, "Beyond the Sublime: The Aesthetics of the Analogy of Being," two parts, *Modern Theology* 21:3 (2005), pp. 367–411, and 22:1 (2006), pp. 1–50. Though such accounts are typically explicitly contrasted with Barth's, it should be evident that the present reading brings Barth within hailing distance of them.

[30] Karl Barth, *Die Kirchliche Dogmatik*, vol. II, *Die Lehre von Gott*, part 1 (Zollikon-Zürich: Evangelischer Verlag A. G., 1940), pp. 14 and 209. (Hereafter KD II/1).

God who encounters us in Jesus Christ – is not such a one as we can appropriate of ourselves."[31] In and of themselves, then, human words and concepts have no capacity for application to God, since God cannot be fit within the totality of creaturely objects and ideas.

This does not entail, however, that concepts cannot be applied to God; it entails, rather, that such application depends utterly upon God's grace. "What we cannot do *of* ourselves," Barth writes, "God can do *through* us. If our intuitions, concepts, and words are in themselves too confined to grasp God, it does not follow that a limit is thereby set for God, as if it were impossible for God to take up a dwelling within these confines."[32] Barth thus claims that the appropriateness of theological concept use depends upon God's act of "*raising* our words to this their proper use, *giving* Godself to be their proper object, and thus *giving* them their truth."[33] Barth explains this "raising" in two steps. He argues, first, that proper knowledge of and speech about God is an intra-triune affair: "first of all and at the heart of the truth in which we know God, God knows Godself: the Father the Son, the Son the Father, in the unity of the Holy Spirit."[34] To know God properly, then, is to participate in God's knowledge of Godself – that is, in the Son's knowledge of the Father. Such participation is possible, according to Barth, because (a) in the incarnation of the Son, a creature has been taken up into God's self-knowledge, and (b) through the outpouring of the Spirit, this creature's taking-up is imparted to others; in this way, "in Godself an event takes place, which is copied, so to speak, in the revelation in which the human person takes part."[35] Insofar as creaturely concepts are thus taken up into God's own self-knowledge, accordingly, they can apply properly to God.

Barth then explains this taking-up in sacramental terms: such taking-up occurs, he claims, "in such a way that God elevates and distinguishes a particular creaturely subject–object relationship

[31] Barth, KD II/1, p. 239.   [32] Barth, KD II/1, p. 239.   [33] Barth, KD II/1, p. 260.
[34] Barth, KD II/1, p. 52.   [35] Barth, KD II/1, p. 54.

(here, a concept application) to be the instrument of the covenant between God, the creator, and the human person as God's creature. God brings about the knowledge of God in the framework of this sacramental actuality, not otherwise and not elsewhere."[36] In consequence of such elevation and selection, human persons, along with their concepts, are "*taken up* into this happening in the Highest, so that God is now the object not only of God's self-knowledge but *also* the object of *human knowing*."[37] To clarify what Barth has in mind here, we might usefully compare his view with Calvin's understanding of the Lord's Supper. Just as concepts cannot contain God, so neither, according to Calvin, can bread and wine contain Christ's body and blood, "as if the body of Christ, by a local presence, were put there to be touched by the hands, to be chewed by the teeth, and to be swallowed by the mouth."[38] While Calvin affirms that one does indeed feed on Christ's body and blood when one partakes of bread and wine, he rejects the idea that Christ could be contained in these elements, since Christ would then be subject to human handling, control, and so forth. The error of those who think that the former affirmation can be accounted for only in terms of such "containment," on Calvin's view, is that "they think they only communicate with [Christ's body] if it descends into bread; but they do not understand the manner of descent by which he lifts us up to himself."[39] Christ's body has ascended, according to Calvin, which means that if one is to feed upon it, one must be raised up to heaven by "the Spirit [who] truly unites things separated in space."[40] Calvin's understanding of the Supper thus maintains, on the one hand, that Christ's body and blood are not contained in the elements of bread and wine, while on the other, that by the power of the Holy Spirit,

---

[36] Barth, KD II/1, p. 60.   [37] Barth, KD II/1, p. 230.

[38] John Calvin, *Institutes of the Christian Religion*, trans. Ford Lewis Battles (Philadelphia: Westminster Press, 1960), IV.xvii.12, p. 1372.

[39] Calvin, *Institutes* IV.xvii.16, p. 1379.

[40] Calvin, *Institutes* IV.xvii.10, p. 1370.

God raises up one's partaking of bread and wine so that one in fact partakes of Christ's risen body and blood.[41] In much the same way, Barth claims that although God cannot be contained in human concepts, God nevertheless raises these concepts up and applies them to Godself. And because this application depends wholly upon God's elevation of certain concepts, it follows, crucially, that human concept users must take up a "standpoint of grace [which] is as such a standpoint of subsequence, which renders impossible any dominion over this object. Knowledge of God is thus not the relationship of an already available subject to an object that steps into its domain and is thereby subject to its laws."[42] In and of themselves, creaturely concepts have no capacity to be applied to God, which entails that such application depends wholly upon God's grace; this being the case, one's use of these concepts must be subsequent to God's appropriation of them and must cling to that appropriation, in consequence of which one can (and must) resist the temptation to equate God with one's preconceptions.

So far, it would appear, so good. It is at precisely this point, however, that a serious objection has been raised against Barth's view. The problem turns on Barth's claim that "our intuition, conception, and speech are placed in a *service* and put to a *use* for which they nevertheless have *no fitness* in themselves and as such," such that there seems to be no intrinsic relationship between our concepts *as ours* and as elevated by God.[43] The problem is this: if creaturely concepts have *no* fitness for application to God – if their meaning as applied to God is wholly discontinuous from their usual meaning – it seems to follow that one has no idea what one is talking about

---

[41] Ascribing such sacramental "realism" to Calvin is somewhat controversial, in spite of the fact that Calvin himself insists that "it would be extreme madness to recognize no communion of believers with the flesh and blood of the Lord … " (*Institutes* IV.xvii.9, p. 1370).

[42] Barth, KD II/1, p. 22.

[43] Barth, KD II/1, p. 218; cf. the discussion of an intrinsic vs. an extrinsic relationship at p. 239. For a thoughtful elaboration of this objection, see Jay Wesley Richards, "Barth on the Divine 'Conscription' of Language," *Heythrop Journal* 38:3 (1997), pp. 247–66.

when one talks about God. That is to say, if the concept "justice" means something completely different when God predicates it of Godself, then one's own application of it to God is either idolatrous or nonsense, as if one were mouthing words in a language one did not, and in principle could not, understand, since the very fact that one understands what one is saying would entail that it is not that which has been taken up by God. It would appear, then, that Barth's attempt to save us from idolatry has come at the cost of rendering theological language meaningless.[44]

This is obviously a serious objection. There is reason to think, however, that it rests upon a misunderstanding of Barth's claims about the fitness or capacity of concepts, as well as a misunderstanding of what it means for such concepts to be "taken up." That is, Barth's concern is not to deny continuity between ordinary concepts and their application to God, but to insist that such continuity is a matter of *grace*, and therefore that the continuity in question cannot be thought of as simply an extension of ordinary concept use, as though one could predict a concept's meaning as applied to God from its meaning as applied to ordinary objects, such that its ordinary meaning would decide in advance its meaning as applied to God. That Barth is willing to affirm *some* continuity, at any rate, is clear: he asserts, for instance, that when God applies human concepts to Godself, "it is not the case that our intuitions, concepts, and words are merely said to have a capacity, so that the use we make of them is still fenced in by the proviso of an 'as if' … It is again not the case that God does something unseemly in allowing and commanding us in revelation to make use of our intuitions, concepts, and words, because these intuitions, concepts, and words, now that they are applied to God, must be alienated from their proper and original sense and use."[45] Indeed, far from tearing them away from their ordinary usage and meaning, the use and meaning of ordinary

---

[44] For an example of a theologian who *does* hold this view, see Victor Preller, *Divine Science and the Science of God: A Reformulation of Thomas Aquinas* (Princeton, NJ: Princeton University Press, 1967).

[45] Barth, KD II/1, p. 257.

concepts are *fulfilled* by their application to God: God applies human concepts to Godself by "*elevating* our words to this their proper use," such that, from the standpoint of their application to God, one can see both their fitness for this application as well as the relative impropriety of other applications; Barth thus writes that, "looking back from divine revelation, we can now say that we use words improperly and figuratively when we apply them within the limits of what is suitable for the creature. When we apply them to God, by contrast, they are not alienated from but *restored* to their *original* object and therewith their truth."[46] It would appear, then, that for Barth there is a perspectival element in the putative continuity between ordinary concepts and their application to God: from the point of view of ordinary usage and meaning, concepts have no capacity for application to God, since one cannot project forward from ordinary usage in order to determine a concept's properly theological meaning; looking back from God's application of a concept to Godself, on the other hand, one can see the latter application as the fulfillment of the concept's ordinary use and meaning, such that, from this point of view, one can see both discontinuity *and* continuity between the two.[47]

2

We can explain Barth's position further in terms of the present proposal, two aspects of which are especially relevant. First, the previous chapter defended an account according to which the

---

[46] Barth, KD II/1, p. 259.

[47] This account of theological analogy thus avoids the standard criticisms leveled against such accounts, for which see, for instance, Kai Nielsen, "Talk of God and the Doctrine of Analogy," *The Thomist* 40 (1976), pp. 32–60; George I. Mavrodes, "On Ross's Theory of Analogy," *Journal of Philosophy* 67:20 (1970), pp. 747–55; Humphrey Palmer, *Analogy: A Study of Qualification of Argument in Theology* (New York: St. Martin's Press, 1973); Victor Preller, *Divine Science and the Science of God*; Robert W. Jenson, *The Knowledge of Things Hoped For: The Sense of Theological Discourse* (Oxford University Press, 1969); and David Burrell, *Analogy and Philosophical Language* (New Haven, CT: Yale University Press, 1973).

normative Spirit of Christ is mediated through a process of intersubjective recognition: by submitting one's beliefs and actions to
the judgments of those who are recognized as knowing how to follow Christ, one learns how to do so; a person is thus recognized
as following Christ if he or she knows how to go on in the same
way as others who have been recognized as knowing how, and a
belief or action counts as following Christ if it is recognizable as
going on in the same way as other beliefs and actions which have
been recognized as such. With respect to concept use, then, the
picture looks something like this: Jesus recognized certain claims
about God as correct and eventually recognized certain persons as
competent judges of such correctness; these persons recognized
certain claims as correct and eventually recognized certain persons, and so on. To count as using (Christian) theological concepts, then, one must implicitly try to carry on this chain, which
means subjecting one's concept use to precedent uses and seeking
this same precedential status for one's own use; in this way, one's
use of theological concepts simultaneously answers to, and carries
on, Christ's normative Spirit. As we shall see, Barth's notion of God
taking up concepts and applying them to Godself can be explained
in terms of this ongoing work of Christ's Spirit, since this Spirit
enters into certain discursive practices in order to conform human
concepts to God. Before turning to this explanation, however, we
need to reiterate some of our earlier claims about meaning, especially (a) that to use a concept is (implicitly) to seek precedential
status for one's use, which entails (b) that the meaning of such a use
is specified by the normative trajectory implicit in precedent uses
as fulfilled by the candidate use, from which it follows (c) that the
meaning of a concept changes, if only slightly, every time a novel
use is recognized as carrying on that trajectory. On this account, to
describe a particular circumstance as "just," for instance, such as a
proposed steepening of the graduated income tax, is to intend for
one's use of the concept to go on in the same way as precedent uses
(to describe, say, the organization of textile workers and the Civil

Rights Act of 1964), and thus to offer one's use as itself precedential for further uses. The meaning of "just" is a product of a series of such precedents, from which it follows that this meaning changes every time a use is recognized.

With these arguments in mind, we can now return to Barth's theology of meaning. Again, Barth claims that God applies ordinary concepts to Godself and that this application can be seen as the fulfillment of these concepts' ordinary usage and meaning. To understand how this might work, consider, first, the meaning of a concept as ordinarily applied. As uses of a concept such as "love" are recognized as correct, the concept's meaning is rendered determinate; hence, if the concept is applied to a parent's feeling for his child, a citizen's commitment to her country, a child's affection for her pet, and so on, and if these applications are recognized as correct, it follows that further applications of the concept will be recognizable as such only if they go on in the same way, and that these precedents thus contribute to the meaning of those applications. It is in view of this determinacy that some concepts can be recognized – retrospectively – as fit for application to God, while others cannot. That is to say, the application of certain concepts to God can be exhibited as the culmination of the normative trajectory implicit in their precedent applications, while not as the culmination of others; this explains why it would be appropriate to apply some concepts, such as "god," "love," and "covenant," to God, but not others, such as "purple," "demon," and "idol." Application to God goes on in the same way as some series of precedents, and not others. Note well, however, that a concept's fitness for application to God can be perceived only by looking back from that application, that is, in view of the candidate trajectory's retrospective recognizability as culminating in its theological application, and not prospectively, as if the concept's meaning as applied to God were something one could predict simply by projecting forward the meaning of the concept as it had been applied in the past. The latter cannot work, not only because the meaning of a concept is constantly changing, but because there is a crucial difference between what an ordinary concept, taken by itself, can say about God, and what a properly theological application of the concept can say. According to the present account, then, there is a sense in which a concept's application to God *fulfills* the normative trajectory implicit in precedent uses, and a sense in which it simultaneously *judges* those uses: in view of a concept's retrospectively-recognizable fitness for application to God, one can see the latter application as the culmination of precedent applications, yet precisely because the concept's theological use fulfills the trajectory implicit in other uses, it can likewise be seen to stand in judgment over them. Consider an analogy: suppose someone learns the concept "white" by applying it to variously whitish objects, and he or she then encounters something purely white. He or she recognizes the latter object *as* white insofar as it can be seen as relevantly similar to other objects to which the concept had been applied, such that the purely white object can be seen as the fulfillment of these applications, yet once the purely white object has been taken into account, it becomes apparent that the other objects to which the concept had been applied fall short of pure whiteness; indeed, set side by side with the purely white object, they may no longer appear very white at all. Something similar could be said of the relationship between the ordinary use of, say, "justice" and its meaning as applied to God: application of the concept to God can be seen as the fulfillment of precedent applications, yet it also provides the standard by which to judge the extent to which such applications measure up to true justice. (It hardly needs saying that an account of theological meaning ought to be able to explain this kind of judgment, yet it is not clear how such judgments could be explained on the supposition of utter discontinuity, since, if "justice" as applied to God means something completely different than in ordinary application, the former would have no critical purchase on the latter; to speak of God's justice as the standard by which to judge creaturely justice would be like saying that the number seven is the standard by which to judge the color brown.)

We can clarify these points by considering a few examples, the first of which is borrowed from Barth himself. The second half of *Church Dogmatics* II/1 is devoted to an account of God's attributes or, as Barth prefers, God's "perfections," the guiding principle of which is that God's attributes must be understood in light of God, rather than God being understood in terms of antecedently constructed categories; as Barth insists, "when it comes to the divine perfections, the relationship between subject and predicate is irreversible."[48] So, for instance, Barth attempts to understand the meaning of "freedom" as ascribed to God as that concept is conformed to Christ by the power of the Spirit, rather than in terms of some prior idea of what "freedom" means. He begins, then, by noting that "freedom," in its ordinary usage, usually carries both a negative and a positive sense: to be free is, on the one hand, "to be unlimited, unchecked, and unconditioned," and, on the other, "to be grounded in oneself and through oneself, determined by oneself and moved by oneself."[49] Barth then reinterprets these senses in light of the concept's application to God: "The freedom of God," he insists, "must be cognized as *God's* freedom, and this means as the matter stands in God, which means, in turn, as God has enacted it. In God, however, it stands in his Son Jesus Christ, and it is just in him that God has enacted it."[50] On this basis, Barth concludes that God's acts are in fact grounded in Godself: "Even in relationship and communion with another," he writes, "God's freedom has its original truth in Godself," because this freedom "has its truth in the inner-trinitarian life of the Father with the Son through the Holy Spirit."[51] Antecedently in Godself, that is, God is a triune communion of love, from which it follows (a) that God's giving of Godself to communion with others is grounded in Godself, (b) that God can give Godself wholly to this communion without giving Godself away, (c) that this giving is not essentially conditioned by the ones with whom God enters into communion,

---

[48] Barth, KD II/1, p. 504.   [49] Barth, KD II/1, p. 339.
[50] Barth, KD II/1, p. 360.   [51] Barth, KD II/1, p. 356.

and (d) that God can let the other *be* other, since God's entrance into this communion is consequent upon the sheer plenitude of God's primary communion-in-Godself.[52] The application of "freedom" to God can thus be seen as the fulfillment of the concept, since the triune God is the unsurpassable example of a being whose will (namely, love) is grounded in, and determined by, itself, and who is therefore free from limits, restrictions, or conditions upon that will. This application likewise stands in judgment over other uses of the concept, in two respects. First, once the concept has been understood in light of its application to God's being-with-us, the inadequacy of certain other understandings of divine freedom becomes apparent, especially those which conceive God's freedom from the world as opposition to or distance from it.[53] And second, once the concept has been fulfilled by its application to God, the inadequacy of certain conceptions of *creaturely* freedom likewise becomes apparent, especially those which portray one as a wholly independent, unconditioned subjectivity, as well as those which picture one as able to give oneself wholly to others without any danger of giving oneself

---

[52] So Barth: "God has the prerogative to be free *without* being limited by God's freedom from external conditioning, since God is also free vis-à-vis this freedom, free to give Godself to this communion and in this communion to enact this *faithfulness*, and just so to be actually free, free in Godself" (KD II/1, p. 341); because God is free in *this* sense, "God can have a real relationship with the world, there can be a real world standing over against God, neither endangered nor annihilated by God's absoluteness but, on the contrary, existing as a world precisely by the power of God's absoluteness" (KD II/1, p. 347).

[53] Barth thus claims that "the concept of God's 'transcendence' can be inserted as a substitute to designate God's essence only if one bears in mind that such transcendence cannot be exhaustively defined in terms of God's antithesis to that which is distinct from God, that it likewise includes God's relationship to and communion with this distinct reality, and thus includes God's 'immanence,' too. If one fails to keep this in mind, one ends up seeing the essence of God according to the fateful guidance of Neoplatonism's abstract understanding of transcendence – which is, however, to see that essence as non-being in its relationship to the being of that distinct reality, and to replace the biblical concept of God with a concept that is easy to recognize as the highest concept of humanity" (KD II/1, p. 341).

away.[54] Barth thus sees the ordinary meaning of the concept "freedom" as both fulfilled and judged by its application to God.

As a second example, consider the meaning of "God"-concepts, especially *El*, *elohim*, and their variants, as these emerged prior to their application to the God of Abraham.[55] The generic concept "god" (*elohim*) seems to have developed through application to objects which were thought to have (or be) "powers" over certain spheres – "local deities," in other words – and "the god" (*El*) appears to have denoted the "head" of these gods. These concepts, in turn, were apparently derived from ordinary concepts for "to be in front," "to be strong," or "to be dreaded." On the basis of these applications, the meaning of the concept "god" was rendered determinate, that is, as applicable to an object that has power over some aspect of one's life, as calling for one's acknowledgment of this power, and so on. This concept was then applied by the ancient Hebrews to the one who made a covenant with Abraham, but, importantly, this application not only carried on the normative trajectory implicit in precedent applications, it also stood in judgment over them. That is to say, both precedent and subsequent applications of the concept "god" were now judged in terms of its application to the one who covenanted with Abraham, to such an extent that the ancient Hebrews eventually concluded that the concept "god" properly applies *only* to this one. The meaning of the concept thus changed: the one to whom the concept "god" was applied was the one who stood in a relation of covenant-faithfulness to a particular people, such that the "being in front" implicit in the concept was now understood as God's faithful leading of God's people, God's gracious precedence in

[54] On these points, see *Die Kirchliche Dogmatik*, vol. iii, *Die Lehre von der Schöpfung*, part 2 (Zollikon-Zürich: Evangelischer Verlag A. G., 1948), §45.2.

[55] On these developments, see Frank Moore Cross, "El," *Theological Dictionary of the Old Testament*, vol. i, G. Johannes Botterweck and Helmer Ringgren (eds.) (Grand Rapids, MI: Eerdmans, 1974), pp. 242–61; and "The Religion of Canaan and the God of Israel," *Canaanite Myth and Hebrew Epic: Essays in the History of the Religion of Israel* (Cambridge, MA: Harvard University Press, 1997), pp. 3–75.

maintaining a covenant with them, and so on. The point is straight-forward enough: when the concept "god" was applied to the one who covenanted with Abraham, its meaning changed, and precedent and subsequent uses of the concept were now judged on this basis. From a Christian point of view, this process culminated in the application of the concept "god" to the one whom Jesus Christ called "Father" (about which a similar story could be told); we will spell this out further in the following chapter, but for now, the point is that in apply-ing the concept "god" to the God of Abraham, the ordinary meaning of that concept was both fulfilled and judged.

This account can be instructively contrasted with a model accord-ing to which the meaning of concepts as applied to God is strictly dictated by previous applications. We find such a model in Gordon Kaufman, who claims that all experience of God is mediated by con-cepts, and that the ordinary meaning of these concepts is strictly normative for their application to God.[56] Kaufman thus claims, for instance, that concepts of God "were each created as our fore-bears sought ways (over many generations) to come to terms with the various issues with which life faced them";[57] such concepts were constructed, then, "to gather up, comprehend, and hold together all reality and experience, all possibilities and imaginings in a meaning-ful connection that can orient human life."[58] In its ordinary mean-ing, accordingly, "god" is a symbol that one uses "to direct attention to what can be called the 'ultimate point of reference' of all action,

---

[56] "The entire vocabulary of the church – including such central terms as God, man, church, reconciliation, prayer, faith – consists of ordinary words from the everyday language of people" (Kaufman, *Essay on Theological Method*, third edn. [Atlanta, GA: Scholars Press, 1995], p. 3). Or again, "there is no such thing as a raw pre-linguistic experience of 'transcendence,' say, as distinguished from the experience of 'ultimacy' or of the 'infinite.' Each of these 'experiences' is shaped, delimited and informed by the linguistic symbols which also name it. Without those symbols to guide our consciousness, these 'experiences' would not be available to us at all" (*Essay*, p. 7).

[57] Kaufman, *In the Beginning ... Creativity* (Minneapolis: Fortress Press, 2004), p. 39.

[58] Kaufman, *In the Beginning*, p. 27

consciousness, and reflection."[59] This ordinary meaning is then supposed to govern the concept's application to (putative) experiences and revelations of God: "In order to function as an ultimate point of reference," Kaufman argues, "God cannot be conceived as simply one more of the items of ordinary experience or knowledge, in some way side by side with the others," from which he concludes that "talk about the *experience* of God involves what philosophers call a 'category mistake,' and should not, therefore, be engaged in."[60] So then: Kaufman begins by claiming that any putative experience of God must be mediated by ordinary concepts, argues that the meaning of the ordinary concept "god" is "ultimate point of reference," asserts that an ultimate point of reference cannot itself stand within one's frame of reference, and thus concludes that one cannot have experience of God. The crucial point, for our purposes, is that Kaufman uses the ordinary meaning of the concept "god" to judge its putative application *to* God, whereas our account uses its application to God to judge the concept's ordinary meaning.

On the present account, then, we can understand the relationship between the meaning of ordinary and theological concept use in roughly the following terms: (a) ordinary concepts are rendered determinate by their application to creaturely objects; (b) the normative trajectory implicit in these applications renders some of these concepts fit for application to God; (c) this fitness is recognizable only retrospectively from a concept's (would-be) application to God; and (d) the concept's application to God both fulfills and judges other applications of the concept.

3

Those familiar with the theological tradition will recognize the preceding account as an example of the so-called analogy of attribution,

---

[59] Kaufman, *In the Beginning*, p. 59.
[60] Kaufman, *Essay*, p. 16, and *In the Beginning*, p. 110.

according to which the proper meaning of a concept derives from its application to God: thus, in Thomas Aquinas's influential formulation, "God prepossesses in himself all the perfections of creatures, being himself simply and universally perfect … So, when we say *God is good*, the meaning is not, *God is the cause of goodness*, or *God is not evil*, but the meaning is, *Whatever good we attribute to creatures, pre-exists in God*, and all in a more excellent and higher way."[61] In an analogy of attribution, then, a single term is predicated of two different objects, but the predicate is proper to one of the objects and is said of the other only derivatively, such that it is predicated of the latter in a way which is related to, but not identical with, its predication of the former. Barth's account could be understood as an instance of this species of analogy, but it is crucial to note that for Barth, the concept of analogy, too, must be understood in light of its application to God: "We can also say that which is to be said about this relationship," he claims, "only with our creaturely-focused words. Likeness, unlikeness, and analogy are in the same way such creaturely words and thus in themselves wholly inadequate to say what is to be said here, where it is a matter of God and the creature."[62] Like "freedom," "justice," and "love," so the meaning of "analogy" must be derived from its application to God. This leads Barth to claim, first, that the meaning of the doctrine of analogy "is already here before our eyes in the doctrine of the justification of the sinner solely through faith," since, if there is an

---

[61] *Summa Theologiae*, 1a, q. 13, art. 2 (trans. Fathers of the English Dominican Province [New York: Benziger Brothers, 1948]); I offer a reading of this material in "Apophaticism in Thomas Aquinas: A Re-reformulation and Recommendation," *Scottish Journal of Theology* 60:4 (2007), pp. 377–93.

[62] Barth, KD II/1, pp. 254–5. Barth is especially critical of understandings of "analogy" which appeal to a quasi-mathematical account of the relationship between God and creatures (as in some formulations of the so-called "analogy of proper proportionality"): given that the relationship depends wholly upon God's grace, Barth insists that "with respect to such algebraic division – and division that we can know and carry out is such algebraic division – it will not do between God and us" (KD II/1, p. 264).

analogy between God and the human person, "how can it be other-wise than that which is posited and created through the work and action of God, which is actual of God and only of God, and thus in faith and only in faith?"[63] One's concepts can indeed apply to God, but this application depends wholly upon God's gracious initiative, from which it follows that one's application of these concepts must be a matter of faith in, and obedience to, God's prior act. Barth thus argues that, "because the human person is and remains human, if his or her intuitions, concepts, and words, in their oh-so-human-ness, are sufficient in virtue of their awakening and conscription to grasp and thus express and establish truthful knowledge of God's being (the one, whole, undivided being of God!), they are this inso-far as in faith in God's revelation, they are formed and expressed in obedience to the direction there given. This is the 'partly,' the *limit* in the concept of likeness and thus the forward boundary of our knowledge of God: as we know God, we should not and will not depart from the grace of revelation. We must not dispense with it. Nor will it become superfluous to us."[64] Just as sinful creatures are made righteous before God solely on the basis of God's grace, so creaturely concepts are applicable to God only on the basis of that same grace. And just as the sheer grace of justification entails that one must set one's faith wholly upon that which God has done, so the grace by which God applies human concepts to Godself entails that one must set one's faith wholly upon that application, which is to say that one must seek to let one's concept use be grounded in, and therefore obediently conformed to, God's prior act.

On this account, then, the analogy of attribution is itself analo-gous to justification by grace received in faith. This is an important departure from most accounts of analogy; another, crucial to the present project, is that analogy is here understood not as bridging a gap between two meanings – one theological, the other ordinary – as if these were separate entities, but as naming the way a normative

---

[63] Barth, KD II/1, pp. 274, 91.   [64] Barth, KD II/1, pp. 265–6.

trajectory changes as a concept is applied in ever-new circumstances. Theological meaning is analogous to ordinary meaning, therefore, not because there is a bridge-like relationship between two different, idea-like "meanings," but because a concept's application to God represents the fulfillment and judgment of the precedent series leading to and from that application.

4

On this account, then, the meaning of a concept as applied to God is both the fulfillment and judgment of its meaning as ordinarily used. Several aspects of this account require clarification. First, if a concept's meaning continues to change as it is applied in new circumstances – as previous sections have argued – how could one possibly know that a particular application represents the concept's unsurpassable fulfillment? To see why this would be a problem, consider again the concept "white": once one has seen a very white object, one perceives objects to which one had previously applied the concept as not quite white. It would appear, however, that one would be entitled to describe an object as *unsurpassably* white only if one had seen the entire series of candidates to which the concept might be applied, yet it is hard to see how a finite being could ever know this to be the case. By what right, then, could one claim that a concept's application to God is unsurpassable? To address this question, consider two possible responses. First, if one accepts the proposition that God (as perfect and as sovereign) is the measure of all other instantiations of that which could be properly ascribed to God – a proposition to which I will not try to entitle myself here – then one would have grounds for claiming that a concept's application to God must be unsurpassable, since that application must be the measure by which all others are judged. One might also respond, as Wolfhart Pannenberg does, by appealing to Jesus' resurrection from the dead: if resurrection is the end of history within history, as the New Testament seems to indicate, then one could claim that in the resurrected one, one has in fact seen the entire series of concept applications, such that future applications cannot surpass these ones.[65] Either way, there are reasons to think of a concept's theological application as unsurpassable, though these reasons are internal to the so-called "theological circle," and thereby subject to certain limitations: at best, they provide internal, rather than external, warrant for theological claims, but such warrant need not be seen as second-rate.[66] (In this connection, it is worth remembering the situation of Neurath's sailors.)

The fact that a concept's application to God functions as an unsurpassable precedent should not be thought to entail, however, that it cannot be applied in novel, unpredictable ways, nor that its meaning does not develop over time. This brings us to a second clarification: the appropriately theological meaning of a concept is not something that simply falls into human hands once God has appropriated it; rather, the properly theological meaning of subsequent uses depends upon their going on in the same way as this particular precedent, which depends, in turn, upon the Spirit's work of carrying on the norm implicit in that precedent. The theological use of these concepts, moreover, has not insulated them from further use in non-theological circumstances, from which it follows that if their meaning is subsequently to be applicable to God, the Spirit must continually repeat the process by which they were initially taken up. To see why this would be the case (and how it works), recall that the meaning of a particular use depends upon the series of precedents onto which one maps it. Hence, the meaning of "freedom" as applied to God depends upon which precedents its use carries on and which among these precedents is normative for the others. If one's use carries on a series of so-called "Cartesian" precedents,

---

[65] On this point, see Wolfhart Pannenberg, *Jesus: God and Man*, trans. Lewis Wilkins and Duane Priebe (Philadelphia: Westminster Press, 1968).

[66] For an elaboration and defense of these points, see Paul Tillich, *Systematic Theology*, vol. I, (Chicago: University of Chicago Press, 1951).

according to which "freedom" is a matter of unconditionedness, and if this series is taken to be normative for the concept's application to God, then it would follow that the latter has been assimilated to the former, and the meaning thus specified would be inappropriate for application to God. On the other hand, if one takes the concept's application to God to be normative for all other applications, and if one thus sees this precedent as their judgment and fulfillment, then one's meaning can stand in conformity to that precedent and so be appropriate for application to God. One's intention to let one's application of a concept be judged by its application to God thus matters, though this intention does not by itself guarantee that its meaning is theologically appropriate, since one could well be mistaken about the meaning of the initial application. That is to say, one has to apply concepts to the initial application in order to let it stand in judgment over subsequent applications – at least if one is to know what one means by them – yet these applications, too, are relevantly "subsequent," which means that they, too, must be judged. We seem, therefore, to be caught in a circle. This brings us back to the claim that the properly theological meaning of a concept has not simply fallen into human hands, in consequence of which one must continue to depend upon the Spirit's work of conforming one's concepts to that meaning. As noted in the previous chapter, one can judge the meaning of any particular concept application by holding it accountable to its precedent application to God, but one cannot judge them all at once.

This brings us to three points about how an application's meaning is made explicit, and so rendered judgeable. It is important to note, first, a point about the grammar of "means"-talk: to say that x means y is to express a normative commitment to the effect that when one says x, one *should* mean y.[67] To claim, then, that an assertion such

---

[67] For a defense of this claim, see Mark Norris Lance and John O'Leary Hawthorne, *The Grammar of Meaning: Normativity and Semantic Discourse* (Cambridge University Press, 1997).

as "God is free" means that God can give Godself wholly to communion without giving Godself away, and that this giving is not essentially conditioned by the relative worthiness of its recipients, is to claim that this is what one *should* mean when one says "God is free." "Means"-talk is prescriptive, in other words, rather than descriptive. In the idiom of the present project, one could thus say that "means"-talk enables one to make a claim about what concepts ought to mean if they are to go on in the same way as the relevant precedents, and that such talk can, accordingly, play a role in carrying on the normative Spirit implicit in those precedents: if one's meaning-claim faithfully explicitates the norm implicit in a series of precedents, it follows that one's claim both depends upon the Spirit and enables still others to depend upon it. This leads to a second point: the paradigmatic means by which one would entitle oneself to such a claim is to exhibit it as standing at the conclusion of a series of precedents, in view of which one can judge the extent to which one's meaning-claim is itself normed by the Spirit's application of the concept. Crucially, though, such assessment is not the sort of thing with which one could ever be finished; unlike the use of an answer key to grade a multiple-choice test, a concept's putative conformity to Christ must be subject to continual reassessment, since, again, the standard by which to make such judgments never falls into one's hands. This brings us to one final point: the fact that the meaning of one's concepts must continually answer to God does not entail that they do not answer to oneself or one's peers; quite the contrary. The properly theological meaning of a concept is the product of a normative trajectory carried on by a series of precedents which are themselves normed by God's being-with-us, and this normativity is carried on by Christ's normative Spirit – yet given that the Spirit is itself carried on through an ongoing process of intersubjective recognition, it follows that meaning's answerability to God is not incompatible with its answerability to human persons, since the norms implicit in one's recognitions have been mediated by, and in turn mediate, the normative Spirit by which meaning is to be judged. The meaning of theological concept use thus turns out to depend upon God's triune activity, yet because Christ's normative Spirit is carried on through the practice of intersubjective recognition, it follows that this dependence is not incompatible with dependence upon creaturely social practices.

***

On the present account, then, a concept is rendered determinate by its application to ordinary objects; the normative trajectory implicit in these applications renders some of these concepts fit for application to God; this fitness is only retrospectively recognizable as such; and the concept's application to God both fulfills and judges other applications of the concept. Given that the meaning of a concept changes each time a new use is recognized, and given further that its meaning as applied to God is only retrospectively recognizable (rather than prospectively predictable) as fulfilling its antecedent meaning, it follows that the application of concepts to God does not entail that God has been subsumed under a predetermined, fixed category. This being the case, it follows that even if one were to deny that a concept's "meaning" (construed essentialistically) could apply to God, this would not entail that human concepts cannot apply to God, nor that God must stand at a distance from whatever one says about God.

Conclusion

We began this chapter by defending a non-metaphysical account of conceptual content: the meaning of a concept is not a matter of its correspondence to an essence-like "meaning," I argued, but the product of its relationship to a normative trajectory implicit in precedent uses of the concept. Given that this trajectory changes, if only slightly, each time a use is recognized as carrying it on, it follows that a concept's meaning is continually changing. This entails that the meaning of a concept is neither fixed, uniform, nor predictable, since some uses will be recognizable only retrospectively as carrying on that trajectory. With this account on board, I then defended an account according to which the Spirit takes up concepts and applies them to God, thereby judging and fulfilling the normative trajectory implicit in their use. Certain concepts are thus retrospectively recognizable as fit for application to God, and the latter application sets an unsurpassable precedent by which all others are to be judged. We can thus understand the meaning of concepts otherwise than in terms of their putative correspondence to an essence-like "meaning," in consequence of which we can avoid the idolatrous consequences of cutting God down to conceptual size without having to insist that God stands at a distance from concept use. So far, then, so good. There are still two sets of metaphysical assumptions, however, for which we need to provide therapy, namely, those related to reference and to truth. To the former we now turn.

4 | Reference and presence

The preceding chapters have defended several elements of a therapeutic response to metaphysics: by elaborating a non-essentialist,
non-correspondentist account of concepts and meaning, and
explaining theological concept use in terms of the Spirit's circulation
through practices of intersubjective recognition, we arrived at the
conclusion that one's rejection of an essentialist-correspondentist
picture of language's relation to God need not be thought to entail
that God stands at a distance from language. In order to complete
the therapy, we must address two further issues, namely, intentionality and truth. This chapter takes up the issue of "intentionality," by which I mean the object-directedness of one's words and
thoughts – the issue, that is, of the very idea that words could have
God as their object.[1] This issue can be further analyzed in terms of
two sub-issues, namely, that of object-*directedness* – here, the use of
words to refer to an object – and of *object*-directedness – the availability of such objects. It turns out that therapy is needed here, too,
since intentionality, like meaning, has long been understood along
essentialist-correspondentist lines and has, accordingly, given rise
to the assumption that the failure of essentialist-correspondentist
metaphysics entails that one cannot intend God with one's words.

[1] Franz Brentano revived the term "intentionality" in his 1874 *Psychology from an
Empirical Standpoint* (London: Routledge and Kegan Paul, 1973), p. 88. Helpful
elaborations – from very different perspectives – can be found in John Searle,
Intentionality: An Essay in the Philosophy of Mind (Cambridge University Press, 1983)
and Daniel C. Dennett, *The Intentional Stance* (Cambridge, MA: MIT Press, 1987).

Metaphysics, intentionality, and homesickness

There are two issues involved in accounting for the putative "about-ness" of God-talk: issues related to the semantical notion of reference – paradigmatically the use of a name to pick out some object – and those related to an object's very availability. Each of these has been understood in essentialist-correspondentist terms at various points in its career, which has made it appear that if God cannot be inscribed within a metaphysical framework, then one cannot refer to God, and God is never available to one.

1

We begin with the more easily stated of the two issues, namely, reference to God. If an object is paradigmatically picked out by a name – as "Aristotle," for instance, refers to Aristotle – is it appropriate to say that God is picked out by the name "God"? To understand the problems involved in theological reference, especially with respect to an essentialist-correspondentist account thereof, it will help to understand why apophatic anti-metaphysicians answer this question with a definitive "No." John Caputo puts the point with characteristic color: "By giving God a name," he argues, "we give the gift of what we do not have. For by naming we risk binding what is named, enslaving it, prescribing to it 'an assigned passion,'" from which he concludes that "if the name of God were actually to hit its mark and so wrench God into manifestation," it would "pu[t] a violent end to God's absolute heterogeneity and holy height."[2] From Caputo's point of view, the use of a name to pick out God would, if successful, amount to God's being bound by that name – but since God cannot be so bound, Caputo concludes that names cannot pick out God. It seems clear that a particular understanding of the semantics of

---

[2] John D. Caputo, *The Prayers and Tears of Jacques Derrida: Religion Without Religion* (Bloomington: Indiana University Press, 1997), pp. 43–4.

naming is implicit in this denial of theological reference; something along these lines is intimated in Jean-Luc Marion's claim that "the concept, when it knows the divine in its hold and thus names 'God,' defines it. Defines it, and therefore measures it according to the dimension of its hold."[3] What seems to be at stake here, for Marion as well as Caputo, is a picture of reference according to which one picks out some object by applying certain concepts to it; to refer to God, on such an account, would be to apply concepts which correspond uniquely with God and just so pick God out. The essentialist-correspondentist model of reference could thus be understood along the lines of what philosophers call a descriptivist theory of names, where the referent of a name is fixed by a set of descriptions. So, on this account, one's use of the name "Aristotle" successfully refers to Aristotle if and only if (a) one's ideas about Aristotle (that he was Plato's student, that he wrote *De Anima*, that he taught Alexander the Great, etc.) suffice to pick out a unique object, and (b) that object is Aristotle.[4] On this account, then, one's use of the name "God" would refer to God just in case (a) one's ideas about God (that God created the heavens and the earth, that God is that than which none greater can be conceived, etc.) suffice to pick out a unique object, and (b) that object is God. The problem is this: if one's ability to refer to God depends upon God's correspondence to one's ideas – and, conversely, upon the sufficiency of one's ideas

---

[3] Marion, *Dieu sans l'être* (Librairie Arthème Fayard, 1982), pp. 26, 44.

[4] Exponents of "descriptivism" include Bertrand Russell (see "On Denoting," *Mind* n.s. 14:56 [1905], pp. 479–93); contemporary descriptivists (of the "two-dimensionalist" variety) include Jason Stanley ("Names and Rigid Designation," in *A Companion to the Philosophy of Language*, B. Hale and C. Wright [eds.] [Oxford: Blackwell Press, 1997], pp. 555–85, and "Rigidity and Content," in *Language, Thought, and Logic: Essays in Honor of Michael Dummett*, R. Heck [ed.] [Oxford University Press, 1997], pp. 131–56), David Chalmers ("The Foundations of Two-Dimensional Semantics," in *Two-Dimensional Semantics: Foundations and Applications*, M. Garcia-Carpintero and J. Macia [eds.] [Oxford University Press, 2004]), and Frank Jackson ("Reference and Description Revisited," in *Philosophical Perspectives 12: Language, Mind, and Ontology*, J. Tomberlin [ed.] [Oxford: Blackwell, 1998], pp. 201–18).

uniquely to pick out God – then theological reference would seem to depend upon God's being fit into a correspondentist framework and, accordingly, being treated as an idol. Caputo, Marion, and other contemporary anti-metaphysicians reject this sort of fitting-in and, in consequence, insist that one's names for God should not be thought to pick God out; such names, rather, are seen as marks of God's "absence, anonymity, or withdrawal," such that "God himself 'slips away' from every name we give Him."[5] It would appear, however, that if the essentialist-correspondentist picture of reference were itself called into question, then one's rejection of metaphysics would not necessarily entail that God must stand at a distance from one's would-be reference to God.

2

This brings us to a second, somewhat more complicated problem, namely, that of the very availability of objects. Here, too, a correspondentist picture has held sway, according to which objects are immediately available to one, prior to and apart from one's application of concepts to them, such that the concept-free perception of an object can (and should) be the means by which concepts are judged.[6] Several famous arguments have been marshaled against this picture, one of which – call it the "This-Here-Now" argument – should suffice to make the relevant point. Kant summarizes an argument along

---

[5] Marion, "In the Name: How to Avoid Speaking of 'Negative Theology,'" in *God, The Gift, and Postmodernism*, John D. Caputo and Michael J. Scanlon (eds.) (Bloomington: Indiana University Press, 1999), p. 29; Caputo, *Prayers and Tears*, p. 43.

[6] Wilfrid Sellars offers a classic description of this picture (which he calls "the Myth of the Given"): it is "the idea that there is, indeed *must be*, a structure of particular matter of fact such that (a) each fact can not only be noninferentially known to be the case, but presupposes no other knowledge either of particular matter of fact, or of general truths; and (b) such that the noninferential knowledge of facts belonging to this structure constitutes the ultimate court of appeals for all factual claims – particular and general – about the world" (*Empiricism and the Philosophy of Mind* [Cambridge, MA: Harvard University Press, 1956, 1997], pp. 68–9).

these lines in the following terms: "without the consciousness that what we think is the same as what we thought a moment before," he observes, "all reproduction in the series of representations would be futile. For then it would be a new representation in each moment and would not in any way belong to the act by which it was produced, and the manifold itself would never constitute a whole, since it would lack the unity that only consciousness can supply."[7] To understand Kant's point, consider the following thought experiment: suppose one aims one's eyes in the direction of a bowling pin, yet one prescinds from any and all conceptual judgments (even implicit ones) about candidate similarities between the content of this and other aspects of one's experience. What would be the content of such a perception? The content cannot be "Lo, a bowling pin," since such an observation obviously involves the application of concepts, but neither can it be "a white patch," "such-and-such shape (say, that of a Russian doll)," or even "a thing," since each of these characterizations makes use of concepts. Hence, in order to avoid smuggling in concepts, we need to reduce our description of the relevant experience to something primitive such as "this-here-now." On the view under consideration, then, one aims one's eyes at the bowling pin, and "this-here-now" names whatever one happens to perceive at that instant. For the sake of argument, suppose one were to grant that such this-here-now-ing requires no concept application. What would follow? Could one *think* about such a concept-less this-here-now? Could one say anything meaningful about it? It would appear not, since this-here-now is, as its name indicates, indexed to a certain temporal and spatial instant, whereas in order to think about this-here-now, one must be able to keep it in mind – at which point it is no longer the *same* this-here-now. Or again, in order to say anything about this-here-now, one must be able to refer back to it – but as soon as one refers to "this-here-now," this-here-now has

---

[7] Kant, *Kritik der reinen Vernunft, Kants Werke: Akademie Textausgabe*, vol. IV (Berlin: Walter de Gruyter, 1968), p. A103.

already changed, and one ends up talking about some *other* this-here-now. (Think about telling someone how many fractions of a second remain on a running stopwatch.) This-here-now cannot be the object of one's thoughts or sentences, accordingly, since such object-hood depends upon the ability to recognize an object as *the same thing* from moment to moment and from perspective to perspective. Indeed, apart from the application of concepts, one has no reason to take multiple "this-here-nows" as being of the same object, in consequence of which a series of this-here-nows could never add up to "a bowling pin" or even "an object." Hence, it would appear that one cannot perceive something *as* something unless one applies concepts to it.[8]

This argument, in turn, has commonly been taken to imply that concepts mediate objects to us, and so stand between us and them: if (a) concept application is necessary to one's perception of objects, such that (b) one cannot perceive objects apart from the concepts one applies to them, it seems to follow (c) that we have no access to objects as they are in themselves, that is, apart from our conceptualization of them, (d) that concepts therefore mediate the world to us, and (e) that, for all we know, the world itself could be entirely different than we perceive it to be. Indeed, Kant himself draws precisely this conclusion: "We have thus meant to say," he claims, "that all our intuition is nothing but the representation of appearance; that

---

[8] Kant's more extended arguments in each of the Transcendental Deductions can be understood as expansions of this point: to perceive an object, one's experiences of that object must be unified; this unity is not supplied by the manifold of sense data; the unity must thus be supplied by the perceiving subject; this is particularly the case, according to the B Deduction, in order that these perceptions be recognizable as one's own. Kant claims that "the *combination* (*conjuntio*) of a manifold can never come to us through sense, and can thus not be contained in the pure form of sensible intuition," from which it follows that if "an *object* is that in the concept of which the manifold of a given intuition is *united*," then to perceive an object, one must "synthetically bring into being a determinate combination of a given manifold, so that the unity of this action is at the same time the unity of consciousness, and through that an object (a determinate space) will be known for the first time" (*Kritik der reinen Vernunft*, pp. B129, B137–8).

the things we intuit are not in themselves what we intuit them to be, nor their relations so comprised in themselves as they appear to us"; hence, "How things stand with objects in themselves and apart from all this receptivity of our sensibility remains entirely unknown to us. We know nothing other than our manner of perceiving them, which is peculiar to us and is not necessarily shared by every being, though surely by every human being."[9] This supposition, according to which one has no concept-free access to objects, in turn encourages us to picture concepts as mediating the world to one, and therefore as potentially standing like a veil between one and the world – as if one's only access to the outside world were conveyed by messengers whose reliability could not, in principle, be checked.[10] One moral that has been drawn from this argument, accordingly, is that one has no access to objects as they are in themselves. This moral is reinforced, in turn, if one accepts a premise which Kant here denies, namely, that the concepts by which objects are mediated are themselves relative to particular historically and culturally contingent circumstances, and that these circumstances reinforce (and are reinforced by) certain relations of power.[11] That is to say, if

[9] Kant, *Kritik der reinen Vernunft*, p. A42=B59; cf. Bxx, A30=B45, A39=B56, A43=B60, A44=B62. To be sure, it is controversial to ascribe a view along these lines to Kant; Terry Pinkard, for instance, claims that skepticism about "objects-in-themselves" is theoretically necessary for Kant, as a way of exempting human freedom from the realm of causation (see his *German Philosophy 1760–1860* [Cambridge University Press, 2002]), whereas John McDowell claims that Kant does not in fact end up with such skepticism (for which see his Woodbridge Lectures, "Having the World in View," *Journal of Philosophy* 95 [1998]).

[10] Davidson describes the picture in these terms in "A Coherence Theory of Truth and Knowledge," *Subjective, Intersubjective, Objective* (Oxford University Press, 2001), pp. 143–4.

[11] For examples of this sort of view, see Paul Feyerabend, "Explanation, Reduction, and Empiricism," in *Scientific Explanation, Space and Time*, H. Feigl and G. Maxwell (eds.) (Minneapolis: University of Minnesota Press, 1962), pp. 28–97; T. S. Kuhn, *The Structure of Scientific Revolutions* (Chicago: University of Chicago Press, 1962); Alasdair MacIntyre, *After Virtue: A Study in Moral Theory* (Notre Dame, IN: University of Notre Dame Press, 1981, 1984) and "Incommensurability, Truth, and the Conversation Between Confucians and Aristotelians about the Virtues," in *Culture*

(a) the world is mediated to one through concepts, (b) one's repertoire of concepts is relative to one's historical and cultural location, and (c) the relevant concepts differ enough from place to place and time to time – if, that is, these differences are "incommensurable" – it would appear to follow (d) that users of one set of concepts see a different world from users of another set, and (e) that there is no way of adjudicating these differences.

On the basis of such an argument, it would appear that a certain correspondentist picture of objects' immediate availability – sometimes referred to as "the metaphysics of presence" – is unworkable. Caputo, again, draws the relevant conclusion: "Every claim to the 'things themselves' is a claim made within and by means of the resources of certain semi-systems, linguistic and otherwise, situated within the framework of a complex set of contextual presuppositions which can never be saturated. There are no things themselves outside these textual and contextual limits, no naked contact with being which somehow shakes loose of the coded system which makes notions like the 'things themselves' possible to begin with and which enables speakers to refer to them and indeed to get themselves in heat about their access to them."[12] Caputo thus insists that there is "no privileged access, no transcendental signified, no hyperessential intuition, no *Ding an sich* to which we have extratextual (extraterrestrial) access," from which it follows that "the thing itself slips away leaving nothing behind, save the name."[13] This is good news, on Caputo's view, for it is precisely an object's unavailability which safeguards it from the totalizing violence of concepts – on his view, that is, to insist that one has no access to objects in themselves is to maintain an object's otherness to, and so freedom from, conceptual grasp. God, too, is thus freed from one's grasp, and one is

and Modernity: East–West Philosophic Perspectives, E. Deutsch (ed.) (Honolulu: University of Hawaii Press, 1991), pp. 104–22; and John Milbank, *Theology and Social Theory: Beyond Secular Reason* (Oxford: Blackwell, 1990).

[12] Caputo, *Prayers and Tears*, p. 17.
[13] Caputo, *Prayers and Tears*, pp. 34, 43.

in turn freed from one's would-be idolatry, for if God is available to one only through the mediation of concepts, then it follows that one has no access to God "in Godself." Concepts thus stand between one and God, and if one remembers this, one will no longer be tempted to think of oneself as standing in immediate, correspondence-like touch with God, and God's absolute otherness will be upheld.

Certain theologians have thus concluded that language stands like a veil between one and God. From a therapeutic point of view, by contrast, one's readiness to move from the premise that objects are available to one only on the basis of concept application, to the conclusion that one is out of touch with these objects' fundamental reality, indicates that one is still in the grip of essentialist-correspondentist presuppositions about what it would mean to be *in* touch with objects. If one were to do without these presuppositions, one's rejection of "concept-free access" would not be thought to entail that concepts stand between objects and oneself, nor that "objects themselves" are ultimately elusive.

***

In rejecting an essentialist-correspondentist picture of theological reference and of God's availability to one, some theologians have denied the possibility that one's words and thoughts could in fact be about God, as well as the possibility that God could be present to one. The rest of this chapter aims to demonstrate that the former rejection need not be thought to entail the latter denials, and to exhibit these denials as a kind of residual attachment to essentialist-correspondentist metaphysics.

Ordinary and theological reference

This section elaborates and defends an account of reference which is fit for theological use, and then explains how words could be thought to refer to God *without* being guilty of essentialist-correspondentist idolatry. The argument proceeds in the following steps: with respect to reference per se, I argue (a) that in order to refer to some object, it is necessary and sufficient that that object be triangulated; (b) that such triangulation turns out to depend upon a prior notion of repeatability-of-reference; (c) that we can explain the relevant repeatability in terms of anaphora (paradigmatically the use of pronouns); and (d) that anaphora can in turn be explained in terms of one's being appropriately treated as inheriting a prior reference commitment. I then explain how, due to God's gracious precedence in Christ and Spirit, one's words could refer to God, too. The aim, again, is to do without the essentialist-correspondentist picture of reference, as well as the attendant sense that its failure leaves one out of touch with God.

1

We begin with the claim that words (and thoughts) count as referring to an object if and only if they pick out one and only one object.[14] The simplest way to get a grip on this claim is to consider the use of singular terms such as "the coffee mug," "the number seven," and so on, terms which purport to pick out an object. In order for such a term to do so, it is necessary, on the one hand, that it pick out at least one

[14] This account of reference is heavily indebted to Gottlob Frege, *Foundations of Arithmetic*, trans. J. L. Austin (Evanston, IL: Northwestern University Press, 1980), §§62ff.; Robert B. Brandom, "The Significance of Complex Numbers for Frege's Philosophy of Mathematics," *Tales of the Mighty Dead: Historical Essays in the Metaphysics of Intentionality* (Cambridge, MA: Harvard University Press, 2002), pp. 277–97, and *Making It Explicit: Reasoning, Representing, and Discursive Commitment* (Cambridge, MA: Harvard University Press, 1994), Chapters 6 and 7; Donald Davidson, *Subjective, Intersubjective, Objective*, and *Inquiries into Truth and Interpretation*, 2nd edn. (New York: Oxford University Press, 1984, 2001); Saul A. Kripke, *Naming and Necessity* (Cambridge, MA: Harvard University Press, 1972, 1980) and "Speaker's Reference and Semantic Reference," *Midwest Studies in Philosophy* 2 (1977), pp. 255–76; Hilary Putnam, "The Meaning of 'Meaning'," *Mind, Language, and Reality* (Cambridge University Press, 1975); Keith Donnellan, "Reference and Definite Descriptions," *Philosophical Review* 75 (1966), pp. 281–304, and "Proper Names and Identifying Descriptions," in *The Semantics of Natural Language*, Donald Davidson and Gilbert Harman (eds.) (Dordrecht: Reidel, 1972), pp. 356–79.

object, since if it did not, it would obviously not succeed in picking something out, and must pick out *only* one object, for otherwise – if a singular term were to move from object to object like a spinning bottle, as it were, without stopping to point at any of them – it would not succeed in picking anything out. How is it, then, that a singular term could meet these conditions? According to one influential approach, it would appear that both conditions can be met by locating an object on a grid, since the point at which a set of coordinates intersect is necessarily a *single* point. One can thus pick out a physical object by locating it on a spatial grid; one can pick out a cardinal number such as "7" by identifying it as the square root of 49, the sum of 3 plus 4, etc.; and one can locate a virtue such as "temperance" by coordinating the convergence of applications of the concept. On this view, the necessary and sufficient condition of picking out one and only one object can be met by locating an object at the convergence of a set of coordinates, which is what Donald Davidson has in mind when he explains objective purport in terms of "triangulation": if one draws a line out from fixed point *a*, this line will intersect with innumerable points, but "is on a line extending from *a*" will not suffice to pick out any one of them. If one also draws a line out from fixed point *b*, however, the point of intersection between the two will locate a single point on the first line, thereby sufficing to specify one and only one object.[15] Hence, if we understand the grids in question as a way of understanding Davidson's notion of triangulation, we can say that triangulation is a necessary and sufficient condition of reference: a singular term picks out an object if and only if it picks out a *triangulated* object.

Much more needs to be said about how such triangulation works, but before elaborating this claim further, it is worth noting that if triangulation is a necessary and sufficient condition of picking out an object, it follows that one can refer to all sorts of objects, including

---

[15] Davidson elaborates a view along these lines in several places, the first of which is in "Rational Animals," *Subjective Intersubjective, Objective*, pp. 95–105.

abstract and fictitious ones. There is no sensible object called "wisdom," for instance, at least not in the same way that there are sensible objects called "bears." One learns the concept "wisdom" by applying it to certain persons and actions, but there is no sensible object "wisdom" in addition to these persons and actions. One can still individuate something called "wisdom," however, because one can pick out the same thing, wisdom, from more than one point of view. In this case, different points of view converge upon the salient features of instances to which the concept "wise" has been applied, and one can identify "wisdom" as that which is picked out by these applications. Hence, if triangulation is necessary as well as sufficient for picking out an object, it follows that one can object-ify (and have in mind) anything that can be picked out from more than one standpoint, including abstract qualities and other "absent" objects such as historical figures or events, complex numbers, and fictitious characters.

Even if triangulation is a necessary and sufficient condition of reference, however, it is not clear whether I have yet said anything that explains how reference works, since it would appear that triangulation needs to be explained just as much as reference does. In order to contribute to an explanation of reference, then, we need some account of how triangulation works; toward this end, it will help if we take a look at two paradigmatic examples of the triangulation in question, namely, intersubstitutability in a non-trivial identity claim and the convergence of two persons' points of view. Consider, first, the triangulation of an object from two persons' points of view. This sort of triangulation occurs, by necessity, when someone learns a concept from another person, since in order to know what the concept applies to, one must be able to pick out the salient features of the surrounding (physical or conceptual) environment. To see how this sort of triangulation works, suppose a mother is trying to teach her daughter the concept "bear." She may take her to the zoo and say "bear" when they are standing in front of one, she may say "bear" while showing her pictures of bears, etc. In each of these instances, there are innumerable non-bear aspects of the environment, such as trees, rocks, and other animals. In order for the girl to learn the concept "bear," therefore, she has to learn what part of the environment counts as "bear" and what does not. She presumably learns this over time by noticing that her mother says "bear" when bears are present, but not when there are trees, rocks, and other objects, but no bears. The point is that in order to learn the concept "bear," the girl must learn to individuate one object as salient, namely, bear-instances, which is to say that the girl learns to pick out a particular object – learns, that is, how to intend her use of the word "bear" to refer to the same thing as her mother's use of the word – by triangulating her responses with her mother's.[16] To be sure, this account faces an obvious problem, but before turning to it, we should consider, briefly, the other paradigm instance of triangulation, namely, intersubstitutability in non-trivial identity claims. Consider the following: the sum of 3 + 4 is identical with the cardinal number between 6 and 8, which is identical with the largest prime number under 10, etc. Given that the sum of 3 + 4 is 7, and given further that 7 is the cardinal number between 6 and 8, it follows that the same object has been located from two different points of view, thereby apparently meeting the necessary and sufficient conditions by which reference might be secured. Insofar as the object picked out on each side of the identity sign is the same object, then, non-trivial identity claims such as these can be said to triangulate a single object.[17]

We can now turn to the problem mentioned above, since both examples fall prey to it. The problem is that both kinds of triangulation still seem to presuppose reference, which means that although they may clarify our understanding of reference, they cannot by themselves explain it. So, with respect to the former example, we

---

[16] For a similar approach, see Davidson, "Meaning, Truth, and Evidence," *Truth, Language, and History* (New York: Oxford University Press, 2005), pp. 47–62.

[17] For arguments to this effect, see Brandom's "The Significance of Complex Numbers for Frege's Philosophy of Mathematics," and Chapters 6 and 7 of *Making It Explicit*.

need some explanation not only of how the mother can refer to bears, but of how the girl's use of the word could be said to refer to the same thing: how can one know, for instance, that she is referring to the same thing as her mother, instead of referring to, say, bear-stages, everything-in-the-world-minus-that-bear, the bearness of which that bear is an instance, etc.?[18] For that matter, how does one explain the reference of "the sum of 3 + 4"? The bottom line is that we still need an account of how the practice of reference can get up and running.

One clue as to the way in which a term becomes a referring term – by which it comes, that is, to pick out one and only one object – can be discerned in the process by which a non-referring, indefinite description can become a referring, definite description. To see how this works, consider a fairly ordinary sentence: "A telemarketer just tried to sell me a magazine subscription, but she wasn't very persuasive, so I told her I didn't want it." Notice two things about this sentence. It is important to note, first, that it begins with an indefinite description – namely, "a telemarketer" – which does not by itself pick out one and only one object, a point which becomes clear if one considers a sentence like "persistence is the key to a telemarketer's success." Crucially for our purposes, however, in the original sentence "a telemarketer" *does* pick out one and only one object, precisely because *the same* telemarketer is picked out by subsequent pronouns which form a chain of reference: "she" and "her" repeat the reference to "a telemarketer." The name for this phenomenon, wherein an expression repeats an antecedent reference without repeating the antecedent tokening, is "anaphora," the paradigmatic instance of which is pronoun use.[19] Because pronouns repeat an

---

[18] Quine's famous claim about the inscrutability of reference can thus be understood as a stage in the present argument, though not as its conclusion; for the claim itself, see *Ontological Relativity and Other Essays* (New York: Columbia University Press, 1969).

[19] I am here following the influential argument of Charles Chastain, "Reference and Context," in *Language, Mind, and Knowledge*, Keith Gunderson (ed.) (Minneapolis: University of Minnesota Press, 1975), pp. 194–269.

antecedent reference in this way, their use in referring back to the referent of an indefinite description serves to pick out the same thing from another point of view. Hence, by repeating the initial, non-referring term, pronouns triangulate a single object, and a referent for the initiating term is specified.

This phenomenon provides us with a clue by which to explain the semantics of reference: expressions which by themselves would not pick out one and only one object can do so if and only if subsequent expressions refer to the same thing – if and only if, that is, they are carried on by an anaphoric chain. To see why this is the case, consider the two paradigmatic instances of putatively referring expressions, namely, demonstratives and proper names. The reference of a demonstrative expression – saying "that!" or "this-here-now!" while pointing at some object – is not in itself repeatable, since a subsequent tokening of "this-here-now" will not pick out the *same* this-here-now. Such demonstrative expressions make some object available to cognition and communication only if they can be repeated, but in order to be repeated, one needs to use an expression other than "this-here-now!"; one needs an anaphoric expression, such as a pronoun, which is designed to refer to whatever its antecedent referred to, thereby rendering the initial reference repeatable. Apart from such repeatability, demonstratives would be unrepeatable and would be unable in principle to pick out an object as "the same again," from which it follows that a demonstrative refers only insofar as its referent can be carried on by an anaphoric chain.

Perhaps surprisingly, the referentiality of proper names likewise depends upon anaphora. On a slightly idealized account, an object receives a name in virtue of a quasi-official dubbing ceremony wherein someone says something like "I hereby name this child 'Anastasia.'" In addition to the fact that one's ability to pick out "this child" depends upon anaphora, a name's ability to pick out the same object depends upon anaphora in a further sense: if one could not use the name as a way of repeating the initial naming, then every subsequent tokening of the word "Anastasia" would be a new naming, in consequence of which the name would not necessarily pick out the same person. Consider an example: "Anastasia took Anastasia's book to the library." Though the second tokening of "Anastasia" appears to repeat the first, their cotypicality does not guarantee that they refer to the same object; it is entirely possible that one Anastasia is doing a favor for another. The point is simple: unless a subsequent tokening of a name is in some respect dependent upon an antecedent tokening – in this instance, the initial dubbing of a child as "Anastasia" – these tokenings will not suffice to pick out an object as the same again. That is to say, unless subsequent tokenings carry on or repeat an initiating reference, there is no reason to think that they refer to the same object; hence, if the use of a proper name does indeed suffice to refer to a single object, it must be the case that subsequent uses of the name repeat the initial reference – it must be the case, that is, that subsequent uses are in the relevant sense anaphorically dependent upon an antecedent naming. It would thus appear that a putatively referring expression such as a demonstrative, a proper name, or a (definite or indefinite) description can succeed in referring only if that expression can be carried on by a chain of anaphoric dependents.

The next step in the argument can be framed as a response to a rather obvious objection: several of the examples adduced in previous paragraphs were supposed to demonstrate that reference depends upon anaphora, yet these examples appear to demonstrate, instead, that anaphor-free utterances *can* repeat a reference to the same object. Consider a variation on the telemarketer example: "A telemarketer just tried to sell me a magazine subscription, but a telemarketer wasn't very persuasive, so I told a telemarketer I didn't want it." I claimed that the repetitions of the indefinite term "a telemarketer" do not suffice to pick out a single object, yet it seems that in some plausible contexts, a competent interpreter would in fact take these terms to pick out one and the same person. Given the right context, that is, it may be clear that the speaker is talking about one and the same person, yet, in apparent contradiction to my argument, he or she does so without the use of an anaphoric chain. Worse, even in the putatively successful version of the telemarketer example (namely, "A telemarketer just tried to sell me a magazine subscription, but she wasn't very persuasive, so I told her I didn't want it"), the use of pronouns does not necessarily guarantee reference back to the antecedent tokening of "a telemarketer," as the speaker's pronouns could be referring to someone else. (As would be clear if, say, the telemarketer were male, though no such clues are necessary.) It might thus appear that, contrary to earlier claims, anaphora is neither necessary nor sufficient for carrying on an antecedent reference.

This objection brings us to an important step in the argument. To see what this is, consider, first, the difference between speaker's reference and semantic reference: suppose someone at a cocktail party identifies her new colleague as "the man in the corner drinking a martini," and that unbeknownst to her the man in the corner – her new colleague – is in fact drinking water.[20] On the semantic level, the woman's sentence refers not to her new colleague but either to no one or to whoever *is* drinking a martini in the corner, yet, in spite of this, the woman herself has nevertheless picked out her new colleague, since it makes more sense to say that she is mistaken about what her colleague is drinking than that she is referring to someone other than the one to whom she intended to refer. The point is that although a speaker can use certain words to refer to an object, a speaker's ability to do so is not necessarily a product of his or her words themselves. To be sure, this does not entail that there is no such thing as semantic reference, though it does suggest something important about how to explain the semantics of reference.

It should come as no surprise that, on the explanation to be defended here, the phenomenon of anaphora should be understood in normative terms: to carry on an anaphoric chain of reference

---

[20] The example is from Donnellan, "Reference and Definite Descriptions"; see also Kripke, "Speaker's Reference and Semantic Reference."

is to intend for one's use of certain words to depend upon certain precedents, where one's use of these words counts as the implicit undertaking of a commitment (a) to inheriting the relevant precedent's referent, whatever that may be, and (b) to using this reference in such a way that one's use of it could stand on one side of an equal sign, so to speak, in an identity claim the other side of which is the precedent reference, in consequence of which (c) still others can inherit the referent by linking up with one's reference to it. We can thus understand the practice of using a name in the following terms: when one uses the name "Aristotle," for instance, one implicitly acknowledges the normative authority of an original use of this word to refer to Aristotle, such that in using the name one inherits the original use's commitment to picking out this particular person. This explains why one cannot identify the referent of "Aristotle" with whatever descriptions one happens to associate with that name, since the one who was Plato's student and wrote *The Nicomachean Ethics*, say, may turn out to be someone other than Aristotle, whereas the name "Aristotle" always picks out Aristotle, just because one's use of that name defers to the one who named him.[21] If everything goes smoothly, accordingly, the use of a name is a way of guaranteeing that one's picking-out goes on in the same way as another's – not, note well, because this guarantee is "in" the name itself, but because one's use of the name implicitly commits one to inheriting the commitments undertaken by precedent uses of it, especially the use of whoever conferred the name upon the object.

A similar story could be told about the other paradigmatic way of inheriting (and so repeating) a reference, namely, the use of pronouns. Consider again the telemarketer example: when one uses pronominal locutions such as "she" and "her" in saying "A telemarketer just tried to sell me a magazine subscription, but she wasn't very persuasive, so I told her I didn't want it," one implicitly commits

---

[21] This account obviously follows that offered by Saul Kripke in *Naming and Necessity*; I spell this out further below.

oneself to inheriting the reference of "a telemarketer," where this commitment should be understood as an implicit claim to the effect that one's further references could stand on the other side of an identity claim from the initial reference, and as licensing others to refer to the initiating reference's referent by using anaphoric locutions to carry on the chain to which one has added a link. On the picture defended here, then, one uses a name or a pronoun by committing oneself to going on in the same way as precedent uses, particularly the precedent use which initiates a chain of reference, and one implicitly claims that others can link up with that chain, and so inherit the reference that initiated it, by going on in the same way as one's own use. Hence, if reference depends upon triangulation, and triangulation depends upon inheritability-of-reference, then reference ends up depending upon the fact that one's use of names and pronouns can inherit the commitments of antecedent references.

2

This way of explaining reference inheritance provides us with a way of understanding the function and importance of locutions such as " … refers to … " Although the antecedent of an anaphoric locution is sometimes obvious – as in, for instance, "Krista returned her book" – this is not always the case; there are times when the relevant antecedent is ambiguous. Consider two examples: "The police officer apprehended the robber; he was wearing a mask" and "I wonder how Steve is doing."[22] In the former, it may not be clear whether "he" is supposed to refer to the police officer or to the robber (though we may assume it is the robber), and in the latter, it may not be clear to which "Steve" the speaker intends to refer. In such cases, one could clarify which antecedent reference one intends to inherit by means

[22] The former example is borrowed from Jason Stanley, for which see his "Hornsby on the Phenomenology of Speech," *Proceedings of the Aristotelian Society, Supplementary Volume* 79 (2005), pp. 131–46.

of a " ... refers to ... " locution: one could thus say, for instance, that "he" refers to the robber, or that the "Steve" one has in mind is "the one who was my lab partner sophomore year," thereby specifying the anaphoric chain one intends one's reference to carry on. Note well, however, that on this account, although one can use descriptions such as "the one who was my lab partner" in order to specify which antecedent reference one intends to inherit, this is not the same thing as explaining reference per se in terms of such descriptions; this account is not liable, therefore, to the kinds of counterexamples customarily adduced against descriptivist accounts.

One further note: theories which explain reference in terms of subsequent tokenings inheriting the reference of an antecedent have been criticized on the grounds that they cannot explain the phenomenon of reference change – when, for instance, a name comes to refer to something other than the object initially picked out by it, as when "Madagascar" came to refer to an island off the eastern coast of Africa, rather than to the section of the mainland to which the name originally referred.[23] In situations such as these, a name is initially given to a particular object, at some point the name is used to refer to some other object, and, eventually, the name comes to refer to the latter instead of the former. If subsequent uses of a name are supposed to inherit the initial reference of the name, how could such changes occur? In order to address this problem, recall the distinction between speaker's reference and semantic reference: someone who intends to use the name "Madagascar" so as to go on in the same way as its initial use may in fact use the name while pointing, say, to some other object, and if subsequent users of the name intend their usage as carrying on this speaker's reference, it follows that they, too, may end up using it to refer to something other than that to which the name initially referred, and eventually, if enough persons use the name in this way, one's interest in using the name to

---

[23] See here Gareth Evans, "The Causal Theory of Names," *Proceedings of the Aristotelian Society, Supplementary Volume* 47 (1973), pp. 187–208.

refer to what others use it to refer to may override one's interest in using it so as to inherit the initial reference. The point, in any event, is that because we have explained reference in terms of what one does with words rather than in terms of words themselves, it is not hard to imagine how such referent change could be explained.

3

I have argued, first, that in order to pick out an object, one must be able to pick out the same object from more than one standpoint (whether these standpoints are those of persons or of intersubstitutable non-trivial identity claims). I then claimed that picking out the same object depends upon the inheritability (and so repeatability) of an antecedent referent, and explained such inheritance in terms of one's commitment to refer to whatever an antecedent referred to. With this account in view, we can turn to the issue of reference to God (or, for convenience, "theological reference"), with respect to which I will argue, first, that reference to God is secured by an anaphoric chain of reference with which God identifies; second, that this chain is itself a work of the Spirit; and third, that this explanation sheds some light on the issues of non-masculinist naming of God and of whether adherents of various religions refer to the same God.[24]

Just as we turned to Schleiermacher to anchor our account of normativity and Barth our account of meaning, so here we turn to Janet Martin Soskice to anchor our account of reference. Soskice's approach is recognizably "therapeutic," since she claims that one's rejection of a correspondentist theory of theological reference – in

---

[24] The account that follows bypasses concerns about the possibility of pointing to God, though it certainly provides reason to think that God can be triangulated (and so picked out). For concerns about pointing to God, see Gordon Kaufman, *God the Problem* (Cambridge, MA: Harvard University Press, 1972), and Robert W. Jenson, *The Knowledge of Things Hoped For: The Sense of Theological Discourse* (Oxford University Press, 1969).

the form of descriptivism – should not be thought to entail that one cannot refer to God. Taking some cues from Saul Kripke and Hilary Putnam, Soskice notes that "reference can take place independently of the possession of a definite description which somehow 'qualitatively uniquely' picks out the individual in question and can even be successful where the identifying description associated with the name fails to be true of the individual in question."[25] As evidence of this, she notes that even if all of one's beliefs about, say, Christopher Columbus turn out to be incorrect – supposing that one could describe him only as "the one who discovered America" or "the one who first realized that the Earth is round" – one's use of the name "Christopher Columbus" would still refer to Columbus himself rather than, say, whoever in fact discovered America. The moral of the story is that "terms can refer independently of unrevisable definitions," and that "reference can take place even where the identifying descriptions associated with a name or a natural kind term fail to be true of the individual in question."[26] An obvious consequence is that it may be possible to refer to God even if one's ideas of God are not themselves sufficient to do so. Soskice accounts for this possibility in two steps. She claims, first, that if one refers to God as "the cause of such-and-such," one's words may pick out God even if they do not *correspond* to God. Soskice here draws an analogy with the picking-out of physical magnitudes such as "heat": one may initially refer to "heat" as "that which causes sensations of warmth," yet the word "heat" refers not to these sensations but to that which causes them – *whatever that might be* – such that one can refer to "heat itself" even if one knows nothing about it.[27] By parity of reasoning, she argues that God can be picked out even if one has no

---

[25] "Theological Realism," in *The Rationality of Religious Belief: Essays in Honor of Basil Mitchell*, William J. Abraham and Steven W. Holtzer (eds.) (Oxford University Press, 1987), p. 111.

[26] Soskice, *Metaphor and Religious Language* (New York: Oxford University Press, 1985), p. 127.

[27] Soskice, *Metaphor and Religious Language*, pp. 127–8.

adequate description of God's essence; Soskice thus refers to God as "the source and cause of all there is," and, in view of various reports of mystical experience of God, as "that which caused such-and-such person's experience."[28] Soskice next argues that such references can be passed along from person to person, in consequence of which even those who lack mystical experience can refer to the cause of another's experience, and those who simply use the name "God" can count as referring to the one dubbed "the source and cause of all there is"; this is possible, according to Soskice, because and insofar as "the speaker is a member of a linguistic community which has passed the name from link to link."[29] The idea here is that one can use a name to refer to an object even if one has no direct acquaintance with it, because one is part of a community some of whose members do have such acquaintance; one can thus use the name "God" to refer to that which others have picked out as "the source and cause of all there is" or as "the one who caused such-and-such experience," even if one is in no position to produce such a picking-out.

Soskice's approach to theological reference could thus be understood as therapeutic, since, by elaborating a non-correspondentist account of reference, she demonstrates that the failure of correspondentism does not necessarily entail that one cannot refer to God. The rest of this section builds on this account by explaining further how God could be picked out, how this picking-out could be passed along from person to person, and how both of these could depend upon God's grace working through Jesus Christ and his Spirit.

4

So then: if one can refer to an object only if one's thought or talk can pick it out as the same again from more than one point of view, and if the paradigmatic way of doing so is by undertaking anaphoric

---

[28] Soskice, *Metaphor and Religious Language*, pp. 139, 152; "Theological Realism," p. 115.
[29] Soskice, *Metaphor and Religious Language*, p. 127.

commitments to inheriting an antecedent picking-out, then we can begin to make sense of theological reference by reconstructing a somewhat idealized account of the way ancient Israelites referred to God – specifically, how an indefinite description became a definite, and so referring, description. Consider: "a god told Abraham to leave his homeland, and this same god made a covenant with him and Sarah, promising to bless them and to be the god of their children." In this example, the one by whom Abraham was called is taken to be identical with the one who made a covenant with him, and it is on this basis that Abraham speaks of God, as when he identifies this God to one of his servants, saying, "The LORD, the God of heaven, who took me from my father's house and from the land of my birth, and who spoke to me and swore to me, 'To your offspring I will give this land,' he will send an angel before you" (Genesis 24:7).[30] Here Abraham identifies the God he has in mind by rehearsing a brief identity claim ("God" is the one who took me from my father's house and who promised this land to my offspring), and then uses an anaphoric locution ("*he* will send an angel … ") to pick out this same God; Abraham thus intends his reference as carrying on (and so inheriting the reference of) a chain of reference that stretches back to a canonical picking-out ("the god who took me from my father's house … "), and he does this by intending a present reference as standing on one side of an identity claim whose other side is a canonical picking-out and its anaphoric dependents. Abraham's servant is enabled to pick out this same God, in turn, by intending his reference as anaphorically dependent upon, and so

---

[30] Scripture translations are from the NRSV. A word on the terms "identification" and "reference": while the terms are not interchangeable, I use "identification" in this subsection to mean something like "a would-be reference that stands on one side of an identity claim the other side of which is a prior reference." One further clarification: I have not here defended the claim that there *is* a God to whom the term "God" might refer. On the present account, however, the term "God" can pick out a single object even if that object were thought not to exist in the real world; in that case, those who so think of God could understand the term to refer to a fictional object, rather than to no object at all.

carrying on, this same chain: so, later in the same story, Abraham's servant directs his prayer to God by saying, "O LORD, God of my master Abraham, please grant me success today" (Genesis 24:12). The servant uses the phrase "God of my master Abraham" as a way of specifying the one to whom he addresses his prayer, and he does this precisely by referring back to a canonical picking-out of God: by setting his reference to God in anaphoric dependence upon a chain of reference that stretches back to Abraham's own reference to God, the servant intends to address his prayer to this same God. We see a similar pattern in subsequent references, as when Jacob intends God as the addressee of his prayer by addressing the one picked out by a series of precedents stretching back to Abraham's canonical reference: "And Jacob said, 'O God of my father Abraham and God of my father Isaac, O LORD who said to me, "Return to your country and to your kindred" ' " (Genesis 32:9). By committing himself to carrying on a chain of reference that stretches back from Isaac to Abraham, Jacob inherits the reference commitment that initiated the chain, and insofar as his reference carries on that chain – insofar, that is, as his reference is intersubstitutable in a non-trivial identity claim the other side of which is the canonical reference – then others will be able to inherit the initial reference by setting themselves in anaphoric dependence upon *Jacob's* reference. An anaphoric chain, stretching back to Abraham's canonical picking-out of God, therefore enables subsequent talk to be about this same God by setting itself in anaphoric dependence upon, in order thus to inherit, that picking-out.

Interestingly enough, Scripture portrays God, too, as referring to Godself by identifying with an anaphoric chain that stretches back to Abraham's canonical picking-out. So when God appears to Moses, for instance, God identifies Godself to him by saying, "I am the God of your father, the God of Abraham, the God of Isaac, and the God of Jacob" (Exodus 3:6). The God who is speaking to Moses identifies Godself as the one who was referred to by Abraham, Isaac, and Jacob, such that the present God's identification of Godself claims to stand on the right side, as it were, of an identity claim whose left side is Abraham's canonical picking-out of God. In this way, God enables Moses to have the right God in mind and implicitly claims that this identification carries on the series of relevant precedents, such that still other references can stand in dependence upon this one; as a result, Israel is now able to refer to the God of Abraham, Isaac, and Jacob as the one who appeared to Moses in the burning bush, who led them out of Egypt, who gave them the law, and so on. Indeed, the God who identified Godself as "the God of Abraham, the God of Isaac, and the God of Jacob" can now refer to Godself as "the LORD your God, who brought you out of the land of Egypt, out of the house of slavery" (Exodus 20:2). Because each subsequent link in this chain is intersubstitutable with precedent links, it follows that as long as subsequent references go on in the same way, they pick out the same God.

We can understand the giving of the divine name in similar terms.[31] The scriptural context is crucial to the present reconstruction, so we quote it at some length: the one who has identified Godself as the God of Abraham says to Moses,

> "The cry of the Israelites has now come to me; I have also seen how the Egyptians oppress them. So come, I will send you to Pharaoh to bring my people, the Israelites, out of Egypt." But Moses said to God, "Who am I that I should go to Pharaoh, and bring the Israelites out of Egypt?" He said, "I will be with you; and this shall be the sign for you that it is I who sent you: when you have brought the people out of Egypt, you shall worship God on this mountain." But Moses said to God, "If I come to the Israelites and say to them, 'the God of your ancestors has sent me to you,' and they ask me, 'What is his name?' what shall I say to them?" God said to Moses, "I will be who I am" ['ehyeh' ašer' ehyeh]. He said further, "Thus you shall say to the Israelites, 'The LORD, the God of your ancestors, the God of

---

[31] For a summary of the vast literature on the subject, see Brevard Childs, *The Book of Exodus: A Critical, Theological Commentary* (Louisville, KY: Westminster John Knox Press, 1974), pp. 60ff.

Abraham, the God of Isaac, and the God of Jacob, has sent me to you': This is my name forever, and this my title for all generations."

(Exodus 3:9–15)

This story has been the subject of endless controversy, but even if we cannot settle the matter here, we can nevertheless use our reconstruction to shed light on a few of its features. First, it is important to note that God's giving of the name is explicitly located within the context of canonical identifications of God: the one here named is the same one who covenanted with Abraham, etc. Second, with respect to the name itself, there is some reason to take it as rendered above, namely, as "I will be who I am." On this view, God identifies Godself as the one who is and will continue to be the one who made a covenant with Abraham and his children, such that "I will be who I am" is just another way of saying "I am and will always be the God of Abraham, Isaac, and Jacob." This is not the only way of understanding the name, of course, but there are a few reasons that speak on its behalf.[32] First, this construal of the name makes sense as a way of reassuring worried Israelites: in response to their concerns about following Moses out of Egypt, it is fitting that God would tell them that God is and will continue to be the one who covenanted with their ancestors. Second, this reading ties in with God's just-mentioned promise to Moses, "I will be with you" (3:12), repeating the same verbal form. Third, this reading explains the apparent parallelism between "I will be who I am" and "I am the LORD, the God of your fathers," since, on the present construal, both names identify God as the one who is and will remain faithful to the covenant with Abraham and his children. And finally, this interpretation makes good sense of the claim that this is God's name down to all generations, since, if God is indeed identifying Godself as the one who is and will forever be the one who covenanted with Abraham,

---

[32] For an argument along these lines, see Terence E. Fretheim, *Exodus* (Louisville, KY: Westminster John Knox, 1991), pp. 63ff.

it follows that this is how God can and should be identified from generation to generation. The present account of reference thus helps explain the giving of the name, precisely since it explains the sense in which names are related to anaphoric chains of reference, as in "the God of Abraham is the one who will be with us as we depart from Egypt."

Ancient Israel thus came to identify God as the God of Abraham, Isaac, and Jacob, the one who led them out of Egypt, the one who gave them the law, and so on; we can understand the New Testament as intending to carry on this chain of reference while developing it in crucial respects. One of the key themes of the entire New Testament, it seems, is that "the God of Abraham, the God of Isaac, and the God of Jacob, the God of our ancestors has glorified his servant Jesus" (Acts 3:13); that the God of Abraham is thus "the one who raised the Lord Jesus" (2 Corinthians 4:14; cf. Romans 4:24 and 8:11), the one who sent Jesus (cf. John 12:44, 13:20, and 15:21), whom Jesus calls "Father" (John 8:54), and "the one who justifies the ungodly" (Romans 4:5). That is to say, the New Testament claims that the God of Abraham, Isaac, and Jacob is identical with the one who sent Jesus, who justifies the ungodly, and so forth, thereby claiming that these references carry on the anaphoric chain that stretches back to Abraham's canonical picking-out of God, even as they constitute a crucial development within it. The crucial development is this: the New Testament claims not only that there is no God other than the God of Abraham, but that there is no God other than the one who sent Jesus; and insofar as God identifies wholeheartedly with Jesus (in the sense discussed in Chapter 1), it follows that *God's* identity is now irreversibly tied to *Jesus'* identity. From a New Testament point of view, accordingly, the chain of reference that stretches back to Abraham has undergone a decisive shift: in consequence of God's identification with Jesus, it would appear that reference to God as the one who sent Jesus stands as a kind of second canonical picking-out, one which carries on the chain that stretches back to Abraham – the chain that prepared the way for this reference – yet which nevertheless can be seen to stand out from it. According to the New Testament, something new has happened. Explaining just what this novelty was – with respect to the anaphoric chain of reference, that is – is the task of the next two subsections.

5

The New Testament claims that the God who covenanted with Abraham, who led the Israelites out of Egypt, and so on, is the one who sent Jesus, who justifies the ungodly, etc. God's identification as the one who sent Jesus is thus supposed to carry on the chain of reference that stretches back to Abraham's canonical picking-out of God, yet there are a few respects in which this identification stands out from the others, the first of which has to do with God's canonical identification as the one who is faithful to the covenant with Israel. The novelty is this: on the one hand, as noted in the previous subsection, God declares Godself to be the one who is and will be faithful to the covenant to all generations, and on the other, the New Testament proclaims that the covenant has been fulfilled in Jesus Christ. Hence, if God identifies Godself wholeheartedly with faithfulness to the covenant, and Jesus Christ is the ultimate fulfillment of this faithfulness, it follows that God identifies Godself wholeheartedly and ultimately as the one who sent Jesus Christ. That is to say, if Jesus Christ is the fulfillment of the covenant, he must also be the fulfillment of God's identity as the one who called Abraham, the one who led the Israelites out of Egypt, and so on. One could thus see God's identification with Jesus Christ as the culmination of all previous references to God, since, from a retrospective point of view, it becomes clear that this is the direction in which all precedent references have been pointing. This identification could likewise be seen to stand in judgment on all prior and subsequent would-be references to God, in that a putative identification of God would now count as correct just in case it could stand on the left side of an identity claim whose right side is God's identification as the one who sent Jesus, who justifies the ungodly, etc.

We will return to this point momentarily, but before doing so, we need to mention a further sense in which God's identification as the one who sent Jesus, who justifies the ungodly, and so forth is thought to stand out from precedent references to God, namely, the New Testament's claim that the one who sent Jesus also sent the Holy Spirit to bear witness to him. As argued above, one's use of certain words does not by itself guarantee that those words pick out a particular object: taken by themselves, neither pronouns nor proper names can be said to refer to a particular object; a pronoun, proper name, or other means of picking out an object is able to do so only if one's use of them is recognizable as inheriting the commitment implicit in a precedent picking-out, where this commitment should be understood as an implicit claim to the effect that one's reference to this object is intersubstitutable with the relevant precedents, such that others could refer to this object by inheriting one's reference to it. Something similar must be said about reference to God, and, as one should by now expect, this should be understood as a work of the Spirit. On the account elaborated here, Christ imparted his normative Spirit to his disciples by training them to distinguish which beliefs and actions would count as following him, and when they had internalized the norms with which to draw such distinctions, he recognized them not only as knowing how to do so, but as able to recognize others as knowing how, too; that is to say, once he had recognized the disciples as knowing how to follow him, others could learn to do so by submitting their practices to the disciples' assessments until they had internalized the relevant norms, at which point the disciples recognized their authority as fellow recognizers, and so on. In this way, Christ's normative Spirit is mediated through a process of intersubjective recognition, and it is this Spirit which enables one to refer to God: on the present account, (a) one intends one's use of putatively referring terms, such as "God," "Father," or "Lord," as referring to God by committing oneself to inheriting the reference of a chain of canonical references that stretches back to Abraham, Moses, and Jesus, (b) one undertakes this commitment by recognizing certain precedent references as authoritative and by trying to go on in the same way – paradigmatically by referring to God in such a way that one's reference is intersubstitutable in an identity claim the other side of which is a canonical picking-out – and (c) one thereby implicitly licenses others both to hold one accountable for this commitment and to refer to God by going on in the same way as one's own reference locutions. One's reference to God thus depends upon one's going on in the same way as a chain of precedent references, and if one's reference is recognizable as doing so, it follows that still others can refer to God by going on in the same way. The chain of reference can thus be thought to carry on a normative Spirit that stretches back to a canonical reference to God, paradigmatically that of Jesus. On the account defended here, then, theological reference is understood to be a trinitarian affair: one refers to God if one's reference is recognizable as going on in the same way as Christ's own reference to God, and one's ability to do so depends upon the work of the Spirit. This is not to suggest, however, that Christians alone are able to refer to God; the following subsection aims to clarify this point.

6

I have discussed two claims which would seem to entail that Christians alone can refer to God: the claim, on the one hand, that Jesus Christ fulfills and judges all precedent and subsequent reference to God, and on the other, that one's ability to refer to God depends in some respect upon the mediation of Christ's normative Spirit. Can this account explain the possibility that non-Christians could refer to this same God? Can it explain, for instance, Paul's apparent recognition that some non-Christian philosophers were talking about God – albeit unknowingly? To see how these questions might be addressed, it is important to note that the present account requires only that one's reference be intersubstitutable in a non-trivial identity claim one side of which is a canonical reference to God. With this requirement in mind, we can understand the referent of non-Christian God-talk in more or less the same terms we have used to explain the possibility of Christian reference. Suppose someone says something like the following: "Praise God from whom all blessings flow." To what or whom has this person directed his or her praise? The mere fact that he or she uses the word "God" does not by itself guarantee that he or she is referring to the same God as anyone else, any more than someone's use of the word "Kevin" would guarantee that he or she were talking about me. Is it possible that this person has referred to the one who sent Jesus, who justifies the ungodly, etc.? In order to answer this question, one would need to learn more about the person's collateral commitments, since his or her understanding of blessings, for instance, as well as his or her understanding of God's nature, may play a role in determining whether his or her reference is recognizable as referring to the one to whom Christians refer, depending on how much these understandings diverge from the content of these concepts as applied to the God who sent Jesus. Most would-be references to God would undoubtedly meet this condition. A second condition might prove more difficult: as Keith Donnellan points out, there is an important difference between "referential" and "attributive" descriptions, where the former is a use of descriptions to talk about a particular object which is picked out on some other basis, while the latter is a use of descriptions to talk about whatever fits the description.[33] Hence, in the example of "the one from whom all blessings flow," a "referential" use of this description would use it to say something about a God whom one has already picked out, such that the words would be directed to that God even if it turned out that that God was *not* the one from whom all blessings flow. An "attributive" use, by contrast, would use the description precisely *as* a way of picking out the relevant object, such that "God," on this use, would refer

[33] On this point, see Donnellan, "Reference and Definite Descriptions."

to "the one from whom all blessings flow – *whoever that may be*." Hence, if the content of the speaker's concepts is recognizable as going on in the same way as their content as applied to the one who sent Jesus and so forth, then an attributive use of "the one from whom all blessings flow" could indeed be thought to refer to that God.[34] If the speaker were to intend this description "referentially," however, it would appear that his or her reference would be recognizable as identifying the one who sent Jesus only if the canonical references upon which his or her reference depends are themselves recognizable as going on in the same way as references such as "the one who called Abraham, who led the Israelites out of Egypt, and who justifies the ungodly," which seems a much narrower standard to meet. There are no rules, in any event, by which one could judge in advance which references will count as referring to the one who sent Jesus, for this, too, is a judgment which is subject to the ongoing recognition of the Spirit, and one's determination about whether a candidate reference counts as a reference to the God of Jesus Christ may involve some trade-offs: if one recognizes a member of another faith tradition as referring to the God of Jesus Christ, then one has little choice but to interpret his or her divergences from recognized precedents as errors of some sort (or as indicative of one's own errors), whereas if one takes him or her to be referring to some other god, then one has no reason to count his or her divergences as errors. We will discuss this point further in the next section.

7

This account is liable to a handful of objections, the most serious of which concerns its relationship to oppressive uses of God-talk.

---

[34] This seems to be the proper construal of William Alston's important argument in "Referring to God," *Divine Nature and Human Language: Essays in Philosophical Theology* (Ithaca, NY: Cornell University Press, 1989).

The objection could be framed in terms of contemporary feminist concerns with the preponderance of masculinist images and names for God: if one's reference to God depends upon one's going on in the same way as precedent references, as the present account claims, it would appear to follow that God-talk can never be liberated from the oppressive uses of the past, since one's very reference to God would implicitly preserve the unjust social arrangements underwritten by those uses. I cannot do justice to this concern until Chapter 6, but for now, I can at least gesture in the right direction by observing that the present proposal supplies rebuttals against two objections commonly raised against non-masculinist language for God.

Conveniently enough, an influential version of each objection has been raised by the same theologian, Robert W. Jenson (with whom this project otherwise has so much in common). Jenson objects, first, to the increasingly common practice of using "God" and "Godself" in place of masculine pronouns such as "he," "his," and "himself": Jenson claims that if "God" is a common name, then "such sentences as 'God sent God's Son' do not establish that the referent of the second 'God' is the same as the referent of the first, or to which divinity this 'Son' is then related. The sentence could, as far as its grammar shows, be the report of a typical polytheistic transaction."[35] On the other hand, even if "God" is thought to be a proper name, the same problems arise: "If someone says, 'Joan sent Joan's son,' this sentence does not in fact establish that the son sent is the son of the person named by the first occurrence of 'Joan.' For of course, there may be and usually are many bearers of the same 'proper' name. Where the initial instance of a proper name has in the semantic context effected a successful identification, its later repetition in place of

---

[35] Jenson, "The Father, He … " in *Speaking the Christian God: The Holy Trinity and the Challenge of Feminism*, Alvin F. Kimel (ed.) (Grand Rapids, MI: Eerdmans, 1992), p. 98. Paul Molnar raised a version of this argument against me in his "The Trinity, Election, and God's Ontological Freedom: A Response to Kevin W. Hector," *International Journal of Systematic Theology* 8:3 (2006), pp. 294–306; this section should suffice as a response.

a pronoun positively suggests that two different persons are referred to. The repetition of 'God,' precisely in a context where this is heard as a proper name, must still most naturally belong to a polytheistic context."[36] Jenson thus concludes that the practice of using "God … God … Godself" in place of "God … he … himself" is polytheistic in nature if not intent, and is therefore nothing less than "the invasion of an antagonistic religious discourse [which] represents a true crisis of the faith that cannot be dealt with by compromise."[37] In response to this, it should suffice to recall my earlier argument to the effect that pronouns themselves are neither necessary nor sufficient to guarantee co-reference with some antecedent picking-out of God, since it is not hard to imagine cases where a second use of a proper name refers to the same person as the first use, just as it is not hard to imagine cases where a pronoun refers to someone other than the immediate antecedent. So the multiply athletic Bo Jackson, for instance, consistently referred to himself by name – as in "Bo knows what Bo has to do tomorrow" – yet no one thought that subsequent tokenings of "Bo" referred to anyone other than the first tokening. Likewise, when someone says "God sent God's Son," no one – not even Jenson – actually thinks that the second tokening of "God" refers to someone other than the first tokening. In light of the foregoing, we might say that Jenson's argument fails to appreciate the distinction between speaker's reference and semantic reference. Then again, if pronouns are not by themselves sufficient to guarantee co-reference with a particular antecedent, it follows that semantic reference is not as unambiguous as Jenson assumes. Jenson seems to think that the use of a pronoun in "Joan sent her son," unlike "Joan sent Joan's son," guarantees that the son in question is Joan's, but this is not necessarily the case, since the use of "her" does not necessarily refer to "Joan": if Joan has no children, for instance, or if the remark in question were to occur during a conversation about how Joan takes advantage of another woman's family, the "her" may either be ambiguous or refer

---

[36] Jenson, "The Father, He," p. 99.   [37] Jenson, "The Father, He," p. 96.

to someone other than Joan. (We could sort this out, of course, by means of a "refers-to" locution.) Similarly, the use of "his" does not by itself guarantee co-reference to God, since the "his" in "God sent his son" could refer, say, to Amoz (Isaiah's father). At the very least, the reference of a pronoun depends upon its relationship to a particular discursive context, though this relationship, by itself, does not determine a pronoun's reference; its reference is determined, rather, by a speaker's normative commitment to inherit a precedent reference and an interpreter's ability to recognize the commitment thus undertaken. This, and not something in one's words themselves, is what enables proper names and pronouns to refer to a particular object, which means that although Jenson may be entitled to his use of masculine pronouns, he has not succeeded in demonstrating that those who avoid such pronouns are not entitled to do so.

This brings us to Jenson's second objection, which concerns the practice of using names other than "Father" to refer to God. His argument, simply stated, is that "Father" cannot be replaced, because (a) it is the term by which Jesus picked out God, and (b) one has no way of knowing whether a candidate replacement would refer to the same God. "That Jesus called on God with 'father' rather than 'mother,'" Jenson argues, "is a fact about the historic person Jesus that we can no more change by decree than we can decree that he was not Jewish, a wandering rabbi, or unpopular with the Sanhedrin. Since the church's address of God is authorized only as the repetition of Jesus' address, this fact about him is determinative for the church."[38] In the usual case, of course, one's reference to some object does not depend upon one's authorization to do so, yet Jenson thinks that in this instance, one can pick out God only by means of the referring term Jesus authorized. He realizes that theological reference thus differs from ordinary reference, but he claims that the use of "Father" to refer to God, like the use of water in baptism, is in this respect simply unlike the use of an ordinary sign: "A sign that belongs to a proper

[38] Jenson, "The Father, He," p. 104.

language, constituted by knowable semantic and syntactic rules, can be replaced in the language by some other sound or mark, following the same semantic rules by which the sign was specified in the first place. But we are not in a position to do this with such signs as the bath of baptism. We are not able to create a different ceremony of initiation – say, the giving of a particular lifelong haircut – and declare that this will now mean what baptism has meant. The reason is that we possess no semantic rules to control the translation."[39] This argument faces a serious objection, however, namely, that Christians *do* translate the name by which Jesus called upon God. That is to say, Christians refer to the one to whom Jesus referred not simply by *repeating* or *transliterating* the noises that he made, but by looking for a word in their language that means the same thing as those noises – they refer to this one, in other words, precisely by *translating* Jesus' word of address. And while some may take issue with particular ways in which this word is translated, no one, least of all Jenson, seems to question the propriety per se of doing so. Jenson could rejoin, of course, that there is a significant difference between translating Jesus' address as "Father" and calling God "Mother," but the mere fact that Jenson accepts the propriety of the former entails that the repetition in question need not be *mere* repetition, as it likewise entails that one's authorization to refer to God extends beyond such repetition. Jenson might nevertheless try to limit these consequences by falling back on another of his influential arguments, namely, his claim that any attempt to address God in non-traditional terms "presuppose[s] that we first know about a triune God and then look about for a form of words to address him, when in fact it is the other way around."[40] This seems not to be true, however, or at least not necessarily so. To see why not, consider a declaration such as the following: "From now on, I will refer to the one whom Jesus called 'Father' as 'Mother.'" Such a

---

[39] Jenson, "The Father, He," p. 107.

[40] Jenson, *The Triune Identity: God According to the Gospel* (Minneapolis, MN: Augsburg Fortress Press, 1982), p. 17.

declaration – the semantics of which is entirely in order – exhibits the fact that one's commitment to a non-traditional way of addressing God need not presuppose that one is picking out God otherwise than in dependence upon Jesus, and insofar as one's use of this address is "referential" (in Donnellan's sense), it follows that even if it were granted that the concept "mother" is inappropriate for God – and I have not granted this – this would mean only that one's use of the concept to refer to God is in some respect inappropriate for doing so, not that one has not referred to this God.[41] The issue, then, is not whether one can refer to God in alternative ways; the issue is whether such alternatives are recognizable as going on in the same way as the relevant precedents and whether these precedents establish a normative trajectory which is necessarily complicit in certain unjust social arrangements. We will return to these issues in Chapter 6; for now, it suffices to demonstrate that the present account provides us with some resources by which to respond to arguments against non-masculinist language for God.

***

We began this chapter by noting a problem: if one's reference to an object depends upon a unique correspondence between one's ideas and the object itself, it seems to follow that if such correspondence is unworkable (at least with respect to God), then one cannot refer to God. The aim of this section was to render this conclusion optional by elaborating and defending a non-correspondentist account of reference, and then explaining how the Spirit of Christ could enable one to refer to God. A problem remains, however: even if one could direct one's words to God, one might still feel alienated from God insofar as (a) one is thought to be in touch with an object only if one enjoys immediate access to its being-in-itself, and (b) one lacks this sort of access to God. To this problem we now turn.

---

[41] Indeed, one's judgment that the concept is inappropriate for application to God depends upon one's taking God to be its purported object.

Seeing through the Spirit

The other issue mentioned in the first section is that concepts are thought to stand like a veil between one and objects (including God), such that one's language and thoughts could never be in touch with – or genuinely about – objects themselves. From a therapeutic point of view, this sense of limitation looks like the residual influence of an essentialist-correspondentist picture of what it means to be in touch with objects; the aim of the present section, accordingly, is to free us from the idea that concepts stand between one and God by elaborating a deflationary account of "being in touch" as this emerges from a de-metaphysicalized notion of concepts.

1

To understand the idea that concepts stand like a veil between us and objects, we must recall the argument of Kant (and others) to the effect that one can neither think nor talk about objects apart from one's application of concepts to them. In light of such arguments, it is commonly claimed that concepts must play a role in perception, at least insofar as perception is supposed to play a role in communication, thought, knowledge, and so forth. Thus far, I would agree. I disagree, however, with the further claim that concepts should be thought to mediate objects to us in such a way that we have no access to objects themselves. The relevant counterclaim is that once concepts have been suitably deflated, it no longer makes sense to think of them as go-betweens, such that one's denial of the correspondentist picture of immediate, concept-free access to objects-in-themselves (or of privileged correspondence between concepts and an object-in-itself, which is the topic of Chapter 5) need not leave one with a sense of distance between "objects-themselves" and "objects-as-one-perceives-them."

There are two characteristic ways in which concepts may come to seem like an intermediary between objects and oneself: on the one hand, insofar as the concept application necessary to perception is thought of as the product of inference, it appears that one has no immediate, inference-free access to the objects of such perception; and on the other, if various persons' concepts differ to such an extent that these persons perceive different worlds, it may appear that perception is irreducibly relative to, and so mediated by, a conceptual scheme, and that one has no access to objects apart from such a scheme. This subsection deals with the former issue by sketching an account according to which concepts are applied non-inferentially, and so immediately, in everyday perception.[42] Toward this end, consider the role concepts play in, say, reading the word "glitter." When children are first learning how to read, they probably learn which concept to apply to each letter – to apply the concept "A" to A, "B" to B, and so on. If they encountered the letters G-L-I-T-T-E-R at this point, they would try to apply the proper letter concepts to each letter, and their teachers would help them do so.[43] Once they have mastered letter concepts, they then learn what sounds to associate with each letter when letters are grouped together into words. (They also learn how to apply the concept "word," of course.) If they encounter the letters G-L-I-T-T-E-R at this point, they will attempt to sound out each letter and then put the sounds together, as their teachers assess their performance. Now imagine that these children have grown up

---

[42] Here I am drawing together some arguments of John McDowell (for which see *Mind and World* [Cambridge, MA: Harvard University Press, 1994] and *Having the World in View* [Cambridge, MA: Harvard University Press, 2009]); Robert Brandom, *Making It Explicit*, Chapter 4; Donald Davidson, "Seeing Through Language," *Truth, Language, and History*, pp. 127–41. I likewise defend a view along these lines in "Attunement and Explicitation: A Pragmatist Reading of Schleiermacher's 'Theology of Feeling,'" in *Schleiermacher, the Study of Religion, and the Future of Theology*, Brent Sockness and Wilhelm Gräb (eds.) (Berlin: Walter de Gruyter, 2010).

[43] A further argument against the idea that concepts stand between us and objects could be derived from the fact that one can so much as learn concepts only by virtue of interacting with a teacher and a shared object; for an argument to this effect, see Davidson, *Inquiries into Truth and Interpretation*.

and become competent readers. How will they respond to the letters G-L-I-T-T-E-R at this point? Once they have mastered the concepts for each letter, and have mastered the way letters work together to produce words, they will simply *see* the letters *as* the word "glitter." For those who are competent readers, that is, letter concepts have become second nature, such that one applies them without having to think about it. In order to arrive at this point, one had to learn how to apply the relevant concepts, but once one has mastered them, one applies them more or less automatically. In fact, once one has become reliably disposed to do so, simply looking at certain letters will cause one to apply the relevant concepts. If one is a competent reader of English, that is, just seeing the letters G-L-I-T-T-E-R will cause one to apply the concept "glitter." As with letters, so with other objects: one initially learns to apply concepts to them by trying to go on in the same way as one's teachers, but once one has mastered these applications, one becomes disposed to apply them non-inferentially whenever one notices the relevant objects. It is this insight that underlies Quine's claim that observability is relative to the training provided by a particular discursive community – a community of skilled musicians, for instance, can hear certain sounds *as* a particular combination of notes; a community of baseball umpires can see certain pitches *as* balls or strikes; a community of wine-drinkers can taste a wine *as* of a certain variety – such that members of these communities apply the relevant concepts without having to think about doing so.[44]

So then: when one has become reliably disposed to respond non-inferentially to certain objects by applying the appropriate concepts, one automatically perceives such objects *as* thus-and-so, without having to deliberate about what concept to apply. Because certain concept applications have become second nature, one sees certain marks as letters, sees letters as words, sees strings of words as

[44] W. V. O. Quine, "Epistemology Naturalized," in *Ontological Relativity and Other Essays*, pp. 69–90.

making a claim, and so on. There are moments, of course, when one's automatic concept application turns out to be incorrect – when, for instance, one accidentally reads a word such as "psychical" as "physical" – and moments when one has to slow down and deliberate over the proper concepts to apply – as when one has to sound out an unfamiliar name such as "Asenath." In such moments, one realizes what one has been doing all along without noticing it, namely, applying concepts. In general, though, nothing goes wrong, and one perceives objects as something or other in virtue of a non-inferential disposition to apply particular concepts, such that, in the vast majority of cases, merely paying attention to an object causes one to apply the relevant concept. Once one has mastered a concept, accordingly, the appearance of whatever it applies to causes one non-inferentially to apply it, in consequence of which one need not think of concept application as introducing an intermediate, inference-like step between an object's presence and one's perception of it.

2

As noted above, observability is relative to a discursive community: if members of a community have been trained to apply certain concepts to certain objects, and if these members have become reliably disposed to respond to these objects by applying the relevant concept, then merely attending to such objects will cause these persons to perceive them *as* something or other. Supposing, then, that one can apply concepts to God (as the previous two chapters have argued); would it make sense to apply this model to one's putative perception of God?[45] To see how this question might be addressed, recall two earlier claims: (a) that to use a theological concept correctly, one's

---

[45] This subsection is heavily indebted to two important works: William Alston's *Perceiving God: The Epistemology of Religious Experience* (Ithaca, NY: Cornell University Press, 1991) and especially the remarkable dissertation of Stephen S. Bush, "Experience and Power: The Theory and Ethics of Religious Experience" (Unpublished PhD Dissertation, Princeton University, 2008).

use must be recognizable as going on in the same way as precedent uses, and (b) that the normative Spirit of Christ's own recognition is mediated through an ongoing process of such recognitions. If one properly perceives some object to be God, therefore, or properly perceives some experience to be an experience *of* God, only if one correctly applies the relevant concept, then we can understand perception of God to be immediate (at least potentially) in two respects. First, though it would be difficult to prove, it is at least thinkable that ancient Israelites, for instance, as well as early Christians were trained to distinguish experience of God from other experiences and thereby became reliably disposed to respond to God's presence by applying the proper concept. So Scripture portrays ancient Israelites, for instance, being trained by patriarchs, prophets, and other leaders to distinguish the true God from false gods, and Jesus training his followers to distinguish between true and false "words of God," true and false works of the Spirit, and so on, and it therefore makes sense to understand at least some perceptions of God as non-inferential, though, again, this is hard to prove. In certain stories, at any rate, it seems as if God's mere presence causes those beholding it to respond by applying some version of the concept "God," just as those who had been filled with Jesus' Spirit seem to have been able to see certain persons *as* filled with that Spirit.[46] This is not to suggest that every candidate perception of God is non-inferential – there are plenty of examples to the contrary – but that non-inferential perception is at least possible, and if one accepts the possibility that God appears to persons or that God speaks, on the one hand, and that persons can be trained to respond to these appearances by non-inferentially applying the appropriate concepts, on the other, then it is probable that God's presence could be observable in the relevant sense. (The fact that one could become reliably disposed to respond non-inferentially in this way would go a long way toward explaining

---

[46] See, among many others, the call narratives of Isaiah and Jeremiah, on the one hand, and the perceptions of the Spirit recorded in Acts, on the other.

the so-called anonymity of the Holy Spirit, since it explains how the Spirit works best, so to speak, when it fades into the background, thereby enabling one to see *through* it.) Perception of God can also be understood as immediate in a further sense: if (a) to perceive God as God is to respond to God's presence by applying the appropriate concepts, (b) to apply such concepts is a matter of their answering to God's revelation in Christ, and (c) to answer to Christ is for one's use of these concepts to go on in the same way as uses which carry on Christ's normative Spirit, it follows (d) that one perceives God *through* God – that is, that one's perception of God is a trinitarian affair, and therefore not external to God.

On this account of perception of God, then, there are two senses in which concepts could be thought not to stand between one and God. On the one hand, concepts need not stand between one and God if it is by God's own activity, through Word and Spirit, that such perception is possible, and on the other, if one can become reliably disposed to respond non-inferentially to God's presence by applying the relevant concepts. In this way, God enables one to see God through God's Spirit, and concepts need not be thought to introduce an intermediate (because inferential) step between God's presence and one's perception of that presence.

3

So far, then, so good: if one can perceive God through God, and if one can become reliably disposed to respond non-inferentially to God's presence by applying the relevant concepts, then the involvement of concepts in such perception need not be thought to introduce an inferential step between God's presence and one's perception of God. This is not the only way in which concepts are thought to introduce an intermediate step, however; as noted, one's perception of objects is sometimes thought to be relative to a conceptual scheme, such that if (a) one perceives objects only through the application of concepts, (b) conceptual schemes differ from person to person to such an extent that persons perceive different worlds, and (c) one cannot appeal to objects themselves in order to adjudicate among these perceptions, it seems to follow (d) that concepts do indeed stand between the world and oneself. That is to say, if one's concepts are incommensurable with the concepts that others apply to God, it would appear to follow that the God one perceives will in fact be incommensurable with the God perceived by others and that concepts thus stand between one and God.

In order to respond to this problem, we must first clarify the relationship between incommensurability and the distance that concepts are alleged to introduce between us and objects. In the sense in which the term is being used here, a set of concepts is incommensurable with another such set if and only if there is no way to map one set onto the other or to map both sets onto a third, where the mapping in question should be understood in terms of interpretability. If sets of concepts were incommensurable in this respect, then it might make sense to think that those who perceive objects through them in fact see incommensurably (and inadjudicably) different objects, such that concepts could indeed be thought to stand like a veil between us and the world.

So then: can sets of concepts be incommensurable in this sense? Donald Davidson famously argued that we can make no sense of the idea of vastly incommensurable conceptual schemes, though both the content and import of that argument have been much debated. Whether or not it ought to be ascribed to Davidson, a version of his argument can be defended in terms of the semantics sketched here. One key to the argument is that language, too, is part of the environing circumstances with which one is constantly trying to cope, just like the objects about which one speaks. This claim is a consequence of Davidson's (and my) abandonment of the idea that the meaning of an utterance is to be understood in terms of its correspondence to a fixed, idea-like "meaning"; one result of this abandonment is that one's interpretation of another's marks and noises must be a product of one's ongoing attempt to make sense of them, testing whether one's interpretation works, and so on, just as one copes with other, non-linguistic aspects of one's environment. Concepts can hardly be thought of as a *tertium* standing between us and the environment, therefore, since their use is itself part of that environment; that is to say, once one has recognized that one makes sense of others' marks and noises in the same way one makes sense of other aspects of one's environment, one has simultaneously "erased the boundary between knowing a language and knowing our way around the world generally."[47] Given that an argument along these lines was defended in the previous chapter, it remains here only to consider how it would apply to the idea of incommensurability: if concept use is neither fixed nor uniform (since, on our account, the meaning of a concept changes every time a novel use is recognized as going on in the same way as precedent uses), it follows that in order to interpret another's marks and noises as concept use, one must try to understand them as carrying on the normative trajectory implicit in the relevant precedents. In order to be recognizable as carrying on such a trajectory, in turn, a candidate concept use must be seen as applying the concept in circumstances relevantly similar to those in which it had been applied in precedent uses, which turns out to mean that one interprets another's marks and noises as concept use only if one can correlate them with environing circumstances (including other marks and noises) to which the concept has been applied. If one cannot understand them as trying to go on in the same way as these precedents, especially with respect to their circumstances of application, one has no reason to count these particular behaviors as concept use (or as an attempt to use a particular concept). That is to say, either (a) one can establish correlations between another's concept use and one's own, in which case (i) the two sets of concepts cannot be understood as incommensurable, (ii) perception's relativity to a conceptual scheme does not amount to persons seeing irreducibly and inadjudicably different worlds, and (iii) concepts need

---

[47] Davidson, "A Nice Derangement of Epitaphs," *Truth, Language, and History,* p. 107.

not be thought to stand like a veil between one and objects; or else (b) one cannot establish such correlations, and one therefore has no grounds for thinking that one has understood what the other person has said.[48]

Consider an example: suppose one can draw some correlation between the circumstances to which another applies a particular concept, yet that concept seems to mean something significantly different from the concept one would apply in those circumstances. Insofar as they apply a concept which is incompatible with the concept one would oneself apply, it may indeed seem that these persons perceive something different than one does – as, for instance, someone who hears "Excuse me while I kiss this guy" when Jimi Hendrix sings "Excuse me while I kiss the sky" has indeed perceived something different than someone who hears the words " … kiss the sky." Likewise, someone who perceived God's presence as *Baal's* presence would have perceived something different than one who perceived it as God's. In cases like these, it makes sense to say that two persons see different objects as a result of the concepts they have been trained to apply. This hardly entails that objects are irreducibly relative to a conceptual scheme, however, since (a) one should judge that the person who hears " … kiss the sky" as " … kiss this guy" has in fact *mis*heard these words, just as the person who perceives God as Baal has misperceived God, and (b) the very possibility of such judgments indicates that the two sets of schemes are commensurable, since taking a perception to be mistaken presupposes common ground by which to recognize it as such, which suggests that the objects perceived are not finally and ineliminably relative to one's conceptual scheme. This claim faces an apparent objection, however: if one's judgment that another person misperceives some object is itself based on one's own perception of the object, how does one know that one's

[48] For an able defense of a claim along these lines, see Jeffrey Stout's *Ethics After Babel: The Languages of Morals and Their Discontents* (Princeton, NJ: Princeton University Press, 1988, 2001).

194

own perceptions are not mistaken? In response, consider, first, that once one's perceptual belief has been appropriately questioned and one considers whether one's disposition to apply a particular concept is correct, one's application of the concept in question is no longer a non-inferential affair. That is to say, once someone suggests that the lyric in question is " … kiss the sky," not " … kiss this guy," one will listen to the song more carefully, consider whether one's previous hearing of it is correct, try to hear it as others do, and so on. This does not entail that one is now engaged in concept-free perception of the song, but as long as one leaves unquestioned a sufficient number of one's other perceptual beliefs, one can suspend one's commitment to one's usual way of perceiving it in order to judge whether that perception is correct. Because non-inferential concept applications can thus be called into question, it follows that one is not bound by whatever misperceptions they might make one liable to. Moreover, it is telling that there is a rather limited range of what might count as a misperception: we can make sense of someone hearing "kiss the sky" as "kiss this guy," but not as, say, "hug that girl"; for a mistake, the latter would be too large, and instead of taking it to be a misperception of "kiss the sky," one would have to interpret it as a perception of something else, as a joke, or as playing a language game other than "report what you hear."[49] This illustrates an earlier point: though we can question any one of our perceptual beliefs, we cannot question them all at once. That is to say, unless one leaves unquestioned a considerable number of other beliefs – beliefs such as "I am hearing the sound 'kïsthəskï,'" "I am a reliable perceiver of sounds in these circumstances," etc. – there will be no reason to think that it is one's perceptual belief about a particular series of noises that one is calling into question. It is only because persons agree on almost all of these

---

[49] On this point, see Wittgenstein's famous discussion of timber sellers in *Bemerkungen über die Grundlagen der Mathematik*, Schriften, vol. VI, G. E. M. Anscombe, Rush Rhees, and G. H. von Wright (eds.) (Frankfurt am Main: Suhrkamp Verlag, 1974), I.149–50.

beliefs that they can disagree about any one of them, and it is for this same reason that the range of meaningful disagreement is quite limited. Hence, given that a whole range of perceptual beliefs must be thought to be correct in order to question any of them, it follows that the range of divergences which can count as misperceptions is limited, and it follows further that it makes no sense to think of these beliefs as divergent or wrong on the whole. If so, the phenomenon of misperception must be a limited affair, which would mean that concepts cannot, generally speaking, stand between one and objects in the way conceptual-scheme-relativists imagine – unless, that is, one simply prefers to hold a radically skeptical view of the matter, which one would be free to do as long as one grounds that view in an alternative understanding of concepts and objects (say, a robustly essentialist understanding). As explained in the first chapter, the present argument suffices only to entitle one *not* to hold such a view; it does not demonstrate that one cannot do so. (This is the difference Richard Rorty has in mind, I take it, when he distinguishes between answering a skeptic and telling him or her to get lost; the present argument should be understood as a species of the latter.)[50] Given that I am committed only to rendering metaphysics optional, not impossible, the weaker argument suffices.

4

Before concluding this section, it is worth considering one of the reasons that someone might still want to retain the picture of concepts

[50] Rorty, "Pragmatism, Davidson, and Truth," *Objectivity, Relativism, and Truth,* Philosophical Papers, vol. I, (New York: Cambridge University Press, 1991), p. 138. This is not to suggest that the stronger claim is indefensible, only that I will not – and need not – advance such a claim here; for a stronger version of the argument defended here, see, for instance, Bjørn Ramberg, "What Davidson Said to the Skeptic or: Anti-Representationalism, Triangulation, and the Naturalization of the Subjective," in *Interpreting Davidson*, Petr Kotatko, Peter Pagin, and Gabriel Segal (eds.) (Stanford, CA: CSLI Publications, 2001), pp. 213–36.

as mediators, namely, the pluralism it apparently underwrites. The idea here, briefly stated, is that if one has access to God only through various conceptual schemes, and if these schemes are incommensurable with one another, then it is reasonable to understand divergences among various faith traditions not as disagreements to be adjudicated (or fought over), but as culturally specific apprehensions of and devotion to one and the same God.[51] In response to this, we should note, first, that it is not clear whether this approach is genuinely pluralistic, since it ends up requiring particular religions to sacrifice whatever ineliminably particular claims they may make about God "in Godself." John Hick thus notes that Christians, for example, would have to sacrifice several beliefs, including "the doctrine of divine incarnation, the satisfaction and penal-substitutionary conceptions of atonement, and ontological doctrines of the Holy Trinity."[52] To require Christians to give up such commitments hardly seems a route to achieving particularity-respecting pluralism, especially since there would be no need to reach for "mediation" and "incommensurability" if adherents of various religions were already willing to sacrifice whichever of their commitments were incompatible with those of other religions. Be that as it may, it is important to point out that one can take others to be justified in holding their beliefs even if one disagrees with them, which entails that one can be a pluralist about epistemic justification even if one is not a pluralist about the putative truth of incompatible claims. To see why this would be the case, consider the fact that epistemic justification is a context-dependent variable, whereas the truth of a proposition is not: so, for instance, an ancient person who held the false belief that the Earth is flat may well have been justified in holding it, since the belief may have cohered with his or her other beliefs, he or she may have had no reason to doubt it, and so on, while another ancient

---

[51] A position along these lines is famously defended by John Hick, *An Interpretation of Religion* (New Haven, CT: Yale University Press, 1989, 2004), though he is not alone.
[52] Hick, *An Interpretation of Religion*, p. 371.

could have held a true belief to the effect that the Earth is round, yet if he or she arrived at that belief by, say, flipping a coin, he or she would not have been justified in holding it. The point is that one can hold others to be justified in their beliefs even if one takes those beliefs to be false, which entails that one can hold adherents of other faith traditions to be justified in holding (what one takes to be) false beliefs, and, indeed, that one has some obligation to *try* to understand them to be justified in holding those beliefs. That may not amount to the robust sort of pluralism that some would hope for, but it may be truer to the commitments of actual believers and thus provide a kind of pluralism that such believers could embrace.

***

One of the problems mentioned above is that concepts are frequently seen as mediating the world to one, such that one seems never to be in direct epistemic touch with the putative objects of one's perception. According to the account elaborated in this section, such a view is at best optional: while concepts are indeed involved in perception, it does not follow that they stand between one and objects, nor that they mediate the world to one. One learns concepts through one's interactions with other concept users and shared objects, and once one has become reliably disposed to respond to these objects by applying the proper concept, one automatically perceives them as such; their mere presence causes one to apply the relevant concept. As long as nothing goes wrong, therefore, the requisite concept application need not be thought to introduce an intermediate step of inference between oneself and the world. Moreover, once one gives up the essentialist-correspondentist picture of conceptual content, it follows that one copes with others' would-be concept use (usually in the form of marks and noises) in the same way one copes with other aspects of one's environing circumstances, and that one counts as understanding another's concept use just insofar as one can correlate it with one's own use, including the circumstances of that use, such that the picture of incommensurable conceptual schemes – and perception as ineliminably relative to such schemes – makes little sense. I likewise defended an account according to which one perceives God by applying the proper concepts, that these applications can become second nature to one, and that the possibility of such application is a work of God's Word and Spirit. Concepts need not be thought to stand between one and God, accordingly, insofar as (a) such concept-use is itself God's work, (b) one can become reliably disposed to respond to God's presence by applying the proper concept, and (c) perception is not relative to incommensurable conceptual schemes.

Conclusion

The intentionality or "aboutness" of language has long been understood along essentialist-correspondentist lines, which has given rise to the assumption that if one's language cannot correspond to God, then one cannot intend God with one's words. This chapter prescribed a therapeutic response to this assumption. We began with the metaphysics of reference: if one's reference to an object depends upon a unique correspondence between one's ideas and the object itself, then it follows that to reject the possibility of such correspondence with God would be to imply that one cannot refer to God. To avoid this implication, I elaborated a non-correspondentist account of reference, according to which one's picking-out of an object depends upon one's inheritance of a precedent commitment, and then explained how the Spirit of Christ enables one to inherit Christ's own reference to God by joining one to a chain of reference that stretches back to him. I then considered a second problem: due to their rejection of immediate, concept-free correspondence, some theorists have concluded that concepts are not only involved in making objects available to one, but that they stand between one and objects, such that one is never in direct epistemic touch with the putative objects of one's perception. From a therapeutic point of view, one's susceptibility to such a conclusion is evidence that one is still in the grip of metaphysics. I thus tried to render this conclusion optional by arguing that although concepts are indeed involved in perception, they need not be thought to stand between one and objects, since (a) once one has become reliably disposed to respond to certain objects by applying a particular concept, one perceives them as such without having to think about doing so, such that concept application becomes immediate (in the sense of non-inferential); (b) once one gives up the essentialist-correspondentist picture of conceptual content, it follows that one counts as understanding another only if one can correlate his or her marks and noises with one's own, in which case the very idea of incommensurable conceptual schemes makes little sense; and (c) once one becomes attuned to the normative Spirit of Christ, one can become reliably disposed to apply certain concepts to God, too, such that one can stand immediately before God precisely in virtue of one's conceptual capacities. In sum, then, I have argued that so long as one does without a metaphysical picture of language, one need not think that one's rejection of metaphysics entails that language is out of touch with God. If I am to demonstrate that language is not necessarily metaphysical, however, a final obstacle remains: the picture of truth as correspondence. To this we now turn.

5 | Truth and correspondence

Preceding chapters have elaborated and defended a therapeutic approach to concepts, meaning, and reference, but if I am to make good on my project of rendering the essentialist-correspondentist picture of language optional, a daunting hurdle still remains, namely, the semantics of truth – daunting, since truth is often understood in precisely correspondentist terms. The problem is this: if the truth of a belief (or statement, proposition, etc.) just is its correspondence to an object's fundamental reality, and if it is inappropriate to think of our beliefs as standing in this sort of relationship to God, then it would appear that our beliefs cannot be true of God.[1] The present chapter aims to render this conclusion optional by defending a non-correspondentist account of truth and then using this account to explain how theological beliefs could be true. The key moves are these: (a) to understand truth in terms of the practice of taking-true, that is, one's judging some belief to be correct on the basis of one's other beliefs, and thus using it to judge still other beliefs; (b) to understand this practice as carrying on the norms implicit in patterns of intersubjective recognition; and (c) to understand the normative Spirit of Christ as entering into and being carried on

---

[1] Throughout this chapter I will use "belief," "statement," "proposition," "assertion," and the like interchangeably, although there is a sense in which I take propositions to be basic, since I think of beliefs in terms of what is believed, statements in terms of what is stated, and assertions in terms of what is asserted. For a view comparable to mine, see William P. Alston, *A Realist Conception of Truth* (Ithaca, NY: Cornell University Press, 1996), pp. 9–22.

through these same practices, thereby supplying the condition of one's possibly holding true beliefs about God.

Truth problems

Theologians and philosophers have traditionally assumed that truth is a matter of correspondence between beliefs, ideas, or words, on the one hand, and extra-mental, extra-linguistic reality, on the other. So René Descartes, for instance, asserts that "*truth*, in its proper signification, denotes the conformity of thought with object";[2] Immanuel Kant takes it for granted that truth is "the agreement of cognition with its object";[3] and Karl Barth remarks that theological claims are true if and only if "our words stand in a correspondence and agreement with the being of God."[4] Countless examples could be adduced, but the point is that theologians and philosophers have tended to accept some version of the so-called correspondence theory of truth, according to which a belief, statement, or idea counts as true if and only if it corresponds to or is isomorphic with an object. I will say more about this theory in a moment, but for now, it is important to note that although most theologians have accepted some version of it, the correspondence theory has been subjected to serious criticism, leading some to reason that if (a) truth is indeed a matter of correspondence, and (b) such correspondence is unworkable (at least with respect to God), then (c) our beliefs and sentences cannot be true of God. In due course, I will try to render conclusion (c) optional by calling into question premise (a), but in order to motivate the alternative account by means of which to do so, and to

---

[2] Descartes, Letter to Mersenne October 16, 1639, in *Oeuvres de Descartes*, vol. II, Charles Adam and Paul Tannery (eds.) (Paris: Librairie Philosophique J. Vrin, 1983), p. 597.

[3] Kant, *Kritik der reinen Vernunft, Kants Werke: Akademie Textausgabe*, vol. III (Berlin: Walter de Gruyter, 1968), p. A58=B82.

[4] Karl Barth, *Die Kirchliche Dogmatik*, vol. II, *Die Lehre von Gott* (Zollikon-Zürich: Evangelischer Verlag A. G., 1940), p. 263.

establish some criteria for that account's adequacy, we need to spend some time considering the problems at issue in premise (b). Toward that end, this section begins by saying more about the correspondence theory and then considering some of the objections it faces.

Before proceeding, a crucial clarification is in order: "the correspondence theory of truth," as I am using that label, refers to a rather narrow family of accounts, each of which is characterized by two claims: (a) that ideas, beliefs, and statements are true if and only if they are isomorphic with that which they are about, and (b) that such isomorphism explains that in virtue of which such beliefs count as true. Absent either of these claims, a view would not count as a correspondence theory in the sense in which the term is being used here. Given that the category "correspondence theory of truth" has sometimes been thought to include any and all "realist" views (according to which a proposition's truth depends in some crucial respect upon how things are with the world), as well as views which deny isomorphism (such as J. L. Austin's) or explanatory purchase (such as John Searle's), it may be wise to use the label "correspond-ent*ist*" to set apart the theory I have in mind.[5] Readers should keep in mind, then, that the correspondence here criticized is of a very specific sort, and that my critique of such correspondence should not be thought to take aim at everything that might go by that name. It should become clear in due course that one can maintain a deflationary (i.e., non-explanatory), non-isomorphistic understanding of correspondence between belief and object, such that an attack on correspondentism need not be understood as an attack on correspondence per se.

---

[5] For the equation of "realism" with "correspondence," see Arthur Fine, "The Natural Ontological Attitude," in *The Shaky Game: Einstein, Realism, and the Quantum Theory* (Chicago: University of Chicago Press, 1986), pp. 112–35; for an account of correspondence without isomorphism, see J. L. Austin, "Unfair to Facts" and "Truth," in *Philosophical Papers*, J. O. Urmson (ed.) (Oxford University Press, 1961); for "correspondence" without explanatory priority, see John Searle, *The Construction of Social Reality* (New York: The Free Press, 1995), pp. 199–226.

1

We begin, then, with perhaps the most famous characterization of truth, namely Aristotle's claim that "to say of what is that it is not, or of what is not that it is, is false, while to say of what is that it is, and of what is not that it is not, is true."[6] Hence, to say *of* something black *that* it is black is to say something true, and to say of it that it is *not* black is to say something false; the vast majority of philosophers, theologians, and ordinary persons would find this sort of claim relatively unexceptionable.[7] Problems arise, however, when this commonsense notion of truth is further explained in terms of an isomorphic relationship between mind and object. To see what this might look like, it will help to consider Aristotle's own explanation, according to which truth is described in terms of the mind's conformity to objects: so Aristotle asserts, for instance, that "actual knowledge is identical with its object," and explains this identicality in terms of a likeness between the form of the knowing mind and of the object known.[8] Aristotle thus claims that the

---

[6] Aristotle, *Metaphysics* IV.7, 1011b25–6. Translations of Aristotle are taken from *The Complete Works of Aristotle*, two volumes, Jonathan Barnes (ed.) (Princeton, NJ: Princeton University Press, 1984).

[7] I am here glossing Aristotle's claim in terms of Alfred Tarski's famous "Convention T," according to which " '*p*' is true if and only if *p*," where the second "*p*" is the assertible content of an utterance, and the first, quoted "*p*" is the utterance itself; hence, the utterance "snow is white" is true if and only if snow is white. For this, see Alfred Tarski, "The Concept of Truth in Formalized Languages," *Logic, Semantics, Metamathematics*, trans. J. H. Woodger (ed.) (New York: Oxford University Press, 1956). Note that although Tarski's understanding has been used by proponents of the so-called "disquotationalist" approach to truth, according to which the truth-predicate can be eliminated from " '*p*' is true" simply by disquoting "*p*" such that to assert that *p* is true is equivalent to asserting that *p*, it is not clear that Tarski himself would accept this approach. For reasons to be discussed below, I, at least, am not advocating such an approach, though I do integrate it into my proposal. For a disquotationalist view, see W. V. O. Quine, *Pursuit of Truth*, revised edn. (Cambridge, MA: Harvard University Press, 1990), §33.

[8] Aristotle, *De Anima* III.5, 430a20; for the characterization as "likeness" (*homoiosis*), see *De Interpretatione* 1, 16a3–9.

mind is "capable of receiving the form of an object; that is, it must be potentially identical in character with its object without being the object," such that one counts as having knowledge of an object only if the form in one's mind matches up with the object's own form; hence, one's putative knowledge of a stone is true if and only if the mind's idea of stoneness is identical with the stone's own stoneness.[9] There are other ways of spelling out the correspondence relation – Bertrand Russell's being the most famous alternative[10] – but the point is straightforward enough: on this view, truth is an isomorphic relationship between mind or propositions, on the one hand, and objects, on the other. This means, in turn, that one's belief about an object is true if and only if it corresponds to the object's form, and that an object is itself true if and only if it corresponds to that same form; it makes sense, accordingly, to speak not only of a true belief, but also of a true friend, a true believer, true love, etc. As Thomas Aquinas claims, "since the true is in the intellect insofar as it is conformed to the object understood, the aspect of the true must needs pass from the intellect to the object understood, so that also the thing understood is said to be true insofar as it has some relation to the intellect."[11] A crucial ingredient of the correspondence theory, then, is an explanatory appeal to isomorphism, and a crucial ingredient of isomorphism is that it so construes an idea's getting its subject matter right that its subject matter can be thought to get *itself* right just insofar as it agrees with this idea. If it did not underwrite such reversals of

---

[9] Aristotle, *De Anima* III.3, 429a15–18, cf. III.8, 431b29.

[10] For which see Russell, "Truth and Falsehood," *The Problems of Philosophy* (Mineola, NY: Dover Publications, 1912, 1999), pp. 86–94. A distinction is sometimes drawn between a correspondence theory and an identity theory, but the distinction is unimportant for our purposes.

[11] Thomas Aquinas, *Summa Theologiae*, trans. Fathers of the English Dominican Province (New York: Benziger Brothers, 1948), Ia, q. 16, art. 1.

polarity, an account would not count as a correspondence theory in the sense under consideration.[12]

As is well known, Thomas adds an important wrinkle to the correspondence theory, arguing that objects as well as human thoughts are true in virtue of their correspondence to the *divine* mind; we will return to this wrinkle, indirectly, in what follows. For now, it suffices to observe that the correspondence (or "correspondentist") theory explains truth as a relation of isomorphism between mind (or propositions) and objects. The problems to be discussed below focus, in turn, on two elements of this account, namely, (a) the appeal to isomorphism between ideas and objects – the appeal, that is, to an account according to which an idea is true if and only if it agrees with its object and the object is itself true if and only if it agrees with this same idea – and (b) the very idea of *explaining* truth in terms of such an appeal, that is, of thinking that such correspondence could be called upon to explain what one is (or ought to be) doing when one takes some belief to be true.[13]

2

One objection raised against this theory – namely, that correspondentism perpetrates violence upon objects – should be familiar enough at this point. The relevant points are summarized by Heidegger, who claims that the decisive turn toward correspondentism occurs with Plato: according to Heidegger, Plato's momentous step is to think of truth as "that which is examined in the examination of the *idea*, as that which is cognized in cognition."[14] This is a momentous step,

---

[12] For a recent defense of a correspondence theory in precisely this "isomorphic" sense, see John Milbank and Catherine Pickstock, *Truth in Aquinas* (London: Routledge, 2001).

[13] On the understanding of explanatory order here assumed, X counts as explanatorily prior to Y in a strong sense just in case X can be understood without appeal to Y, but not vice versa; in a weak sense just in case Y can be understood in terms of X.

[14] Heidegger, "Platons Lehre von der Wahrheit," *Wegmarken, Gesamtausgabe* vol. IX (Frankfurt am Main: Vittorio Klostermann, 1976), p. 225.

Heidegger thinks, since taking it enabled Plato to "think all beings according to 'ideas' and evaluate all reality according to 'values,'" and so "to establish the metaphysical ground of beings upon 'the human person.'"[15] Irrespective of whether this is an accurate reading of Plato, Heidegger's point is clear enough: by defining truth in terms of the correspondence between one's ideas and a thing's fundamental reality, one may end up identifying that fundamental reality with one's ideas about it, thereby making oneself its ultimate measure and cutting it down to the size of one's categories. The danger, then, is that if one understands truth in terms of an isomorphism relation between one's ideas and an object's fundamental reality, such that one identifies the truth of, say, a cat with one's idea of felinity, the truth of a woman with one's idea of femininity, and so on, then one may make one's antecedent ideas the measure of these objects and thereby do violence to them. It is not hard to see, accordingly, why some have claimed that beliefs about God cannot be thought to be true – or false, for that matter – since, if one's theological beliefs count as true only if they stand in this sort of correspondence relation to God, then a God of whom one's beliefs could be true would be an idol. Barth thus speaks for many when he remarks that "because the human person is and remains human in this relationship, his or her intuitions, concepts, and words as such, as his or her own, are not only partly, but wholly and completely *inadequate* to denote God," since "there can be no likeness between our word, which as such intends creaturely being, and the intended being of God."[16]

A second objection could be called the "no independent access" problem. The problem receives memorable formulation by Kant, who observes that, on the correspondence theory, "my cognition, in order to count as true, should correspond with the object. Now I can, however, compare the object with my cognition only insofar as

---

[15] Heidegger, "Platons Lehre von der Wahrheit," p.236.
[16] Barth, *Kirchliche Dogmatik* II/1, pp. 265, 253.

I *cognize* it. My cognition shall thus confirm itself, which, however, is not nearly sufficient for truth. For since the object is outside of me and the cognition in me, I can always judge only whether my cognition of the object corresponds with my cognition of the object."[17] The problem, it seems, concerns the very possibility of relating a belief to something strictly external to it. (By such "strict externality," I have in mind a picture according to which one is supposed to enjoy belief- and concept-free access to objects; to be clear, then, the objection holds only against a view which requires such access, rather than, say, the real existence of objects outside of beliefs.) Suppose I say "this apple is red," and that I want to determine whether my state- ment corresponds with some bit of extra-linguistic reality – some bit of reality, that is, that I can get a grip on independently of my beliefs, for otherwise it would appear that I am comparing beliefs with other beliefs rather than with something external to them. So then: can I identify something as an "apple" apart from my beliefs? Can I identify something as "red" apart from such beliefs? It would appear not, since, as argued in the previous chapter, one's percep- tion of an object necessarily involves one's application of concepts to it, and concept application is a species of belief formation. If so, then it is not clear how one could compare one's beliefs with some- thing strictly external to them, since one's epistemic grip on such would-be externalities is dependent upon one's beliefs. This conclu- sion, in turn, is thought to underwrite a further objection to the correspondentist theory, namely, that it fails to explain truth, since the entities to which true statements allegedly correspond are them- selves the (apparently circular) product of this theory, and as much in need of explanation as the theory itself. As P. F. Strawson remarks, "of course, statements and facts fit. They were made for each other. If you prise the statements off the world you prise the facts off it too; but the world would be none the poorer. (You don't also prise off

---

[17] *Immanuel Kants Logik: Ein Handbuch zu Vorlesungen*, Gottlob Benjamin Jäsche (ed.) (Königsberg: Friedrich Nicolovius, 1800), pp. 69–70.

the world what the statements are about – for this you would need a different kind of lever.)"[18] The objection, simply stated, is that if one has no belief-free way of individuating the states of affairs to which true statements correspond, and if these belief-laden individuations must themselves be true or false, it follows that the correspondentist theory's alleged primitives ("facts," "states of affairs," and the like) are themselves as much in need of explanation as the theory itself – and, indeed, at precisely the same point.

This brings us to a final objection, raised in a famous passage of Gottlob Frege: "Can one not stipulate," he asks, "that truth obtains when there is a correspondence in a certain respect? But in which? What must we then do in order to decide whether something were true? We must assess whether it were true that, say, a representation and a reality corresponded in the stipulated respect. And with that we stand again before the same kind of question, and the game can begin anew. So this attempt to explain truth as correspondence fails. Just so every other attempt to define truth fails. For in a definition one spells out certain characteristics. And when applied to a particular case it would always come up whether it were true that these characteristics obtain. So one goes around in a circle."[19] To see what Frege has in mind, suppose I claim "John Calvin wrote the *Institutes*," and that I think a claim should be judged to be true if and only if it stands in a correspondence-relation to whatever it is about (that is, that standing in such a relation is a necessary and sufficient condition of a claim's being true, and that one's taking some claim to be true is thus to be explained in terms of one's judging these conditions to have been met). In order to determine whether the claim is true, on this account, I must judge whether the specified relation in fact holds. My judgment about whether this relation holds is itself either true or false, however, such that this judgment, too, is true if

[18] Strawson, "Truth," *Aristotelian Society Supplement* 24 (1950), pp. 129–56.
[19] Frege, "Der Gedanke: Eine logische Untersuchung," *Beiträge zur Philosophie des deutschen Idealismus* 2 (1918–19), p. 60.

and only if it stands in a certain relation to whatever it is about – and my judgment about whether it does so is itself true if and only if it stands in a certain relation … and so on. Frege then generalizes the objection, claiming that a regress threatens *any* substantive (i.e., necessary-and-sufficient-condition-specifying) definition of truth, whether the correspondence theory or something else, since the judgment that a belief meets these conditions – however specified – would itself have to be judged to meet them, and so on. Hence, given that any substantive definition of truth will apparently run into the very same regress, Frege concludes that truth cannot be defined – or, better, that one's taking a belief to be true cannot be explained in terms of a substantive understanding of truth.

***

The correspondentist theory of truth runs into three problems: it runs into the problem, first, of explaining how to compare beliefs with something strictly outside belief; second, the problem of an infinite regress of truth judgments; and third, the problem of cutting objects down to the size of one's ideas. Problems such as these have led some to deny truth altogether; thus John Caputo celebrates the (apparently) Derridean claim that "there is no truth beyond the truth one 'does,' the truth one 'makes' of oneself, *facere veritatem*, in one's heart, by confessing it," just as Nietzsche famously claimed that "truth" is nothing but "a moveable army of metaphors, metonymies, anthropomorphisms, in brief an aggregate of human relations which have been poetically and rhetorically inflated, transferred, and decorated, and which after long use have been regarded by a people as canonical and binding."[20] The correspondence theory likewise faces serious problems as a way of understanding the truth of theological

---

[20] John D. Caputo, *The Prayers and Tears of Jacques Derrida: Religion Without Religion* (Bloomington: Indiana University Press, 1997), p. 290; cf. *On Religion* (London: Routledge, 2000), pp. 109–18; Friedrich Nietzsche, "Über Wahrheit und Lüge im aussermoralischen Sinne," *Werke: Kritische Gesamtausgabe* III/2, Giorgio Colli and Mazzino Montinari (eds.) (Berlin: Walter de Gruyter, 1973).

beliefs, since it is hard to see how human beliefs could be said to stand in an isomorphic relationship to God – unless, that is, "God" were just an idol. Then again, if truth is not necessarily correspond-entistic, one could affirm the possible truth of theological beliefs without thinking of God as an idol. This is the therapeutic strategy to be pursued in the remainder of this chapter.

The practice of taking-true

As we have seen, one of the issues facing not only the correspond-ence theory but all of the substantive alternatives is that they run into serious problems as explanations of the practice of taking some belief to be true. The solution to this problem – or at least the solution to be proposed here – is to invert the customary order of explanation, so that instead of using a substantive theory to explain the practice of taking-true, we can use the practice of taking-true to explain whatever needs to be explained about the concept of truth. The point of this section, then, is twofold: (a) to explain truth other-wise than in terms of an isomorphic relationship between beliefs and objects; and (b) to lay the groundwork for an account of the Spirit's work of conforming beliefs to Christ.

1

So what is one doing when one takes a belief (proposition, thought, etc.) to be true? We find a first clue in the very form in which beliefs are expressed. If someone asserts "this apple is red," his or her asser-tion can be analyzed into two parts: that which the assertion is about (*de re*), and that which the assertion says about it (*de dicto*); hence, in asserting "this apple is red," one asserts *of* this apple *that* it is red, where the of-clause specifies what the assertion is about and the that-clause specifies that which is said about it. It seems obvi-ous and uncontroversial that one takes such an assertion to be true only if one takes that which is said of some object to be correct – if, for instance, the apple in question is indeed red. In order to explain taking-true, therefore, we need some explanation of how assertions can be about objects, and of how one judges their correctness. The previous chapter elaborated an account of the former, so this section need explain only the sort of correctness-taking involved in judging an assertion to be correct. (Readers should keep the previous chapter's account in mind, however, for otherwise they are liable to misinterpret what follows as a defense of coherentism. It will appear coherentistic, that is, just to the extent that one assumes that beliefs either mediate the world to one or stand at a remove from it, contrary to the account defended in Chapter 4.)

According to the relatively uncontroversial notion of truth mentioned in the previous section, a belief is true if and only if it gets its subject matter right, and Chapter 4 already accounted for the "subject matter" element of that notion. How is it, then, that one determines whether a belief gets its subject matter right? On the account to be defended here, one judges a candidate belief to get its subject-matter right on the basis of one's other beliefs (as these are bound up with objects).[21] Consider two examples: "The traffic signal is red," and "The Declaration of Independence was written by Thomas Jefferson." With respect to the first example, if one can see the traffic signal in question, one will take the belief to be true of that signal just in case one perceives it to be red, where one's perception

---

[21] Here I am drawing upon both "deflationary" and "minimalist" accounts of truth, representative examples of which include Arthur Fine, "The Natural Ontological Attitude"; Robert Brandom, *Making It Explicit: Reasoning, Representing, and Discursive Commitment* (Cambridge, MA: Harvard University Press, 1994); Paul Horwich, *Truth* (Oxford University Press, 1999); Donald Davidson, "A Coherence Theory of Truth and Knowledge," in *Subjective, Intersubjective, and Objective* (New York: Oxford University Press, 2001) and *Truth and Predication* (Cambridge, MA: Harvard University Press, 2006); Scott Soames, *Understanding Truth* (Oxford University Press, 1999); Wilfrid Sellars, *Science and Metaphysics: Variations on Kantian Themes* (London: Routledge and Kegan Paul, 1968); and Dorothy Grover, *A Prosentential Theory of Truth* (Princeton, NJ: Princeton University Press, 1992).

depends upon a background of taken-for-granted beliefs: the belief that a certain object is a traffic signal, that one perceives it to be red, that one is a reliable perceiver of redness in the present circumstances, etc. On the other hand, if one cannot see the signal in question, one may nevertheless take the belief to be true if, say, one trusts another's claim to that effect. This kind of trust comes to the fore in an example such as the second: "The Declaration of Independence was written by Thomas Jefferson." One cannot appeal here to one's firsthand acquaintance with the subject matter in question, since one is not in position to perceive the writing of the Declaration; hence, if one takes this claim to be true, one does so on the basis of one's trust in the reports of others. If one has read something to this effect in a textbook, for instance, or if one thinks it unlikely that the many persons who take this claim to be true are mistaken, then one may oneself take it to be true even if one has no firsthand acquaintance with that which the claim is about. (The difference between the two kinds of example should not be overstated, since, on the one hand, both depend upon one's use of taken-for-granted beliefs to judge whether a candidate belief gets its subject matter right, and on the other, both turn out to require one to trust others. This is more obvious in the latter example, but one's judgment that a traffic signal is red likewise requires one to trust, for instance, the judgments of those who taught one concepts such as "traffic signal," "red," and so on.) These examples thus indicate two basic features of the practice of taking-true: one judges whether a candidate belief is true on the basis of one's other beliefs, and one's judgment to this effect often depends upon one's trust in others' judgments.

To understand these features correctly, it is crucial to reiterate two of this book's central claims, namely (a) that the judgments involved in the practice of taking-true are to be understood in terms of the norms implicit in non-inferential responsive dispositions rather than in terms of explicit deliberation, and (b) that in the overwhelming majority of cases, there is no interval between beliefs and what they are about, in consequence of which (i) one need not choose between so-called realism and coherentism, and (ii) one need not construct a theory that explains how such an interval might be bridged. Given the importance of these points, a bit more elaboration may be in order. First, it is worth repeating that even if a belief is judged true or false on the basis of other beliefs, this does not imply that one is locked inside one's beliefs, since, as the previous chapter argued, beliefs need not be thought to stand between one and the world, nor as standing at a remove from it. There is reason to think, moreover, that the vast majority of one's beliefs must be correct, not least because beliefs and objects seem to have been made for one another, from which it would follow, again, that beliefs need not be thought to stand at a distance from that which they are about.[22]

Second, the fact that truth-taking is here explained in terms of a candidate belief's relationship to other held-true beliefs should not be taken to imply that truth is simply a matter of coherence, nor that truth is not objective. On the present account, to take a belief to be true is to take it as getting its subject matter right, which means that one's so taking it could turn out to be wrong by one's own lights. Given a sufficient background of collateral beliefs which one continues to take true, one can recognize instances in which a particular belief which one took to be true is in fact false. Someone might believe, for instance, that the US Constitution contains the words "separation of Church and State." This is a belief about an object, and it should be held true only if it gets that object right. In view of certain other beliefs, therefore, such as believing *of* a copy of the US Constitution *that* it is a reliable copy, coming to believe *of* that copy *that* it does not contain the words "separation of Church and State," and so forth, a person might come to the realization that his or her original belief was false. On this account, then, one assesses the truth or falsity of a belief in terms of its congruence with other held-true

---

[22] For an argument along these lines, see Donald Davidson, "A Coherence Theory of Truth and Knowledge" and "Afterthoughts," *Subjective, Intersubjective, Objective.*

beliefs, but this does not entail that whatever one *takes* to be true *is* true; whether a particular belief is true depends, rather, upon how things are with that which the belief is about. A belief's truth-value is thus an objective matter, though this objectivity is here understood in light of the practice of taking-true (rather than vice versa). That is to say, if one claims "this apple is red" – claims *of* the apple *that* it is red – the correctness of one's claim depends upon how things are with the apple, not with one's claim about it. This being the case, insofar as one takes the claim to be true, one accordingly takes it that it would be true even if one had not claimed it to be such, even if no one had ever made a claim about it, and indeed, even if every claim ever made about it were wrong. Given a certain belief, therefore, its truth depends upon how things stand with what is believed, not upon one's believing it. Note well, however, that this does not entail that one could then reverse the polarities, as it were, in order to claim that the object is itself true just insofar as it conforms to one's belief. To see why not, consider the following: suppose one claims that a particular circle was drawn using black ink. If the circle was in fact drawn with black ink, it follows that one's claim is true, but not that the circle is *itself* therefore true. As a general rule, the fact that a claim is true of an object does not entail that the object would fall short of its own truth if it were not, so if closer examination revealed that the circle was actually blue, this would mean only that one's claim was untrue, not the circle itself. This is not to suggest that such reversals are never warranted – consider the proposition that a circle is true just insofar as each point on the circle is equidistant from its center – but it seems obvious that reversible beliefs constitute at best a small fraction of the total number of beliefs that would be true of any given object, and, therefore, that such reversibility is not implied simply by one's taking a belief to be true. Far from it.

Finally, it is important to note that the distinction between a candidate belief and the beliefs by which it is assessed is ever-shifting. One might take it for granted, for instance, that the Constitution says something about the separation of Church and State, and may on this basis reject the proposition that students in public schools should be required to pray, yet one may later have reason to question whether one's belief about the Constitution is in fact correct, and may assess this belief in light of still other beliefs. This sort of fluidity is important, since it explains the ability to question even one's "core" beliefs, which means that the present account does not entail that the beliefs in terms of which other beliefs are judged are themselves immune to doubt. Again, we can test every one of our beliefs, just not all at once.

The fact that truth is objective in this sense – the fact, that is, that a belief's truth is distinct from one's taking it to be such – helps explain further why truth should be distinguished from epistemic justification (as argued in the previous chapter). Consider again someone living in ancient times who happened to believe that the Sun revolves around the Earth. Supposing that this belief cohered with the rest of his or her beliefs, and supposing further that he or she had no reason to doubt it, he or she was within his or her epistemic rights to hold it. Yet this does not entail that the belief was true, since, if one accepts a Copernican picture of the universe, one holds a contrary belief to the effect that the Sun does *not* revolve around the Earth. The truth of one's belief about the Earth's relationship to the Sun depends upon how things are with the Earth and the Sun, whereas one's justification for holding a given belief depends upon circumstances such as one's historical context, the collateral beliefs available to one, etc. One can take it, therefore, that someone who holds a false belief is justified in doing so, just as one can take it that someone who holds a true belief may not be so justified, precisely because the truth of a belief depends upon its getting its subject matter right, not upon the circumstances of the one believing it. This is not to suggest, however, that truth and justification are entirely distinct, since one's first-personal present-tense judgments about a belief are indeed made in view of its coherence with one's other beliefs. The standard by which one judges an ancient person's belief about the Earth, for instance – as well as his or her justification in holding it – is supplied by one's own beliefs about the matter. This entails that one's first-personal pursuit of truth is inseparable from one's pursuit of justification, though this does not mean that one cannot pursue truth precisely by pursuing justification.[23] I will return to this point below.

2

Further consideration of the two features mentioned above – namely, that one judges a candidate belief on the basis of one's other beliefs, and that one's judgments to this effect depend to some degree upon one's trust in others' judgments – will provide us with resources by which to explain further what one is doing when one takes a belief to be true. First, to judge that a belief is true is to take it that it could appropriately be used to judge other beliefs: on the present account, one judges the possible truth of a belief on the basis of other beliefs which one recognizes as true, which means that if the candidate belief is itself recognized as true, it contributes to the standard by which still other beliefs might be recognized as such. To take some belief to be true, accordingly, is to take it that other beliefs could appropriately be judged in light of it. For example, if one takes it to be true that a particular traffic signal is red, that belief can combine with other taken-true beliefs (such as the belief that one ought to stop one's car at red traffic signals) to lead one to judge that one ought to apply the brakes. We can understand our earlier discussion of a belief's getting its subject matter right in these terms, too: to take a belief about some object to be true is to take it as a standard by which other beliefs about *that object* should be judged. So, in taking it that "this apple is red" is true, one takes it that certain other beliefs are either true or false: trivially, that it is not true that the apple is

---

[23] I am here siding with Akeel Bilgrami, Bernard Williams, Michael Dummett, and others against Rorty's claims in "Is Truth a Goal of Enquiry? Davidson vs. Wright," *Philosophical Quarterly* 45:180 (July 1995), pp. 281–300.

not red; less trivially, in combination with other beliefs (that it is a certain sort of apple, for instance), that the apple is ripe. Moreover, if one takes it to be true *of the apple* that it is red, one takes it that the truth of this belief (i.e., the fact that the apple is actually red) does not depend upon whether anyone actually believes it to be the case. Taking some belief to be true can thus be understood as taking it to be suitable for judging the correctness of still other beliefs about an object. Moreover, since held-true beliefs are taken to be suitable for judging other beliefs about an object, it follows that if one holds a belief to be true, one takes it that it is suitable for judging not only one's own, but others' beliefs about the object, too. That is to say, if one takes it to be true *of* a particular traffic signal *that* it is red, one takes it that insofar as others hold contrary beliefs, their beliefs must not be true, that further judgments they make on the basis of their belief may likewise be erroneous (such as, for instance, that they need not apply the brakes), and so on. To be sure, the taken-true belief can itself turn out to be erroneous, though one's recognition of this fact will depend upon still other beliefs which one continues to take true. The point is simply that when one takes some belief to be true, one takes it to be suitable for judging one's own and others' beliefs about the object in question.

This point leads us to the second feature mentioned above, but before turning to it, we should note an apparent exception which turns out to illustrate the claim: it is not uncommon for one to take another's assertion to be true, yet never use it to judge other beliefs – indeed, to take it to be true knowing well that one will never so use it. If a computer programmer, for instance, whom I recognized to be an expert in his or her field, were to inform me of some obscure bug in the code for Linux, and if none of my beliefs were incompatible with his or her claims, I would probably take his or her claim to be true, yet I may likewise take the information to be useless to me. It seems likely, in fact, that one may be more willing to take a belief to be true precisely insofar as one has no intention of ever using it to judge other beliefs, since little of consequence hangs on it. (By contrast, if someone were to inform me that there was a fire at my child's school, I would be much more concerned to determine whether the claim is in fact correct.) This apparent counterexample could easily be accommodated by the present argument, since the latter claims only that in taking a belief to be true, one takes it to be suitable for judging other beliefs, not that it must be so used. Beyond this, however, it seems that the example actually illustrates the point, since it indicates a significant correlation between the standard a candidate belief must meet in order to be taken-true, on the one hand, and the likelihood of the belief being used in judging other beliefs – especially beliefs that one cares about – on the other.

Our account of taking-true as taking a belief to be suitable for judging other beliefs sheds light, in turn, upon the second feature mentioned above, namely, the trust involved in judging whether a belief is true. On this account, one judges the truth of a candidate belief on the basis of one's other beliefs, and if the belief is recognized as correct on this basis, it contributes to the standard by which still other – and others' – beliefs may be judged. In asserting a belief which one takes to be true, accordingly, one implicitly claims that this belief ought to play a similar role in others' judgments; in asserting a belief, therefore, one implicitly petitions one's auditors to recognize the belief's authority over their judgments, and thereby undertakes responsibility to them for the correctness of that belief – responsibility, that is, for getting one's subject-matter right. To understand how this works, consider a claim such as "I was late because I got locked out of my house." By asserting that one's lateness was due to one's being locked out, one implicitly claims a kind of authority for one's assertion: one claims, on the one hand, that others can take one's claiming of it as sufficient reason to take it to be true, and on the other, that they can use this belief to judge still other beliefs (about, for instance, whether one's tardiness is blameworthy). At the same time, by implicitly petitioning others to take one's assertion to be true, one likewise undertakes responsibility for the assertion's actually being correct. One thus renders oneself appropriately liable to certain sanctions if it turns out that one's assertion is false: so, if it turns out that one was lying about the reason for one's lateness, one may be appropriately punished both for one's lateness and for representing a known falsehood as if it were true. Then again, one may be sanctioned simply inasmuch as one's assertions are no longer taken seriously: if others take it that they cannot rely upon the correctness of one's claims, they will not accept one's asserting them as reason enough to take them to be true. Absent such reasons for doubt, however, it would appear that the passing of truth claims from person to person is a regular (and practically unavoidable) occurrence.

One's judgment about whether a particular claim should be accepted on another's authority can be understood, in turn, along lines similar to those used to explain judgments about whether a candidate belief is true. There is the judgment, first, which one makes with respect to the content of the assertion: does one have any collateral beliefs related to this content? If so, do they suffice to determine whether one should take it to be true? Short of this, do they at least incline one to accept or reject it? Second, as we have seen, there is a judgment about what hangs on the assertion: if nothing seems to hang on it, one may take it to be true even if one has little reason to do so, whereas if a good deal hangs on it, one may take it to be true only if the assertion can pass some relatively stringent tests. And finally, central to the present discussion, there are one's judgments about the asserter him- or herself, which one makes on the basis of one's collateral beliefs about him or her: does one have reason to believe that he or she might not be telling the truth, either wittingly or unwittingly? That is, does one have reason to think that he or she might be lying, or to think that he or she might not actually know what he or she is talking about? If one's collateral beliefs about the speaker lead one to question whether his or her assertion is true, one may decide not to take his or her word for it. When one of my high school students came up to me one morning and told me that airplanes had crashed into the World Trade Center and Pentagon, for example, I held off on taking his claims to be true – not because I thought he was lying, but because, on the one hand, one of my collateral beliefs about high school students was that they are sometimes too ready to believe things they hear, and on the other, a lot hung on whether this information was correct. It turned out that he was telling the truth, unfortunately. The point is that one uses one's collateral beliefs about a person and about the content of their claims to judge whether to accept these claims as true. And while this might sound like a second-class way of coming to hold a belief, it is important to realize that we do this sort of thing all the time, and that we do not usually consider a belief to be second-rate just because we have taken someone else's word for it. If I have no first-hand acquaintance with the Great Wall of China, for instance, but my sister returns from China and tells me that the picture on a certain postcard is of the Great Wall, I will in turn believe that the picture is of the Great Wall, just as her own belief that the edifice in question is the Great Wall depends upon her trusting someone else's claim to that effect, and so on. Indeed, as I mentioned above, even beliefs which one takes to be true on the basis of first-hand acquaintance with a particular object can be seen to depend upon trusting others, since one's judgment that a certain apple is red, for example, involves trust in those who taught one the concepts "apple" and "red." At the very least, if one were to prescind from ever taking someone else's word as sufficient reason to accept a belief as true, one's world would be *severely* restricted.

The point about taking beliefs to be true on the basis of one's trust in others raises questions about whether such beliefs count as one's own, as freely held, and so forth, but before turning to these questions, we need to say a few more things about the way such trust works. Trusting another's assertion as grounds for one's own acceptance of its content is a species of recognition: by making an assertion, one implicitly claims that it would be appropriate for others to take it to be true and that one should be accorded the status of truth-teller, one of the "us" who contributes to the circulation of information. By making assertions which purport to express a true belief, that is, one thereby seeks recognition of one's belief (as true) and of oneself (as one whose assertions should be taken true by others), just as one concomitantly undertakes responsibility for getting one's subject matter right. And if one takes another's assertion to be true, one may oneself assert it, thereby implicitly claiming that others should likewise take it to be true, and so on. To take a belief to be true is thus to recognize it as (potentially) appropriate for passing on to others, which can in turn help us understand what one is doing when one takes a belief such as "The Declaration of Independence was written by Thomas Jefferson" to be true: one is taking another's word for it, who him- or herself took someone else's word for it, and so on, in a chain of taking-true that may in fact reach back to those with firsthand (or near first-hand) acquaintance with the actual writing. Then again, it is neither necessary nor sufficient that a chain stretch back to those with firsthand acquaintance, since, on the one hand, those with first-hand acquaintance are not necessarily correct, and, on the other, one commonly takes beliefs to be true even if no one has such acquaintance (consider beliefs about, say, the extinction of dinosaurs). The bottom line is that by offering a belief to others as true, and by oneself taking others' beliefs to be true, a vastly wider range of beliefs is made available to one, thereby enriching the store of beliefs by which one judges still other beliefs.

The picture of taking-true that emerges thus looks something like this: one judges a candidate belief to be true on the basis of other beliefs already taken-true, and if one takes the candidate to be true, it contributes to the standard by which still other beliefs can be taken as such. To take a belief to be true is thus to confer a kind of recognition upon it. One's taking of another's word for it that a particular belief is true is likewise a kind of recognition, since one thereby confers authority upon him or her and holds him or her responsible for getting his or her subject matter right. The latter kind of recognition underwrites the practice of communicating beliefs from person to person, thus enriching the world of each.

3

With this account on board, we can now understand truth-talk as a way of making explicit that which is implicit in the ordinary practice of truth-taking. Explicit judgments about truth, of the sort involved in one's saying *of* some proposition *that* it is true, serve several important functions, which is to say that truth-talk is not merely redundant, nor should it be entirely "deflated."[24] First, as a near-consensus of philosophers following Quine have noted, the use of the truth predicate is important in allowing one to say something about a range of sentences all at once, as well as to talk about claims at a level of generality otherwise unavailable.[25] Second, the truth predicate enables one to make explicit one's taking of another's claim to be true. It is in this context that one can see the importance of the so-called disquotational property of truth-talk: as is well known, to assert that "snow is white" is true is simply to assert that snow is white, that is, to free the initial statement from its quotation marks, thereby turning it from a mentioned to a used statement. This is one of the roles truth-talk plays in conversation: if someone says, "the traffic signal is red," and someone else responds, "that's true," he or she makes explicit that the statement in question is in some respect his or her own; that is, he or she expresses his or her commitment to *using* the belief in judging other beliefs, instead of merely *ascribing* the belief to the original speaker. One's use of the truth predicate in such instances should therefore be construed not (or not simply) as a way of describing a belief, but as a way of oneself undertaking a

[24] For an example of such a view, see F. P. Ramsey, "On Facts and Propositions," in *The Foundations of Mathematics*, R. B. Braithwaite (ed.) (London: Routledge and Keegan Paul, 1931).

[25] For an argument to this effect, see Anil Gupta, "A Critique of Deflationism," *Philosophical Topics* 21:2 (1993), pp. 57–81.

commitment to its content. Finally, the fact that one can use truth-talk to make explicit the commitments implicit in one's holding of certain beliefs may not add anything to the content of those beliefs, but it allows one to stand in a different relationship to that content. It opens up the space within which one's implicit judgment about some belief (namely, that it is true) can itself be judged, thereby allowing one to decide whether one should in fact take the belief to be true and to distinguish between what one takes to be true and what is in fact the case. By rendering one's judgment about a belief itself susceptible to judgment, therefore, one can come to stand in a different relationship to it: one can come to see oneself as standing behind the belief (or not), thereby making it possible for one to recognize the belief as one's own, to identify with it, and to see it as freely held. Hence, given the number of beliefs one inevitably holds on the basis of one's trust in others, the importance of explicit truth-talk can hardly be overstated, since, in enabling one to achieve self-consciousness about one's beliefs, one is likewise able to consider the extent to which one should stand behind them. Consider a simple example: suppose one has always believed that the American Revolution was justified, and one believes this because that is what others have claimed ("that's just what we believe"). If one has never decided for oneself whether one ought to hold this belief, it is not clear whether one would continue to hold it if one were to think for oneself about it – it is not clear, that is, that the belief is truly one's own. By making explicit the fact that one takes this belief to be true, one can judge one's believing of it: one can suspend one's belief in it, so to speak, in order to determine whether one could find one's way back to holding it. If one can, then even if the content of the belief has not changed, one's relationship to it has, since one has now explicitly reclaimed it as one's own. (We will return to these points in the following chapter.)

***

Rather than appealing to a substantive notion of truth, I have made sense of truth in terms of the practice of taking a belief to be true.

Part of the appeal of this explanation is that it manages to uphold the objectivity of truth judgments without appealing to any *tertium* outside of beliefs and their subject matter (such as an isomorphic relationship between the two): to judge that a belief is true is to judge that it gets its subject matter right, and one judges a candidate belief to get its subject matter right by determining whether it goes on in the same way as precedent beliefs which one judges to be correct. It is true, of course, that the objects which beliefs are about are often outside of one, but since there is no interval between beliefs and objects, there is no need to choose between answering to objects and answering to beliefs, nor any need to establish a theoretical bridge between the two. Moreover, this account enables us to avoid Frege's regress, since, unlike explanations which depend upon substantive understandings of truth, the view defended here does not try to explain truth-taking in terms of the necessary and sufficient conditions which would have to be met by any candidate for truth; on our account, rather, the norm by which to assess such truth-takings is implicit in one's non-inferential responsive dispositions rather than explicit in a set of rule-like conditions, which entails that a regress of explicit condition-meeting need not follow.

Once we have explained truth in terms of taking-true, however, there is a way in which we can rehabilitate a substantive notion of truth. In the previous chapter, I argued that anything which one can triangulate, one can pick out, and anything which one can pick out can be an object of thought, talk, and so forth. If one can pick out "true" from more than one point of view, accordingly, it can be an object of thought, from which it follows that if one wants to develop a theory of truth or a set of claims about correspondence, one can do so. On the account offered here, one could pick out "true" by triangulating the intersection of several uses of the term, just as one can triangulate "wise," "love," and so on. A collateral benefit of pursuing the present approach, accordingly, is that it avoids the problems usually associated with the correspondence theory while providing a way of rehabilitating correspondence-talk (albeit as an explanatory latecomer).

In sum, we can make good sense of the truth of a belief in terms of its getting its subject matter right *without* trying to explain that getting-right in terms of a substantive theory; we can explain it, rather, in terms of one's implicit judgments about what is and is not true. If we begin with these judgments, we can explain the way truth works, we can explain the objectivity of truth, and we can even use this account as the basis of a substantive theory. And we can do all of this without correspondentism, since we have avoided explanatory appeals to isomorphism and, indeed, argued that our account neither entails nor supports isomorphism's characteristic reversal of polarities between the truth of a belief and an object's own truth. Truth need not be seen, then, as complicit in metaphysics or violence. This fact has obvious implications for an account of theological truth, to which we now turn.

The truth of God-talk

Several of the problems facing an account of theological truth (enumerated in the first section of this chapter) revolve around the difficulty of explaining how one's beliefs could possibly correspond to God. Although some theologians have taken these difficulties to warrant their rejection of objectivity, or to underwrite their acceptance of either subjectivist or so-called pragmatist understandings of truth, the approach to be defended here is to explain the possible truth of a theological belief in terms of the Spirit's work of conforming one to Christ. Toward that end, this section elaborates an account of Christ as the truth and of the Spirit's work of enabling one's beliefs to participate in this truth.

1

The argument of this section can be seen as an elaboration (and defense) of several key claims from the best recent treatment of the subject, namely, Bruce Marshall's *Trinity and Truth*. Marshall's first move, following Donald Davidson, is to deny the putative explanatory value of the correspondence theory, and yet to insist that this denial should not be thought to entail an anti-realist attitude toward truth, according to which "truth" would be redefined as, say, that which one is justified in believing.[26] Marshall claims that truth is saved from such anti-realism in virtue of the "intrinsically veridical nature of belief," that is, the fact that it makes no sense to suppose that a person's beliefs could be massively in error. Marshall's argument here, briefly stated, is that if one's understanding of an utterance depends upon one's ability to correlate it with the conditions in which it is uttered – a claim I defended in Chapter 3 – it follows that one could not so much as make sense of such utterances apart from their being true in the vast majority of cases. Moreover, if one does without the picture according to which concepts stand between objects and oneself – as discussed in the previous chapter – it follows that one's commitment to the view that beliefs can be compared only with other beliefs need not be thought to collaterally commit one to a sort of truth-less, solipsistic idealism. The moral of the story, then, is that one's rejection of correspondentism need not be thought to leave one out of touch with objects, nor, indeed, to eventuate in a wholesale denial of truth. In the idiom of the present project, Marshall's approach thus qualifies as a species of therapy.

Marshall's account of specifically *theological* truth is built upon these claims, yet he insists that here some additional factors must be taken into consideration. The truth of one's belief that Jesus is risen, for instance, depends upon something more than what the belief means and how things are with the world; it depends, too, upon *grace*: "the truth of the belief that Jesus is risen," Marshall argues, "cannot be automatic. The content of the belief itself seems to preclude the possibility that the relations of the rest of humanity

---

[26] For these claims, see Bruce D. Marshall, *Trinity and Truth* (Cambridge University Press, 2000), especially pp. 233–8.

to the risen Jesus could be brought about save by Jesus' own action. Any element necessary for such relations to be met must, it seems, depend in some way upon Jesus' own action."[27] That is to say, "if the risen Jesus is not at all at the disposal of creatures, then creatures will have whatever they need in order to acquire a certain relation to him only because he wills that they have it … Were it otherwise, then we could know the risen Jesus regardless of whether he wanted us to – he would be cognitively at our disposal."[28] Marshall insists, therefore, that the truth of a theological belief is a matter of grace, and that this grace is a matter of Jesus himself establishing the possibility of such truth. This brings us to the key element of Marshall's account, namely, his claim that the truth of one's theological commitments turns out to depend upon one's conformity to Christ: according to Marshall, the truth of one's theological beliefs depends upon one's standing in a grace-dependent correspondence relation to Christ, which relation is necessary for any of one's beliefs to be true of God. He argues, accordingly, that "the correspondence to the Father at which the triune God aims by granting us true beliefs about himself is available to us only as a participated likeness of the incarnate Word's own perfect conformity to the Father," such that "the created persons affected by the truth-bestowing action of the Trinity may themselves be seen as truth-bearers. As whole selves, they can become 'true' when the action by which the triune God enables them to have the relevant true beliefs brings about their conformity to the risen Christ."[29] The truth of a theological belief thus seems to differ from that of an ordinary belief, since the truth of a statement such as "the traffic signal is red" depends upon only two factors – namely, what the statement means and how things are with the world – whereas the truth of a theological belief such as "Jesus is risen" adds a third factor, namely, that the believer correspond to Christ. (Obviously, Marshall is here discussing truth in a fairly

---

[27] Marshall, *Trinity and Truth*, p. 247.   [28] Marshall, *Trinity and Truth*, p. 248.
[29] Marshall, *Trinity and Truth*, pp. 270 and 268.

robust sense; below I clarify the sense in which a theological belief to which one merely assents could also be true.) Marshall concludes, therefore, that "we cannot group divine and created conditions together under a single notion of 'condition,' and so cannot suppose that 'sufficient conditions' means the same thing in each case."[30]

Marshall realizes that this move comes at a price: "The cost is obscurity," he writes, since "we cannot conceive of uncreated truth conditions except by qualifying and negating elements in our concept of created truth conditions, which avoids the suggestion of competition but denies us a clear concept of the truth-bestowing role of divine action. As a result we have no clear way now to explain how two elements which we take to be necessary to the concept of truth, at least for one belief – Tarski-style truth conditions and the action of the risen Jesus – fit together in a single concept, even though we are committed to thinking that they have to do so. The best we can do is block the suggestion that they are positively incompatible."[31] Marshall's critics have seized upon this point as evidence that he ends up introducing a dualism between ordinary and theological truth, but the critique fails to follow Marshall's argument through to its culmination, where he sketches a Trinitarian account of *all* truth, thereby claiming, implicitly, that although the relationship between ordinary and theological truth may seem obscure from the point of view of ordinary truth, it is not so from a theological point of view.[32] Marshall claims, that is, that an account of ordinary truth cannot do justice to the truth of theological beliefs, but not vice versa, such that it is a mistake to accuse him of introducing a dualism between the two. Importantly for our purposes, moreover, Marshall claims that once ordinary truth is seen from a theological point of view, it is possible to understand an account of such truth as explaining precisely *how* God brings beliefs into conformity with Christ: "An

---

[30] Marshall, *Trinity and Truth*, p. 258.   [31] Marshall, *Trinity and Truth*, p. 258.
[32] For Marshall's arguments to this effect, see pp. 280ff.; for the relevant criticism, see Pickstock and Milbank, *Truth in Aquinas*, pp. 1–6.

account of truth, meaning, and belief like Davidson's might – now that the coincidence of true beliefs with those whose truth conditions are met has been christologically secured – be taken to describe the mechanism by which the Spirit accomplishes this."[33] The account that follows could be taken, in part, as an attempt to explain further how this might work.

Marshall thus outlines a therapeutic account of truth, three elements of which are crucial: (a) an account of ordinary truth which denies correspondentism without thereby denying that truth consists in a belief's getting its subject matter right; (b) a trinitarian account of theological truth according to which truth depends upon one's being conformed to Christ by the power of the Spirit; and (c) an account of the unity of (a) and (b) in terms of (b). I am largely in agreement with Marshall on each of these matters, though my way of arriving at these claims – and elaborating them – differs in some respects from his. The previous section could rightly be seen as elaborating a version of (a), whereas the remainder of this section elaborates versions of (b) and (c).

2

To proceed, then, we need to say a bit more about what it would mean to claim, with Marshall and much of the tradition, that Jesus Christ is the truth.[34] The previous section argued that to take a belief to be true is to take it as getting its subject matter right, and that taking it as such is recognizing its authority to judge other beliefs. So what might it mean to say of a person, namely Jesus, that he is the truth? On the account offered above, it would mean that one takes him to get his subject matter (that is, the one he calls "Father") right, and that one recognizes his normative authority to judge beliefs and actions related to this subject matter. This construal seems plausible, since,

---

[33] Marshall, *Trinity and Truth*, p. 281.
[34] Cf. John 14:6, to take the most obvious example.

on the one hand, Christians have traditionally taken Jesus to get his subject matter right, seeing him as God's very Word and Image, and on the other, they have taken him to have normative authority over every God-related belief and action. We can understand Jesus as the truth, moreover, not only inasmuch as he tells one true things about God, but in that his very being, as being-in-obedience, "gets God right," and this being-in-obedience is the standard by which everyone else's being is to be judged. The relevant conformity to Jesus, therefore, would be a matter not only of holding true beliefs about God, but of internalizing the norms by which Jesus judged what counts as following him: as Schleiermacher argued, one becomes God's child by being conformed to Christ's image, one is conformed to this image as one internalizes Christ's normative Spirit, and one internalizes this Spirit as the norms implicit in Christ's own recognition of certain persons and performances are transmitted to one through a chain of intersubjective recognition stretching back to Christ himself. We have been over these points again and again, but their importance here can hardly be overstated.

With these points in mind – and, indeed, on their basis – we can say more about the possible truth of beliefs about God. From a Christian point of view, one can say that theological beliefs about God, Jesus Christ, humanity, and so forth should be taken to be true only if they get their subject matter right, that they count as getting their subject matter right only if they are conformed to Christ, and that they are recognizable as such on the basis of other beliefs that carry on a normative trajectory stretching back to him. In terms of our preferred order of explanation, we can arrive at this understanding by proceeding through the following steps. We begin with the practice of taking a commitment to be true: one judges whether a theological belief is true on the basis of other beliefs which one takes to be true, and if the candidate belief is taken to be true, it contributes to the basis in terms of which still other beliefs may be judged. One of the central ways in which one may come to hold a theological belief to be true, in turn, is to take another's word for it: if one takes a belief to be true, one may propose it to others for belief, thereby implicitly recognizing them as recognizers of the truth and seeking their recognition of the belief in question as well as of one-self as a competent taker of truth. Through such transactions, one comes to acquire a stock of taken-true beliefs. The second step is to understand the Spirit's role in this process. The normative Spirit of Christ, on our account, is the Spirit implicit in Jesus' recognition of certain performers and performances as following him, and this Spirit is carried on through a process of intersubjective recognition: further performers and performances are recognized as going on in the same way as those which were recognized by Christ, on the basis of which still others can be recognized, and so on, thereby carrying on the normative Spirit of Christ's recognition. We can understand the Spirit as playing a similar role in the practice of taking theo-logical beliefs to be true: one judges a candidate belief on the basis of other beliefs one takes true, and if the belief is taken to be true, it contributes to the basis in terms of which still other beliefs can be taken as such. The norm according to which a belief's possible truth is assessed is thus mediated through an ongoing process of recogni-tion. Likewise one's recognition of others as competent recognizers of truth: by taking someone's assertions to be good reason to affirm some belief, one confers upon them a kind of authority and treats them as undertaking a correlate responsibility, and one's recognition of them is itself a judgment for which one is responsible. In this way, the practice of recognizing certain beliefs to be true (and recognizing certain persons as competent recognizers of truth) carries on a nor-mative trajectory, and we can understand this trajectory as carrying on the normative Spirit of Christ's own recognition. This brings us to a final step: if we think of the normative trajectory thus mediated as stretching back to Jesus' own recognition of certain performers and performances, it follows that by rendering one's beliefs answer-able to beliefs that carry on this trajectory, one's beliefs answer to the Spirit of the one who is himself the truth. That is to say, if (a) Jesus Christ gets God right, as it were, and is therefore the one to whom all beliefs about God must answer, (b) he himself recognized certain beliefs as correct and certain persons as competent recognizers of such correctness, and (c) the normative Spirit according to which he assessed beliefs is carried forward through an ongoing practice of intersubjective recognition, it follows (d) that by judging candidate beliefs in terms of beliefs which carry on his Spirit, one's beliefs can be judged by, and in turn carry on, this Spirit.

Consider an example. Suppose someone takes it to be true that Jesus Christ is Lord. On the present account, one takes this to be true on the basis of one's other beliefs: one may believe, for instance, that the testimony of others (including Scripture) is trustworthy, and may in consequence believe that Jesus Christ claimed to be God's image, that God raised Jesus from the dead, that this raising amounts to God's affirmation of Jesus' claim, and so on.[35] In view of beliefs such as these, one may take it to be true that Jesus is Lord. If so, one takes this belief to contribute to the standard in terms of which still other beliefs can be assessed – other beliefs about Jesus, for example, but also beliefs about how one should conduct one's life, what one's attitude toward other would-be lords ought to be, and so forth. Taking it to be true that Jesus is Lord, accordingly, should play a role in one's transformation into God's child, insofar as more and more of one's beliefs and actions are brought into conformity with

---

[35] With respect to the normativity of Scripture: Scripture has long been recognized as both carrying on and standing in judgment over judgments about what counts as following Christ, which seems to mean that one counts as going on in the same way as Christ just in case one's performances are recognizable as carrying on the normative trajectory implicit in a series of precedents which not only includes Scripture, but which itself recognizes the authority of Scripture. (To be sure, one's interpretation of Scripture must itself go on in the same way as that which was recognized by Christ, and this should be understood in terms of an interpretation's recognizability as going on in the same way as precedent interpretations that carry on his normative Spirit. Scripture does not replace the Spirit's work, in other words; it is taken up into it. I elaborate a complementary account of scriptural interpretation in my "Postliberal Hermeneutics: Narrative, Community, and the Meaning of Scripture," *Expository Times* 122:3 [December, 2010], pp. 1–12. See, too, the account defended by Schleiermacher, *Der Christliche Glaube*, §§128–30.)

one's belief about Jesus' lordship. (We will return to this point in the following subsection.) One's taking the belief to be true likewise serves as a link in a chain of precedent testimony to it: just as one's acceptance of this belief likely involved taking another's word for it, who likely took yet another's word for it, and so on, so upon accepting this belief to be true, still others can take one's word for it. We can thus understand the taking-true of a particular belief in terms of a wider process of recognition, and understand this process as itself the work of the Spirit, insofar as these recognitions carry on (and are carried on by) the normative Spirit of Christ's own recognition. A similar account could be given of the recognition of claims such as "you are forgiven," "God's love is a refining fire," and "Jesus appeared to me in a dream," though the point should already be clear enough.

On this account, then, the truth of a theological belief is understood in terms of its conformity to Christ, and a belief counts as so conforming only if it goes on in the same way as beliefs which he recognized, that is, beliefs which carry on the normative Spirit implicit in a trajectory of precedent beliefs stretching back to him. An important consequence thus emerges into view, namely, the reconciliation of so-called "epistemic" and "non-epistemic" accounts of truth. An account is *epistemic*, on this distinction, insofar as it explains truth in terms of epistemic justification or warranted belief – usually in an attempt to avoid truth skepticism – whereas an account is *non-epistemic* if it maintains that the truth of a proposition is objective and therefore need have nothing to do with what one has access to, good reason to believe, etc. The present account maintains both objectivity and a connection with epistemic justification, since, on the one hand, the truth of a candidate belief is to be judged solely on whether it gets its subject matter right, and yet, on the other, the belief's subject matter sent its own Spirit, as it were, to indwell one and guide one into all truth, and if that Spirit is carried on through a community's recognitive practices, it follows that beliefs' answerability to their subject matter is compatible with, and indeed mediated by, one's answerability to one's peers. As argued in Chapter 2, the objectivity of a particular normative commitment is administered by those whom one recognizes, in consequence of which (a) objectivity need not be equated with "a view from nowhere," and (b) that which is central to epistemic justification, namely reason-giving, and that which is central to most understandings of truth, namely objectivity, should be seen as working together – for a theological account of truth, at any rate.

3

Several aspects of this account require further elaboration, beginning with the relationship between faith and truth. To be sure, there is an elementary sort of faith involved in taking another's word for some belief, but this is not the only kind of faith relevant to taking theological beliefs to be true. A second kind of faith has to do with one's wholehearted identification with certain beliefs. To understand what this means, consider again the claim that Jesus is Lord. On one level, one's affirmation of this belief involves seeing it as the standard by which still other beliefs might be judged, yet at this level, all that is involved may be "mere intellectual assent."[36] The belief that Jesus is Lord would be no different, at this level, than the belief that water is clear or that George Washington was the first president of the United States. Yet in order to account adequately for the truth of beliefs such as "Jesus is Lord," something more is needed, namely, some explanation of one's *involvement* in that truth. On the present account, we can understand the requisite involvement as coming in two flavors, identification and transformation, each of which involves the explicitation of one's relationship to one's beliefs. (There is an important relationship between identification and transformation, on the one

---

[36] For a searching critique of such assent, see, for instance, Rudolf Bultmann, "Theology as Science," in *New Testament and Mythology*, Schubert Ogden (ed.) (Philadelphia: Fortress Press, 1984).

hand, and justification and sanctification, on the other, but I cannot spell it out here.) First, one's involvement in this truth has to do with one's identification with certain beliefs – that, say, Jesus is Lord or that one is forgiven. As mentioned earlier, by engaging in truth-talk – that is, saying of some belief that one takes it to be true – one's commitment to it becomes explicit and, in consequence, itself susceptible to judgment. If one believes that Jesus is Lord, for example, but one has never judged for oneself whether one stands behind this belief, it may not be clear whether the belief is one's own, rather than something one happens to be stuck with. By making the belief explicit, one can stand in a different relationship to it: one can consider one's reasons for holding the belief, can decide whether to continue believing it, and so on, and while these decisions may not change the content of one's belief, they can change one's relationship to it: the belief may become more recognizably one's own, and one can thus explicitly identify with and commit oneself to it. (More on this in Chapter 6.) What Karl Barth said of one's faith in Jesus Christ applies to this sort of identification, too: "Faith," he writes, "realizes nothing new, it invents nothing; it finds only that which is already the case for the one who has faith as for the one who has not. It is only the person's active decision for it, only his or her active acceptance of it, only his or her active taking part in it. The person him- or herself steps into a relationship to it." As a result of this decision, the object of a person's faith "stands not only in a relationship to the person, but the person him- or herself enters into a relationship to it."[37] Likewise, when one has decided for oneself to hold some theological belief, one can see oneself as standing behind it, can see the belief as self-expressive, and can thus identify with it. This is one aspect of the "something more" necessary to an account of one's involvement in theological truth.[38]

---

[37] Barth, *Die Kirchliche Dogmatik*, vol. IV, *Die Lehre von der Versöhnung*, part 1 (Zollikon-Zürich: Evangelischer Verlag A. G., 1953), p. 829.

[38] This is also a way of understanding the "something more," over and above know-how, that Chapter 2 mentioned as necessary to counting as a follower of Christ.

The other aspect has to do with one's transformation by the truth. As mentioned above, to affirm that Jesus is Lord is to take that belief as contributing to the standard in terms of which other beliefs are to be judged. This entails that one *should* judge other beliefs in terms of this one, which is to say that by taking this belief to be true, one undertakes a belief whose outworking would include the transformation of several of one's collateral beliefs (including beliefs about one's actions and attitudes); so, for example, if one believes that Jesus is Lord, one should no longer take oneself to be one's own lord, nor the government, nor one's peers, insofar as the latter lordships are incompatible with the former. One is not always aware, however, of the ways in which one's collateral beliefs would be judged by a particular belief, nor is one always interested in becoming aware of such judgments. Hence the importance, once again, of explicitation: by making explicit not only one's affirmation of a particular belief but its relationship to other beliefs, one exhibits the extent to which one's commitment to Jesus' lordship would require changes in those beliefs (and other collateral commitments). In this way, one can judge one's commitments in light of one's belief in Christ, thereby opening up the possibility of ever-greater conformity to him.

Taking one's theological beliefs to be true can thus involve more than mere intellectual assent, since one can (and, on a Christian account, should) both identify with and be transformed by this truth. This is not to suggest, however, that Christians alone can make true statements about God or hold true theological beliefs. First, assuming that the meaning of a statement such as "Jesus is Lord" is recognizable as going on in the same way as the relevant precedents, the statement is true irrespective of who is saying it (Christian or otherwise). That is to say, if one takes it that Jesus is in fact the Lord, then Jesus is Lord irrespective of anyone's claiming him to be such; from this, it follows that when someone says "Jesus is Lord," he or she has said something true – even if he or she does not believe it. Assuming, then, that non-Christians can say true things about God, can they themselves take these statements to be true (without thereby ceasing to be non-Christians)? To be sure, someone who not only believed that Jesus is Lord but wholeheartedly identified with this belief would already count as a Christian, but what about someone who merely assents intellectually to this belief – does it make sense, on our account, to imagine someone assenting to this belief while remaining a non-Christian? On the present account, his or her recognition of this belief as true depends upon his or her collateral beliefs, which seems to indicate that there are a number of plausible circumstances in which mere assent would be possible: his or her collateral beliefs could be such that he or she takes this belief to be true, but, say, not important, or he or she could take it to be true but not be ready to identify with it, or not want to follow him, etc. It seems possible, then, that a non-Christian could take a belief such as "Jesus is Lord" to be true while remaining a non-Christian, a possibility even easier to imagine with beliefs that are less centrally and distinctively Christian – and less apparently demanding of self-involvement – such as "the one who created the universe is fundamentally loving." One's status as a recognized recognizer of such truth, however, depends upon one's being reliably able (and inclined) to judge candidate beliefs' truth in a way that carries on the normative Spirit of Christ's own judgments, which seems to suggest that although the truth of a statement does not depend upon its role in a particular form of life, one's ability to recognize it as such ultimately may.[39]

It is also worth clarifying, in this connection, the relationship between ordinary and theological truth. One of my overall goals is to explain the semantics of theological discourse in such a way that one would no longer be tempted to think that there must be

---

[39] I am here siding with George Hunsinger (see his "Truth as Self-Involving: Barth and Lindbeck," in *Disruptive Grace: Studies in the Theology of Karl Barth* [Grand Rapids, MI: Eerdmans, 2000], pp. 305–18) over against George Lindbeck (*The Nature of Doctrine: Religion and Theology in a Postliberal Age* [Louisville, KY: Westminster John Knox, 1984]) – or, more charitably, with Lindbeck's "Response to Bruce Marshall" (*The Thomist* 53 [1989], pp. 403–6) over against *The Nature of Doctrine*.

a gap between God and language, and one of my key strategies for achieving this goal has been to explain how the "supernatural" can become "natural" (to borrow Schleiermacher's slogan), that is, how the semantics of ordinary discourse could be fit for God-talk, and how God-talk could thus enter into ordinary discourse without thereby being cut down to size. I have, accordingly, explained ordinary truth in terms of the norms implicit in taking beliefs to be true, and then explained theological truth in terms of the normative Spirit of Christ carrying on – and being carried on by – this same process as it stretches back to Christ's own recognition of certain beliefs and persons. There is, accordingly, no gap between ordinary and theological truth, since we can understand theological truth as entering into the processes whereby ordinary truth is recognized, though it is crucial to realize that theological truth is not thereby *reduced* to ordinary truth.

4

A second set of clarifications has to do with the role of propositions in this account. On the one hand, it is important to point out that although my account focusses largely on the possible truth of the content of a belief or assertion – that is to say, its propositional content – it is not liable to the objections commonly raised against "propositionalism."[40] First, though my account focusses on propositional content, this by no means entails that theology has thereby been reduced to such content. It should be obvious that one can focus one's attention on propositions without thereby committing oneself to such reductionism, but in order to avoid misunderstandings, something further ought to be said. Propositions have been

---

[40] For a critique along these lines, see Donald Evans, *The Logic of Self-Involvement* (London: SCM Press, 1963); Lindbeck, *The Nature of Doctrine*; and Kevin Vanhoozer, *The Drama of Doctrine: A Canonical-Linguistic Approach to Christian Theology* (Louisville, KY: Westminster John Knox, 2005), pp. 266–78.

privileged here for two reasons: (a) although propositions are not the only kind of God-talk, nor are they the only kind with cognitive content, there are well-known ways of explaining the content of other kinds of speech act precisely in terms of their relation to propositional content; hence, one can understand the meaning of a prayer in terms of the propositional content that would count as an answer to it, the meaning of a command in terms of what propositional content would have to be brought about to count as obeying it, the meaning of a hope in terms of what propositional content would fulfill it, etc. Hence, there is reason to accord *explanatory* privilege to propositions, since an explanation of propositions opens the door to explaining other varieties of speech act. Propositions have also been privileged because (b) one's taking a particular belief, action, or attitude to be Christ-following is itself rendered judgeable precisely by putting its content into propositional form: one can determine whether one's treatment of the poor, for instance, conforms to Christ only insofar as one can make judgments about that treatment, and one's ability to think about this treatment just is one's ability to consider its propositional content. For these reasons, then, it makes sense to accord relative privilege to propositions – relative, that is, to their explanatory value.

This brings us to a second clarification: although my account takes propositions to be explanatorily basic to understanding other speech acts, propositions themselves are to be understood in terms of their role in normative social practices: on this account, one recognizes various performers and performances as correct simply by treating them as such, but one can make these implicit recognitions explicit – and so render them judgeable – by treating one's treatment of them as itself correct or incorrect, which is just to consider their propositional content. This means, on the one hand, that one is not left out of the picture, so to speak, simply because propositions are taken to be explanatorily basic, since propositions, too, are the product of (and susceptible to) a community's normative social practices, and it means, on the other, that the practice of rendering a belief or act's content judgeable should be understood as recontextualizing rather than decontextualizing it, that is, as bringing one part of one's practical repertoire to bear on another part, rather than as moving from social practices to something outside of them.[41]

Finally, some have objected to propositionalism on the grounds that it seeks to gather all knowledge into one point of view, thereby dominating or totalizing that which is known; as an antidote, these objectors remind us that an object can and must be seen from a variety of vantage points, including that of poetry. In response to this objection, we should note, first, that a proposition need not be literal; if one says, for instance, that God is a shelter in the storm, one is speaking both metaphorically *and* propositionally. The category of propositions is thus distinct from the category of the literal, and this distinction should be kept in mind when recommending multiple points of view. Beyond this, however, there is no reason to disagree with the recommendation of these objectors, since there is no reason either to limit propositions to one kind of discourse, nor any reason to limit discussion of an object to one such discourse. That is to say, positively, that one's talk of God, like one's talk generally, need not be limited to a single, usually scientistic, discourse, and there is nothing in the present discussion to suggest otherwise. Just as a game of baseball is endlessly describable in different languages, using different discourses (e.g., the discourse of physics, of aesthetics, of history, of sociology, of myth, and of statistics), each sentence of which could equally claim to be true, so much more can God be described – and praised – in all sorts of languages, discourses, and styles, none of which need be thought to compete with any other. There is no discourse, accordingly – least of all theology – which should claim to speak God's own language about Godself, to the exclusion of other discourses.

---

[41] For an argument along these lines, see Brandom, "Heidegger's Categories in *Sein und Zeit*," *Tales of the Mighty Dead: Historical Essays in the Metaphysics of Intentionality* (Cambridge, MA: Harvard University Press, 2002).

One last point in this connection: it may appear that this account is still liable to one of the objections raised at the outset, namely, that it ends up measuring God in terms of human beliefs and ideas, since it portrays such beliefs as (potentially) getting God right. In response to this charge, it is crucial to note that God's measure, as it were, precedes and stands in judgment over every human measure, since, on the present account, a proposition counts as getting God right only if it conforms to God's incarnate Word by the power of God's normative Spirit. God's measurement is thus prior to any attempt to think or speak about God, both in the sense that God measures such thought and speech, and in that it is precisely this measurement that enables one to think or speak rightly of God. Moreover, although there is a sense in which a human standard here becomes the measure by which the putative truth of a theological belief is judged, this does not entail that God has illicitly been subjected to the violence of being measured, since, on the present account, God has determined to include human persons in the mediation of God's own measurement, such that, on the whole, human measurement need not be thought incompatible with God's own. To be sure, a danger lurks here, namely, that of identifying human truths as God's and then using them to judge God (and one another), but the present account provides at least two significant theoretical resources by which to resist this danger, namely, its commitment to the priority of God's judgment and its insistence that the standard by which God judges does not simply fall into human hands. Both of these points have been sufficiently discussed already.

∗∗∗

A belief about God is true, then, if it gets Christ's subject matter right, and it gets Christ's subject matter right if it goes on in the same way as precedent beliefs which have been recognized as getting it right. Hence, if one says "God justifies the ungodly," one's statement is true if it gets its subject matter right, and it is recognizable as such if it carries on the Spirit of precedent beliefs. Precedent beliefs can go wrong, of course, but we can make sense of such going-wrong only on the basis of a vast amount of going-right. In light of the claim that beliefs about God are true just in case they get Christ's subject matter right, accordingly, and that one's judgment to this effect depends upon the work of the Holy Spirit, we can say that theological truth is a trinitarian affair. Hence, if (a) the Spirit of Christ enters into and is carried on by ordinary practices of taking-true, and (b) the latter can be understood in non-correspondentist, non-metaphysical terms, it follows (c) that the loss of correspondentism need not be thought to entail a loss of theological truth.

Conclusion

This chapter considered several of the problems facing a correspondentist theory of truth, and then sketched an alternative which avoids these problems by reversing the usual order of explanation – that is, by using the ordinary practice of taking-true to explain "truth," rather than using "truth" to explain the practice of taking-true – and then used this same account to explain how theological beliefs could be true. That is to say, by (a) understanding truth in terms of the practice of taking-true – that is, one's (usually implicit) judgment, on the basis of one's other beliefs, that a candidate belief is correct, and (b) understanding the normative Spirit of Christ as entering into and being carried on through this practice, we arrived at a non-metaphysical account of theological truth according to which (c) a belief about God is true if it conforms to God's Word, and (d) it is recognizable as so conforming if it goes on in the same way as precedent beliefs which are recognized as such by the Spirit. The bottom line is that truth need not be thought of in correspondentist terms, from which it follows that here, too, the semantics of ordinary language does not entail that God must stand at a remove from human talk of God. There is a sense, then, in which this chapter's argument completes the project of this book, since I have now elaborated and defended non-metaphysical accounts of God, language, and their relationship, in consequence of which one need no longer be haunted by the ghost of essentialist-correspondentist metaphysics. It remains only to say something further about why this argument matters.

6 | Emancipating theology

I have been arguing that theology needs to be freed from metaphysical assumptions about God and language, and the preceding chapters have aimed to secure this freedom by elaborating an alternative account of each. One of my central claims, simply stated, was that so long as one remains bound to essentialist-correspondentist presuppositions about language and its relation to God, it will seem as if one has to choose between fitting God into a metaphysical framework, on the one hand, and insisting that God stands at a remove from creaturely language and experience, on the other. To be freed from these presuppositions, then, and so from the sense of alienation they beget, I defended a non-metaphysical understanding of both ordinary and theological discourse: by explaining semantical notions such as concept use, meaning, reference, and truth in terms of the norms implicit in the practice of recognition, explaining the mediation of Christ's normative Spirit in terms of these same recognitive practices, and using the latter to explain the semantics of God-talk, I concluded that there need be no distance between God and language. The preceding account thus aimed to emancipate theology from its captivity to certain metaphysical assumptions. The aim of this final chapter is to make explicit the extent to which theology, thus emancipated, is itself emancipating, in that (a) it funds a robust notion of "expressive freedom," and (b) it provides critical and constructive resources for movements of liberation.

Expressive freedom

We begin, accordingly, by making explicit the preceding proposal's commitment to (and underwriting of) "expressive freedom." Such freedom can be understood as a species of autonomy – understood, that is, in terms of one's ability to see one's doxastic and practical commitments (or "beliefs and actions," for short) as due to one – where this being-due-to-one can itself be understood in terms of one's standing in a certain relationship to one's peers. On the picture that emerges, freedom turns out to depend upon one's being constrained by communal norms which are themselves recognizable as due to one, and norms count as such just insofar as they are carried on by capacious patterns of mutual recognition.

1

To get an idea of why one would think of freedom along these lines – and what such freedom looks like – it will be helpful to rehearse a brief historical narrative, beginning with the movement Charles Taylor labels "Reform," namely, the late-Medieval/early-Modern "drive to make over the whole society to higher standards," a drive rooted in "a profound dissatisfaction with the hierarchical equilibrium between lay life and the renunciative vocations" that had become prevalent in Medieval Christendom.[1] Advocates of Reform were concerned that the higher life called for by the Gospel had come to be seen as a special vocation to be practiced by the elite, rather than as a vocation to be lived out by all Christians. Reformers aimed to combat such two-tiered Christianity by insisting that the so-called "higher life" is demanded of every Christian, and by putting into effect all sorts of disciplinary measures by which to ensure that Christians would live up to its demands. This movement thus plays a key role in Taylor's explanation of the rise of a "disciplinary

[1] Taylor, *A Secular Age* (Cambridge, MA: Harvard University Press, 2007), pp. 61 and 63.

society" which contributed, in turn, to the eventual development of secularism, but for our purposes, what is crucial about Reform emerges into view when its rejection of two-tiered Christianity came into conflict with the then-prevailing assumption that members of an entire society could be counted "Christian" (in the relevant sense) solely on the basis of that membership. To understand how this conflict arose, consider that the Reformers insisted that the higher life is demanded of every Christian, and accordingly rejected the idea that certain Christians, such as monks, could relieve others of these demands by "carrying" them. Implicit in Reformers' rejection of two-tiered Christianity, then, is an insistence that the Christian life must be one's own, yet this insistence seems to be at odds, at least potentially, with the assumption that a person could be counted a Christian simply in virtue of his or her birth into a particular society, since it is not always clear whether or to what extent such persons' putative Christianity counts as their own. This became evident once certain conditions changed and more and more persons born into "Christian" societies began to wonder whether their faith was in fact *their* faith, or whether it was instead a kind of historical accident – something that happened to them, as it were, rather than due to them – which wondering led, in turn, to questions about what *would* make one's faith count as one's own.

I cannot do justice here to these developments, but for present purposes, it should suffice to trace how some shifts in the epistemic landscape prepared the way for these questions, and how these questions, in turn, eventually elicited a novel account of the freedom or "mineness" of one's faith.[2] (Several steps of this story were rehearsed

---

[2] On these points, in addition to Taylor's *Secular Age*, see J. B. Schneewind, *The Invention of Autonomy: A History of Modern Moral Philosophy* (Cambridge University Press, 1998); Robert B. Pippin, *Modernism as a Philosophical Problem: On the Dissatisfactions of European High Culture* (Oxford: Blackwell, 1991, 1999); Jeffrey Stout, *The Flight from Authority: Religion, Morality, and the Quest for Autonomy* (Notre Dame, IN: Notre Dame University Press, 1981); Alasdair MacIntyre, *After Virtue: A Study in Moral Theory* (Notre Dame, IN: Notre Dame University Press, 1981, 1984); Karl Barth, *Protestant Theology in the Nineteenth Century: Its Background and History*

in Chapter 2, so I can afford here to be brief.) To begin with, at the time of the Protestant Reformation, the potential conflict between claims about the necessary "mineness" of faith, on the one hand, and the assumption that one could be a Christian simply by being born into a particular society, on the other, remained largely invisible, because the vast majority of persons within the relevant societies took themselves to be Christians. The situation started to shift, however, as epistemic conditions changed. Two changes should suffice to illustrate this shift. First, Reformation and Counter-Reformation polemics seem to have played a crucial role in altering conditions of belief, not just because they led to a revival in skepticism, but because their mere existence ended up putting certain kinds of claim on a different epistemic footing: in a context in which the authority of tradition was itself at issue, it would beg the question to appeal to tradition as a means by which to justify one's claims *about* tradition. For this reason, there was a shift in the prevailing conditions of belief, away from the taken-for-granted justificatory authority of tradition and toward "thinking for oneself," the aim of which is to avoid believing anything simply because it is what one has been taught, what one has always believed, etc.[3] This aim contributed, in turn, to a series of further shifts in the conditions of belief, since it led generations of philosophers and theologians to consider what it would mean to think for oneself and under what conditions this is possible. For most of these thinkers, it seemed evident that one counted as thinking for oneself about some doxastic or practical commitment only if one could offer reasons for it, but this raised an obvious problem: if one counts as thinking for oneself about a commitment only if one gives reasons for it, it follows that one is thinking for oneself about such reasons only if one gives reasons for *them*,

(Grand Rapids, MI: Eerdmans, 2001); Terry Pinkard, *German Philosophy 1760–1860* (Cambridge University Press, 2002); and Jürgen Habermas, *The Philosophical Discourse of Modernity*, trans. F. Lawrence (Cambridge, MA: MIT Press, 1987).

[3] See Kant's famous 1784 essay, "Was ist Aufklärung?" *Kants Werke: Akademie Textausgabe*, vol. VIII (Berlin: Walter de Gruyter, 1968), p. 35.

and so on. The commitment to thinking for oneself thus seems to eventuate in a dilemma: either one is set off on an infinite regress of reason-giving, or else one appeals to a "foundation" in order to stop the regress. Candidates for the latter include appeals to Scripture, experience, and natural law, but such appeals came to grief in the face of critical philosophies such as Kant's, which argue (a) that appealing to such foundations represents a would-be abdication of one's responsibility to think for oneself, and (b) that these founda-tions can do the work asked of them only if they exert normative force without themselves being subject to norms, yet the normative force they exert depends, necessarily, upon their being subjected to norms, since it depends upon our interpretive and inferential capacities. Those committed to thinking for themselves thus had lit-tle choice but to face the other horn of the dilemma, namely, the threatened regress; the inescapability of this threat came clearly into view by the time of the so-called *Grundsatzkritik* of the 1790s, to which some responded by trying to shore up the old foundations, others by claiming that it illustrated reason's ultimate inadequacy and a consequent need for faith, and still others by giving up on the project of "thinking for oneself." Most important for the story I am telling, though, are those who were unsatisfied with such responses and so developed new ways of accounting for freedom, such as Kant, Fichte, Hegel, Schelling, the Schlegels, and Schleiermacher. For our purposes, it should suffice to consider only the response proposed by Schleiermacher, particularly since (a) his proposal draws exten-sively on, and overlaps considerably with, the views of his peers, and (b) I already discussed some elements of his response in Chapter 2.

[margin note: Kantian critique of foundat.]

2

To bring Schleiermacher's proposal into focus, it will help to say a bit more about a then-common understanding of freedom, accord-ing to which one counts as free with respect to some commitment only if one legislates it to oneself, and one counts as so legislating it only if one can offer sufficient reasons for it. Freedom is thus understood as a kind of autonomy: in Kant's famous formulation, one's will counts as free if and only if it "gives the law to itself," such that it "is not merely subject to the law, but so subject that it must be seen as *giving the law to itself* and just so as subject to the law (of which it can consider itself the author)."[4] Such freedom seems to require, first, that one be able to detach oneself from one's beliefs, deeds, and attitudes in order to determine whether one can and should reattach oneself to them, for without this sort of space between one's behavior and one's judgments about it, it would make little sense to inquire whether a creature could see itself as authoring its behavior; the creature would simply do what it does, and the issue of whether it legislates its behavior could not so much as arise for it. (This is not to say that it would lack every kind of freedom, only the sort of freedom under consideration.) The first condition thus involves some capacity for self-consciousness with respect to one's beliefs and deeds, where this self-consciousness should be understood as the capacity to make judgments about them. A second condition emerges from consideration of these judgments, namely, that one counts as free with respect to some belief or action just insofar as one can justify it, that is, offer sufficient reasons for it. The idea here is that unless one can give reasons for one's commitments, there is no reason to think that the commitment is undertaken intentionally, nor any way of determining whether the commitment is due to one rather than merely given to one, since one has not established a connection between it and that which would show that one could legislate it to oneself, namely, reasons. This leads to a third point: the reasons one offers on behalf of one's commitments must themselves be subject to normative assessment, for otherwise, if *anything* offered as a reason were necessarily to count as such, the reasons thus given could not be regarded as justifying a commitment, as legislating it, and so on.

---

[4] Kant, *Grundlegung zur Metaphysik der Sitten, Kants Werke: Akademie Textausgabe*, vol. IV (Berlin: Walter de Gruyter, 1968), p. 431.

Reasons would not be reasons, in other words, unless offered for the sake of justifying some commitment, yet if one cannot distinguish good from bad reasons, there is no reason to think that they could be called upon to justify anything – but if the norms by which one's reasons are to be assessed are not themselves self-legislated, then one's alleged autonomy with respect to one's commitments turns out to depend, ultimately, upon something heteronomous. We thus face a dilemma: if the norms by which one's reasons are to be assessed are not self-legislated, then autonomy ends up collapsing into heteronomy, yet if they are supposed to be self-legislated, then either these norms must be normed solely by oneself, in which case whatever one thinks is right *is right*, or else they are liable to assessment by some extra-subjective norm, in which case one's autonomy rests, again, on a heteronomous foundation.

Schleiermacher can be understood as providing a novel response to this problem, though it should be remembered that several of his contemporaries were working along similar tracks.[5] Schleiermacher's response consists of two key claims, the first of which is that normativity must be *implicit* in one's non-inferential responsive dispositions before it can be made *explicit* in reason-giving, judgments, and so on. The idea here, recall, is that one's attunement to circumstances is norm-laden prior to any explicit decision one might make about which norms to apply, how to apply them, and so forth, and that such attunement is a product of one's becoming reliably disposed

---

[5] Schleiermacher's ethical works attest to the fact that he understood himself to be responding to this problem; so in his *Brouillon*, for instance, he tries to explain how one could see one's commitments as due to one – as "that in the formation of which I am included" – when everywhere it is the case that "the individual always enters with his or her action into that which has already become; his or her action is thus a carrying-on, and that which has-become has not come about through him or her" (*Brouillon zur Ethik* 1805/06, Hans-Joachim Birkner [ed.] [Hamburg: Felix Meiner Verlag, 1981], 34th and 90th Hours). Or again, in his 1812/13 *Ethik*, he frames his discussion in terms of an opposition between "objective necessity and original action" (*Ethik* 1812/13, Hans-Joachim Birkner [ed.] [Hamburg: Felix Meiner Verlag, 1981], p. 170).

to respond according to the practices of one's community. This prioritization of implicit over explicit normativity provides some help in avoiding the threatened regress, since it signals a decisive shift in the prevailing understanding of a right, and so free, relation to one's commitments: the crucial issue is no longer whether one can explicitly reason about each of one's commitments, and only in this way be free with respect to them, but whether the norms by which one would judge such reasoning – that is, the norms implicit in social practice – are themselves recognizable as one's own or as self-expressive – as "that in the formation of which I am included"[6] – where such self-expressivity depends upon the kind of community one is a part of, rather than upon reason-giving per se. For one to stand in the right sort of relationship to one's commitments, in other words, is for the norms by which they are constrained to be recognizably self-expressive, and since these norms are themselves implicit in social practices, it follows that one's relationship to these commitments is caught up in one's relationship to the society whose practices they are; as Schleiermacher puts it, freedom thus depends upon "the identity of objective necessity and inner self-determination as invention, which has mostly to do with the kind and manner of one's community."[7]

This is a complicated claim, elaboration of which will bring us to Schleiermacher's second key argument, but before turning to it, we need to clarify a few points. First, I had been talking about freedom as one's ability to identify a belief or action as due to one in virtue of one's giving reasons for it, yet Schleiermacher's prioritization of implicit normativity seems to suggest that reason-giving has no bearing on freedom. In response to this, it is important to note that Schleiermacher should be understood as re-prioritizing, rather than eliminating, such reason-giving, and, indeed, that reason-giving remains significant, for unless one can offer explicit reasons

---

[6] Schleiermacher, *Brouillon*, 34th Hour. [7] Schleiermacher, *Ethik*, p. 176.

for at least *some* of one's commitments, there would be no reason to construe *any* of them (including those implicit in attunement) as responsive to norms.[8] It is likewise important, however, to understand why Schleiermacher would resist the idea that one stands in the right relation to one's commitments only if one can explicitly justify them: on the one hand, the practice of reason-giving must itself depend upon a background of implicit norms, for otherwise, the practice would be set off on an infinite regress of reason-giving; and on the other, it is hardly unimaginable that one would be justified in holding a commitment even when one's explicit justification is inadequate – as when an expert chicken-sexer justifies his or her sexings by appeal to some visual cue, for instance, when in fact they depend upon a difference in scent, or when someone's failure to justify his or her commitments is indicative of a lack of confidence, rather than a lack of justifiability – which seems to indicate that explicit reason-giving is not a necessary condition of such commitments being justified. That is to say, what finally counts is whether one stands in a right relationship to the appropriate norms, but this need not be established by giving an explicit account of the relationship in each case. There is good reason, accordingly, to explain one's justification for holding a commitment in terms of something other than explicit reason-giving, and Schleiermacher provides such an alternative by appeal to the norms implicit in social practices. Key # 2

The centrality of social practices brings us to Schleiermacher's second key argument, consisting of a series of claims about how one must relate to such practices – and how these practices must be shaped – in order for one to relate freely to one's doxastic and practical commitments. We can begin by rehearsing some claims from

---

[8] So Schleiermacher claims, for instance, that "whoever has not considered his or her most recent actions cannot guarantee that his or her next acts will be truly human nor exhibit humanity's worth … To consider the humanity in oneself and, when one has once found it, never to lose sight of it, is the only secure means by which to remain on its holy ground" (*Monologen, Kritische Gesamtausgabe* 1/3: *Schriften aus der Berliner Zeit 1800–1802*, Günter Meckenstock [ed.] [Berlin: Walter de Gruyter, 1988], p. 16).

Chapter 2. On the Schleiermacherian model elaborated there, one intends one's use of a concept (or other normatively constrained performance) to be recognizable as such by those whom one recognizes as users of it, and one intends this by trying to use it in the same way as precedent uses which are recognized as correct. One's recognition of certain persons and performances thus confers authority upon them, such that one's answerability to them is a consequence of one's acknowledgment of them – that is, their authority to assess one's performances depends upon one's recognition of that authority. On Schleiermacher's account, moreover, the norm to which one answers is not only authorized by one's recognition of it, it is also constituted by that recognition, since the norm in question is a product of the trajectory implicit in uses one recognizes as precedential: if one's performance z is intended as going on in the same way as x and y, then z is to be assessed in terms of a normative trajectory implicit in the series x and y – but because x and y count as precedential only in view of one's recognizing them as such, it follows that one's recognitive commitment plays a role in constituting the norm by which one's performance is to be judged. And finally, if one's own use of the concept is recognizable as correct, it carries on the normative trajectory implicit in precedent uses, which means that it contributes to the norm according to which still other uses might be judged. In using a concept, in other words, one not only confers authority upon uses which one recognizes as precedential, one seeks this same authority for one's own use, such that one's performance ought to contribute to the very norm by which that performance was itself normed. On this model, accordingly, the norm by which one is constrained is authorized, carried on, and shaped by one's own recognitions and performances, which means that these norms are at least potentially recognizable as self-legislated. Schleiermacher thus claims that "each particular formation [of that which has been given to one] must as such endeavor to bring it before others for recognition and recognize the sphere of their formation; and this in its unity completes the essence of sociality, which consists in the recognition of alien property in order to let it be opened up, and in the opening-up of one's own property in order to let it be recognized."[9] "My" norms can thus be "ours," and "our" norms can be "mine."[10] That is to say, one can see oneself as determining these norms' authority over one, as constructing them, administering them, and contributing to them, from which it follows that performances constrained by these norms can be seen as self-legislated. Schleiermacher claims, accordingly, that a *free* community must be characterized by "a reciprocal action that is interwoven among all the participants, but one that is also fully determined and made complete by them," such that "the impetus to community … is satisfied in each person through all and in all through each person."[11]

This understanding of normativity, in turn, implies that in order to be free with respect to one's commitments, the communities of which one is a part must be characterized by (a) openness to novel, individual expressions, and (b) mutuality – they must be characterized, that is, by patterns of recognition that are both capacious and reciprocal. With respect to the former, Schleiermacher claims that a community "forms only a mediating mass, out of which each receives his or her cognition of individuality, and in which he or she places his or her individuality for others to cognize"; this being the case, one can "find oneself in" a community just to the extent that it "provides one with increased leeway for individuality."[12] A

---

[9] Schleiermacher, *Ethik*, p. 265.

[10] An obvious allusion to Hegel's famous description of *Geist* as "I that is *We*, and We that is *I*" (*Phänomenologie des Geistes* [Hamburg: Felix Meiner Verlag, 1988], pp. 108/127), though we find precisely the same thought in Schleiermacher, who insists that in a norm-circulating community, "the common will emerges from the individual, and the individual from the common" (*Ethik*, p. 314).

[11] Schleiermacher, "Versuch einer Theorie des geselligen Betragens," in *Schriften aus der Berliner Zeit, 1796–1799 Kritische Gesamtausgabe* I/2, Günter Meckenstock (ed.) (Berlin: Walter de Gruyter, 1984), p. 169; *Kurze Darstellung des theologischen Studiums* (1830), *Kritische Gesamtausgabe* I/6, Dirk Schmid (ed.) (Berlin: Walter de Gruyter, 1998), §166.

[12] Schleiermacher, *Ethik*, pp. 77, 175.

community supports self-expressive freedom, accordingly, only if its "highest tendency" is "the formation of an art treasury by which the attunement of each is formed and in which each deposits his or her distinct attunement and the free presentations of his or her way of being attuned."[13] That is to say, a community of free expression must be characterized by a range of recognized performers and performances sufficiently broad and diverse to enable each person to see his or her own contributions as recognizable expressions of the community's practices, and see these as contributing, in turn, to a still wider variety, thereby opening up further horizons of expression. Once a sufficiently rich, textured recognitive pattern has been established, accordingly, the self-expressions of each continually open up new possibilities of expression for all.

In view of Schleiermacher's earlier claims, moreover, it is not hard to see how such patterns would be established. Here it is important to remember Schleiermacher's distinction between that which is retrospectively recognizable as carrying on a normative trajectory and that which could be prospectively foreseen as doing so – as that which appears, from one point of view, as "the emergence of something novel, without precedent," and yet, from the other, as "built up from something already available."[14] To see how this explains expressive freedom, consider again a simple example: suppose someone suggests "5" as a candidate for carrying on the series "1, 2, 3, 4 … " From a retrospective point of view – looking back, that is, over the series "1, 2, 3, 4, 5" – it may look as if it were self-evident and predictable that this is the way the series would go on, but from a prospective point of view, things look different, since the series itself does not decide how it should be carried on; it could just as well have been carried on with "1" or "3" or any number of other candidates, which entails that, prospectively speaking, the series' continuation is unpredictable. This entails, in turn, that when a candidate

[13] Schleiermacher, *Ethik*, p. 122.
[14] Schleiermacher, *Kurze Darstellung* (1830), §78.

is recognized as carrying on the trajectory, it affects what it means to do so – and since the recognition of future candidates further determines what it means to "go on in the same way," it follows that this "same way" cannot be determined in advance. An expression counts as carrying on a normative trajectory, therefore, not because it was prospectively predictable, but because it is retrospectively recognizable as such. This entails, on the one hand, that one's constraint by norms does not amount to determination by them (in the sense of strict determinism), since the norm implicit in a series of precedents leaves open the possibility that the series will be carried on in novel and unpredictable ways. On the other hand, the fact that these expressions are retrospectively recognizable as carrying on a trajectory explains how they can be both novel *and* meaningful, since one can see novel expressions as the conclusion of a series of precedents. One's constraint by precedent not only does not foreclose the possibility of novel expressions, therefore, it supplies a condition of the possibility that others will be able to understand (and imitate) them. Consider again the example of language: linguists have demonstrated that the vast majority of sentences one utters have never before been uttered in the history of the language, which is to say that novelty is the rule in language use.[15] Yet, for the most part, language users have no trouble either producing or understanding such utterances, precisely because we can recognize them as going on in the same way as a certain set of precedents.

Schleiermacher thus claims that novel expressions "preserve the mobility" of a norm and "make room for other ways of framing it": because the normative trajectory implicit in a series of precedents changes every time a new expression is recognized as carrying it on, and since such changes are the rule rather than the exception, it follows that novelty is continually opening up the possibility of still further novelty.[16] As a result of being constrained by precedent,

---

[15] Noam Chomsky, *Aspects of the Theory of Syntax* (Cambridge, MA: MIT Press, 1965).
[16] Schleiermacher, *Kurze Darstellung* (1830), §203.

accordingly, one can produce novel expressions, and as a result of such expressions, a whole range of further expressive possibilities is introduced. In this way, the texture of a community's recognitive patterns is constantly being enriched, thereby opening up more and more space for persons' expressions to be both recognized by their community and recognizable as *self*-expressive.

It is thus crucial that the communities one recognizes be characterized by a set of broad and richly textured recognitive patterns. Taken by itself, however, this condition is insufficient; it is also necessary that these patterns be the product of mutual recognition – rather than, say, only of an elite hierarchy's recognitive attitudes – for otherwise, the norms thus instituted would ultimately be legislated by "them" rather than "us" or "me." For this reason, Schleiermacher argues that in a community of free expression (in this case the Church), there must be no fixed distinction between recognizer and recognized, authorizer and authorized, or priest and layperson, for "each is a priest in that he or she draws others to him- or herself in the field for which he or she has particular aptitude and in which he or she can present him- or herself as a virtuoso," and "each is a layperson, in that he or she follows the art and ways of another where he or she is an alien in religion." In such a community, accordingly, "each follows that power in others which he or she feels in him- or herself, and with which he or she also rules over them."[17] Each person should thus recognize others and in turn be recognized by them, as a result of which the contributions of each member of the community would be affirmed and each would see the norm underlying this affirmation as his or her own. On Schleiermacher's account, then, a

---

[17] Schleiermacher, *Über die Religion: Reden an die Gebildeten unter ihren Verächtern, Kritische Gesamtausgabe* I/2, p. 270; cf. the *Brouillon*, where Schleiermacher recommends a form of sociality where "in one's own manner of presentation, each becomes to the other a teacher" (65th Hour), and the *Ethik*, where he claims that "the individual, as organ of reason, can only give him- or herself up to the community insofar he or she receives him- or herself back from the community with the recognition of the totality" (p. 31).

community of free expression must be characterized by patterns of recognition broad and richly textured enough to acknowledge the self-expressive performances of each individual, and these patterns must themselves be the product of mutuality.

We can thus understand Schleiermacher as providing a helpful response to the question with which we began, namely, how to account for the "mineness" of one's faith without precipitating an infinite regress of reason-giving, on the one hand, or grounding that "mineness" on that which is not finally recognizable as one's own, on the other. On the present reconstruction, Schleiermacher proposes a threefold response: he claims, first, that normativity should be understood primarily as a matter of that which is implicit in social practice rather than explicit in reason-giving; second, that whether these norms are due to one should be understood primarily in terms of one's relationship to the community whose practices they are; and third, that such communities enable free self-expression only if they are characterized by patterns of recognition that are both mutual and open to all sorts of novel, individual expressions. Schleiermacher claims that one can see oneself in the norms implicit in such a community's practices, and can likewise see oneself in beliefs and actions that are constrained by these norms.

3

Schleiermacher thus provides a helpful way to think about the "mineness" of one's faith commitments, yet his proposal faces some rather obvious difficulties. This subsection addresses three such problems, though my response to the third leads into (and depends upon) the argument of the subsequent section. A first problem centers on the appeal here to autonomy and related notions of subjectivity. The problem, it seems, is that an individual's putative autonomy depends upon all sorts of apparently heteronomous conditions, including others' recognition (or "interpellation") of one *as* a subject and the normalizing effects of such recognition, which seems to suggest that autonomy is at best relatively latecoming, and at worst a kind of false consciousness.[18] In response to this problem, it is important to note, albeit briefly, that the objection seems to presuppose – and be haunted by – an inflationary picture of subjectivity, and that it is only in consequence of this presupposition that subjectivity seems so elusive. Be that as it may, it should be clear that the preceding account of autonomy does not require that one's subjectivity precede one's recognition as a subject. Quite the contrary: on this account, one is constituted a subject precisely in being recognizable as participating in various social practices, just as one's autonomy depends upon one's standing in a particular relationship to wider patterns of recognition.[19] Hence, although "Cartesian" models of subjectivity may be rendered untenable by this sort of objection, this should not be taken to entail that there is no such thing as subjectivity, since there are other defensible ways of construing the matter.

Concerns might also be raised about this account's emphasis on the "mineness" of faith, particularly since the Christian tradition has overwhelmingly insisted that one's faith is due to God's grace rather than to oneself. To address this concern, it is important to observe, first, a seeming paradox at the heart of Christian belief: according to the New Testament's claims about the new covenant, that which is strictly external to one and due solely to God's grace, namely, the possibility of following Christ, must become one's own possibility and therefore recognizable as due to one. Talking about this paradox, Karl Barth claims that although the possibility of following Christ depends wholly upon God's sovereign grace, this sovereignty

---

[18] For a claim along these lines, see Michel Foucault, "Two Lectures," in *Power/Knowledge: Selected Interviews and Other Writings 1972–1977*, Colin Gordon (ed.) (New York: Pantheon Books, 1980); and Judith Butler, *Excitable Speech: A Politics of the Performative* (London: Routledge, 1996).

[19] On this point, see also Robert B. Brandom, "The Structure of Desire and Recognition: Self-Consciousness and Self-Constitution," *Philosophy and Social Criticism* 33 (2007), pp. 127–50; and Robert B. Pippin, *Hegel's Practical Philosophy: Rational Agency as Ethical Life* (Cambridge University Press, 2008).

"wills to triumph not as a mechanical force, nor by moving the unmovable from without, nor to lord itself over puppets or slaves, but to triumph in true servants and friends, in their own free decision for God." Hence, "instead of merely playing with the human person, merely moving and using him or her, merely bypassing him or her as if he or she were an object, God elevates him or her to be a subject, awakens him or her to genuine individuality and independence, frees him or her, and makes him or her a king, so that God's own kingship obtains even in this form and revelation."[20] Hence, though human faithfulness depends wholly upon God's sovereignty, Barth and many others insist that this dependence is compatible with human autonomy. This raises an obvious question, however, namely, how one's act of following Christ can rest wholly upon God's grace, yet nevertheless be undertaken freely, or, conversely, how one's freely undertaken Christ-following could be due wholly to God's grace. These questions have been the subject of endless controversy, and countless answers have been proposed, including some which simply deny one side of the paradox. Determinists of a non-compatibilist variety, for instance, argue that freedom is an illusion and thus dissolve the apparent paradox, whereas non-compatibilist libertarians dissolve the paradox by claiming that it is one's dependence upon grace that is the illusion.[21] By far the most popular answer, however, has been some species of compatibilism, according to which dependence upon God's grace is not incompatible with human freedom. Beyond this, compatibilist doctrines vary widely: one popular approach is based upon an account of human desire being freely drawn toward that which is most desirable; another upon the claim that divine and human agency lie on different planes and so cannot compete with one another; yet another

---

[20] Barth, *Die Kirchliche Dogmatik*, vol. II, *Die Lehre von Gott*, part 2 (Zollikon-Zürich: Evangelischer Verlag A. G., 1942), pp. 195–6.

[21] Zwingli and Spinoza are commonly seen to exemplify the former approach, and Kant the latter.

upon God's miraculous act of giving a person either a new will or a new-every-moment ability to follow Christ. For present purposes, it should suffice to demonstrate that Schleiermacher's proposal funds one such variety of compatibilism.

To understand this account, recall, first, Schleiermacher's understanding of what it means to follow Christ. This cannot simply be a matter of doing and saying what Jesus did and said, since, on the one hand, one is not called to repeat all of his words and deeds (such as saying of oneself, "I am the way and the truth and the life," or dying on a cross), and on the other, one has to be able to follow him in circumstances that he himself never directly faced. Rather, to follow Christ is to undertake doxastic and practical commitments which go on in the same way as (rather than simply repeat) commitments he recognized. Following Christ is thus a normative affair. Moreover, although some of one's beliefs and actions could follow Christ accidentally, it would appear that in the robust, new covenant sense, to follow Christ is to do so intentionally and devotedly, that is, to try to go on in the same way as those whom he recognized, and to do so out of commitment to him and the one he called "Father." From this angle, too, following Christ turns out to be a normative affair, since one can intend to follow him only if one has some idea of what it would mean to do so and a commitment to doing so correctly. To follow Christ, then, is to intend for one's beliefs, actions, and attitudes to go on in the same way as those which Christ recognized as doing so.

So then: how can such following be due wholly to God, yet nevertheless recognizable as due to one? The first step in answering this question is to explain how this kind of following is due to God. On Schleiermacher's account, God redeems one by attuning one to Godself, and God does this by incarnating this attunement in Christ and mediating it to one through his Spirit. Every moment of Christ's life enacts his devotion to God, such that Jesus Christ's being just is this enactment, both in history and in the triune life. By incarnating this devotion, Jesus contributes one of the necessary conditions of redemption: a human life has now been wholly devoted to God in fulfillment of the covenant, as a result of which the redeemed state has been perfectly realized in human history. Then, in order to mediate this state to others, Jesus sends his Spirit, thereby contributing redemption's other necessary condition. The Spirit is the one who is supposed to fill one's heart with Christ's devotion, to guide one into all truth, and to be Christ's own presence in and to one; on Schleiermacher's account, this Spirit is to be understood, in the first instance, as the Spirit of Christ's normative assessments, the Spirit by which Christ's devotion could become his followers' own. Christ conveyed this Spirit to his followers, on this view, by first telling them what they should say and do, by correcting their mistakes, and so on. As a result of this process, the disciples eventually began to understand what it meant to follow him, and so internalized the norms according to which he assessed their performances, even if they frequently failed to live up to those norms. And once Jesus recognized them as competent to make such assessments, he recognized their authority over others' beliefs and actions, such that one could now learn to follow Jesus by submitting one's beliefs and actions to the disciples' normative assessments. Once a person had been recognized by the disciples as knowing how to go on in the same way, still others could learn how to do so by submitting their beliefs and actions to that person's assessments. In this way, the norms according to which Christ assessed whether one was following him were passed along to others, which is (a way of understanding) the means by which Christ conveyed his normative Spirit to them. This Spirit always comes to one from without, accordingly, both because it was sent by Christ and because it must be mediated to one before one can internalize it and mediate it to others, from which it follows that the possibility of faith is supplied – objectively and subjectively, as it were – by the triune act of God: Christ incarnates perfect faithfulness in human history, thereby supplying the objective possibility of faith, and he imparts his Spirit to one, thereby supplying its subjective possibility.

This brings us to the second step, namely, to say more about how one's faith, thus dependent upon God's prior act, can nevertheless be recognizable as due to one. On Schleiermacher's account, one receives Christ's normative Spirit by submitting one's judgments and performances to those whom one recognizes as knowing how to follow him; one's recognition of these judgments and performances thus confers upon them their authority over one.[22] One's recognitive attitudes thereby demarcate certain persons and performances as authoritative precedents, and one learns how to follow Christ by trying to go on in the same way. By trying to go on in the same way, in turn, one implicitly claims that one's performances and judgments should themselves be recognized as carrying on the normative trajectory implicit in these precedents, in consequence of which still others could carry on the Spirit of Christ by going on in the same way as one's own performances and judgments. The norm by which one is constrained is not only authorized by one's recognition of it, accordingly, but is shaped and administered by one's performances and judgments. Christ's normative Spirit is thus recognizable not only as one's own, but as in some respect due to one, since one's judgments and performances contribute to its meaning and authority. We can thereby explain the compatibility between the grace-dependence of one's faith and that faith being one's own, since the possibility of such faith depends wholly upon God's provision in Christ and Spirit, yet that Spirit's normative force – and so one's grace-dependent faith – can be seen as self-legislated, since one's expressions and judgments contribute to its authority, meaning, and administration.

This brings us to a final concern: what if one's judgments and performances are not recognized by one's community? That is, what if communities fail to achieve the twin conditions of mutuality and

---

[22] Naturally, insofar as Christ's norms reflect God's will, there is a sense in which they are objectively authoritative; in the present connection, we are dealing only with their authority *for* the one over whom they may in any event *be* authoritative.

openness to individual self-expression – would this entail that its members are not (and cannot be) free? That their faith cannot be fully their own? An adequate response to these questions will move us out of the realm of theory and into that of critique – the subject matter of the next section – but before concluding this section, it is worth noting that several theorists, most notably Hegel, would argue that a norm-circulating community cannot be entirely devoid of mutuality and openness (though it could misunderstand itself as if it were), or that if some community were so devoid, it would necessarily be self-defeating – that is, such a community could not be maintained. The argument underlying this claim is complicated even by Hegel's standards, but we can summarize its logic in a few steps. First, if the authority of one's judgments cannot be a "given," it follows that it, too, must be subject to judgment; this entails, among other things, that there can be no a priori, privileged claims to authority. If there can be no privileged claims to authority, however, it follows that there are likewise no a priori grounds by which to establish whose judgments ought to count in determining which claims to authority are valid. This entails, in turn, that there are no non-arbitrary, non-question-begging grounds by which to exclude some persons' judgments about which claims ought to be recognized. A claim to authority, accordingly, is valid as such a claim (rather than a disguised use of force) only if it is recognized by those to whom it will apply, which means that when one proposes some normative standard, one implicitly seeks recognition from those upon whom it will be binding, which is to say that one recognizes *their* authority. The very practice of using norms is thus based upon relations of mutual recognition, and Hegel's phenomenology aims to demonstrate this by showing how patterns of <u>asymmetrical rec</u>ognition end up planting the seeds of their own undoing. According to Hegel's ambitious argument, then, there is no norm-circulating community totally devoid of mutuality, or if there were, it could not be sustained as such a community. Even if Hegel is right that communities cannot be completely devoid of mutuality and openness, however, their relative lack of these characteristics could still leave certain persons unable to identify with the norms implicit in their practices. It seems obvious, therefore, that we need to spend more time considering whether and how the present account might fund a critique of asymmetrical and/or narrow patterns of recognition. The next section aims to meet this need.

**

According to the present proposal, the possibility of one's faith being recognizable as one's own depends upon one's relationship to the community whose practices one carries on: on this account, one can see one's commitments as one's own if the communal practices they carry on are themselves one's own, and the latter count as such if (a) they are broad and richly textured enough that a wide array of potentially self-expressive performances can be recognized as carrying them on; (b) one contributes to their authority, meaning, and administration; and (c) they are the product of mutual recognition. This account thus raises the stakes on the following section's subject matter, namely, how such communities can be achieved and how inadequate communities can be critiqued.

Struggling for emancipation

The previous section argued that the norms implicit in certain Christian practices can be emancipating insofar as they fund self-expressivity, but this raises some obvious and important issues: many persons have been silenced by the prevailing norms, and many others simply do not feel at home with them; as a result, these persons find it hard to see their theological commitments as self-expressive or as due to them. Then again, some persons see these norms as self-expressive even though they are in fact oppressed by them, while others fail to see oppressive norms *as* norms, since they have taken on an air of self-evidence or naturalness. This section makes explicit the present account's resources for dealing with these issues.

1

One of the central problems facing any account of theological language, but especially one which takes intersubjective recognition as its explanatory primitive, is the disturbing fact that some persons' voices are simply not recognized. As Elizabeth Johnson points out, women "have been robbed of the power of naming, of naming themselves, the world, and ultimate holy mystery, having instead to receive the names given by those who rule over them," and they are surely not alone.[23] The authority of women and others to contribute to "our" God-talk has often gone unrecognized, as a result of which they have become "theologically invisible."[24] To be sure, this silencing is not always overt, since the non-recognition at issue can also take the form of recognizing a person's voice only if it reinforces certain norms. So a woman's voice may be recognized, for example, when she says something about child-rearing, but not when she speaks her mind on other issues. Rebecca Chopp thus argues that "until we change the values and hidden rules that run through present linguistic practices, social codes, and psychic orderings, women, persons of color, and other oppressed groups will be forced – by the language, discourses, and practices available to them – into conforming to ongoing practices, to babbling nonsense, or to not speaking at all."[25]

---

[23] Elizabeth A. Johnson, *She Who Is: The Mystery of God in Feminist Theological Discourse* (New York: Crossroad, 1992, 2002), pp. 26–7; similar sentiments are expressed by Mary Daly, *Beyond God the Father: Toward a Philosophy of Women's Liberation* (Boston: Beacon, 1973), pp. 7–8.

[24] Elisabeth Schüssler Fiorenza, "Breaking the Silence – Becoming Visible," in *The Power of Naming: A Concilium Reader in Feminist Liberation Theology*, Elisabeth Schüssler Fiorenza (ed.) (Maryknoll, NY: Orbis, 1996), p. 162.

[25] Rebecca Chopp, *The Power to Speak: Feminism, Language, and God* (New York: Crossroad, 1991), pp. 6–7.

The issue is not only that some persons' voices have not been recognized, however; it is that many persons find it hard to identify with at least some elements of the prevailing God-talk; these persons may thus feel a sense of alienation, of not quite being at home with theological language, and of not seeing it as self-expressive. That is to say, if certain regions of God-talk are controlled by normative concepts and images which exclude certain persons from identifying with them, it can be hard for these persons to see such talk as theirs or as capable of expressing their devotion to God.[26]

Nor are these problems limited to God-talk, since they appear to play a role in perpetuating unjust social arrangements, being called upon to justify these arrangements and to free their beneficiaries from having to defend their privilege. So masculinist imagery, for instance, is thought to be isomorphic with masculinist hierarchy – this is what Mary Daly has in mind when she claims that "if God is male, then the male is God"[27] – just as this imagery is called upon to justify that hierarchy. Likewise, in a society where whiteness is seen as colorlessness, "color-blind" imagery may be isomorphic with white privilege, just as this imagery can be called upon as a way of reinforcing the status quo and undermining resistance.[28] The non-recognition of certain persons and certain ways of speaking about God can thus serve to perpetuate and justify unequal power relations.

[26] To take but one example, consider Carol Christ's oft-cited observation that a woman "may see herself as like God (created in the image of God) only by denying her own sexual identity and affirming God's transcendence of sexual identity. But she can never have the experience that is freely available to every man and boy in her culture, of having her full sexual identity affirmed as being in the image and likeness of God" (Carol P. Christ, "Why Women Need the Goddess: Phenomenological, Psychological, and Political Reflections," in *Womanspirit Rising: A Feminist Reader in Religion*, Carol P. Christ and Judith Plaskow [eds.] [San Francisco: HarperOne, 1992], p. 275).

[27] Daly, *Beyond God the Father*, p. 19.

[28] For an argument to this effect, see James Cone, "God is Black," in *Lift Every Voice: Constructing Christian Theologies from the Underside*, Susan Brooks Thistlethwaite and Mary Potter Engel (eds.) (Maryknoll, NY: Orbis, 1998), pp. 115–26.

These problems are made considerably worse, in turn, by two further factors, each of which will be considered at greater length below. To get an idea of what these are, consider Mary Daly's claim about the oppression of women in the Church: "The exploitative caste system could not be perpetuated," she argues, "without the consent of victims as well as of the dominant sex, and such consent is obtained through sex role socialization – a conditioning process which begins to operate from the moment we are born, and which is enforced by most institutions ... This happens through dynamics that are largely uncalculated and unconscious, yet which reinforce the assumptions, attitudes, stereotypes, customs, and arrangements of sexually hierarchical society."[29] The situation described by Daly thus includes two factors which further entrench patterns of non-recognition. They are further entrenched, first, in consequence of the fact that these norms are commonly recognized as legitimate even by those from whom recognition is being withheld, such that these persons end up justifying (and internalizing) the very recognitive patterns by which their voices and contributions are excluded. So, as Pierre Bourdieu observes, "the symbolic efficacy of words is exercised only insofar as the person subjected to it recognizes the one who exercises it as authorized to do so, or, what amounts to the same thing, only insofar as he or she is ignorant of the fact that in submitting to it, he or she has contributed, through his or her recognition, to its authority."[30] This is related to a second factor, namely, the fact that these patterns come to seem self-evident or natural. Again, Bourdieu: the discourse of non-recognition "is a structured and structuring medium," he writes, "tending to impose an apprehension of the established order as natural (orthodoxy) through the imposition of masked – and thus

<hr/>

[29] Daly, *Beyond God the Father*, p. 2; cf. Anne E. Carr, *Transforming Grace: Christian Tradition and Women's Experience* (New York: Continuum, 1988); and Elisabeth Schüssler Fiorenza, "Breaking the Silence," pp. 169–70.

[30] Bourdieu, "Le langage autorisé: Note sur les conditions sociales de l'efficacité du discours ritual," in *Ce que parler veut dire: l'économie des échanges linguistiques* (Paris: Librairie Arthème Fayard, 1982), p. 119.

misrecognized – systems of classification and of mental structures that are objectively adjusted to social structures."[31] That is, certain patterns of non-recognition, having been reproduced over and over again through generations, are no longer noticed as such; they come to be seen, if at all, as simply the way things are, as natural – and once the prevailing pattern of recognition has become "naturalized" in this way, it can be maintained without any overtly coercive activity on anyone's part.

Again, I will say more about these problems in the following subsections, but for now we need to consider an influential solution elicited by them, namely, the attempt to denaturalize these patterns by emphasizing the distance between God and God-talk. Elizabeth Johnson's claim typifies this approach: "human words, images, and concepts," she argues, "with their inevitable relationship to the finite, are not capable of comprehending God, who by very nature is illimitable and unobjectifiable." From this, Johnson infers that "absolutizing any particular expression as if it were adequate to divine reality is tantamount to a diminishment of truth about God," for if no finite expression can be adequate to the Infinite God, then to treat any such expression as exclusively adequate is to treat God as finite, that is, as an idol.[32] Johnson thus claims that God's transcendence, combined with the limitations of finite human language, entails that no particular strand of God-talk can be privileged over others – much less seen as *naturally* privileged – since all human talk, as human, necessarily falls short of God. Johnson concludes, accordingly, that "the tenacity with which the patriarchal symbol of God is upheld is nothing less than a violation of the first commandment of the Decalogue, the worship of an idol."[33] Against this perceived idolatry, theologians such as Rebecca Chopp have appealed to a "God behind God" whose

---

[31] Bourdieu, "Sur le pouvoir symbolique," *Annales: Histoire, Sciences Sociales* 32:3 (May–June 1977), p. 410.

[32] Johnson, *She Who Is*, p. 112. See also Chopp, *The Power to Speak*, p. 32; Carr, *Transforming Grace*, pp. xvi, 156; and Daly, *Beyond God the Father*, pp. 21–2, 29.

[33] Johnson, *She Who Is*, p. 39.

invocation "creates possibilities of emancipatory transformation for all," in consequence of which God-talk would no longer be limited to certain voices and expressions, but would be fundamentally open to a plenitude of contributors and contributions, thereby opening up possibilities for the flourishing of all persons.[34] The goal is thus to achieve a wider recognition of voices, "to affirm mutuality, maturity, and human potentiality not only in terms of gender but also in terms of class, culture, race, and religion ... [so as] to enable all kinds of people to affirm themselves as whole human persons, chosen and loved by God, and partaking of the divine reality."[35]

The attractiveness of this solution is obvious – and it is equally obvious that the present proposal cannot adopt such a solution, since I have spent the last several chapters defending an account, one of whose theoretical aims was to eliminate this sort of distance between God and language. This should not be taken to entail, however, that we are left empty-handed in response to oppressive social patterns, since "distance" is not the only way to resist such patterns. (Nor is it clear, as a matter of historical fact, that such distance serves to loosen the grip of any particular discourse about God, since it is precisely this distance which has led some theologians to insist that God-talk must be authorized by the hierarchy.) I have already argued that, on my account, there is indeed an inexhaustible plenitude of correct statements which one could make about God, from which it follows that "distance" is at best a sufficient, but not necessary, condition of affirming such plenitude. This is not the only resource provided

[34] Chopp, *The Power to Speak*, pp. 7, 23.

[35] Elisabeth Schüssler Fiorenza, "Feminist Spirituality, Christian Identity, and Catholic Vision," in *Womanspirit Rising*, p. 140. It is important to note that these goals are commonly formulated in terms of self-expressivity. Thus Rebecca Chopp: "Women will be forever strangers unless their words and their voices revise the social and symbolic rules of language, transforming the law of ordered hierarchy in language, in subjectivity, and in politics into a grace of rich plenitude for human flourishing" (*The Power to Speak*, p. 2); Elisabeth Schüssler Fiorenza: "They seek for a new voice, a 'common language' that could express the meaning and significance of 'trying to be in our souls'" ("For Women in Men's World," in *The Power of Naming*, p. 3).

by my account, however, as the following discussion of recognition, disrespect, and emancipation aims to show.

2

One of the difficulties facing any attempt to overcome patterns of non-recognition involves explaining how one could come to see that one's voice has been silenced – and so, in turn, to resist that silencing – when the only available structures within which to recognize one's voice are the very structures that have enforced one's silence. Over against the usual practice of appealing to distance in order to address this difficulty, the account to be defended here appeals to fissures *within* these patterns, particularly as these are disclosed by experiences of disrespect.

As a rough-and-ready way of framing this account, consider a sketch of some developments in critical theory, broadly construed, over the past hundred years. Such a story might begin with a range of figures who take aim at what we might call the domestication of alterity – that is, the fitting of otherness into a predetermined order and the correlative readiness to countenance otherness only insofar as it conforms to that order – and the conceptual and physical violence perpetrated and underwritten by such domestication. Representative examples of this critique include Karl Barth's *Epistle to the Romans*, Martin Heidegger's *Being and Time*, Theodor Adorno's *Negative Dialectics*, and Emmanuel Levinas's *Totality and Infinity*.[36] Relevant differences aside, each of these figures aimed to interrupt a totalizing order, and so loosen its grip, by proposing a means by which something radically other might show up: so Barth points to the infinitely qualitatively different God who shows up only at the

---

[36] Karl Barth, *The Epistle to the Romans* (Oxford University Press, 1933); Martin Heidegger, *Being and Time* (New York: Harper and Row, 1962); Theodor Adorno, *Negative Dialectics* (London: Routledge and Kegan Paul, 1973); Emmanuel Levinas, *Totality and Infinity: An Essay on Exteriority* (Pittsburgh, PA: Duquesne University Press, 1969).

limits of all creaturely possibility; Heidegger seeks to relativize the taken-for-granted, and so apparently ultimate, horizon of beings by interrogating the possibility of being-not; Adorno identifies "instrumentalizing reason" as the source of violence and so looks to Art as providing possibilities which transcend, and so call into question, such reason; and Levinas seeks to disrupt would-be totalities by pointing to a prior ethical "call" or claim made by the face of the Other. The first step in our story, then, is a series of attempts to critique the totalizing order by appeal to that which is exterior to it.

The second step is a critique of these critiques. The basic argument here, some variety of which is advanced by Derrida, Foucault, Bourdieu, and Butler, turns upon the pervasiveness of the totalizing order and the consequent illusoriness of claims to critique that order from a point which transcends it.[37] The claim, simply stated, is that the intelligibility and relativizing force of these critiques depend upon their being brought within the bounds of the criticized totality, since, apart from certain conditions of belief, certain discursive practices, and certain pre-reflective dispositions, a critique mustered from the standpoint of a putatively order-transcending "other" would neither make sense to one nor get a grip on one's imagination. The effectiveness of these critiques thus seems parasitic upon certain prior conditions to which they must be assimilated, in consequence of which their appeals to exteriority appear to depend upon a kind of false consciousness. Indeed, such appeals may serve unwittingly to reinforce the very order they aim to upend, since they give one the illusion of having transcended the totality while remaining within

---

37 See Michel Foucault, "Two Lectures," and "Nietzsche, Genealogy, History," in *Language, Counter-Memory, Practice: Selected Essays and Interviews*, Donald F. Bouchard (ed.) (Ithaca, NY: Cornell University Press, 1977); Judith Butler, *Excitable Speech*; Jacques Derrida, "Violence and Metaphysics: An Essay on the Thought of Emmanuel Levinas," in *Writing and Difference*, trans. Alan Bass (Chicago: University of Chicago Press, 1978), and *Positions*, trans. Alan Bass (Chicago: University of Chicago Press, 1981); and Pierre Bourdieu, *Outline of a Theory of Practice*, trans. Richard Nice (Cambridge University Press, 1977), and *Language and Symbolic Power* (Cambridge, MA: Harvard University Press, 1991).

its bounds. The moral of the story, on this view, is that critics and critiques cannot take up a standpoint outside the totality from which to criticize it. This is not the end of their story, however; rather, the claim that one cannot take up a transcendent standpoint correlates with a shift in the focus of critique, from a focus on interruptive appearances of alterity to a focus on rendering visible the ways in which power is carried on and enforced by all sorts of unnoticed practices, through which certain social arrangements come to seem natural and so require no explicit acts of coercion in order to maintain their force. I will say more about the nature and target of this critique presently, but for now, we need note only that the aim of Foucault's genealogies, Derrida's deconstructions, Butler's arguments about performativity and interpellation, and Bourdieu's claims about the power relations written into one's *habitus* is precisely to unmask the putative naturalness of these social arrangements.

This brings us to a third step in our reconstruction, which consists of a series of critiques raised against this denaturalizing approach, the common thread among which is that the mere unmasking of certain practices and conditions as products of power-laden, culture-involving histories, and so as unnatural, does not amount to a *critique* of these practices, nor does it supply any resources with which to move beyond them. A version of this objection is raised by Nancy Fraser, Jürgen Habermas, and Martha Nussbaum.[38] From this vantage point, critics who insist upon the inescapability of conditionedness end up either cultivating a sort of nihilistic resignation to unjust social arrangements, or else their critique of these arrangements is funded by normative capital borrowed from other sources (usually the much-scorned Western liberal tradition). Third-step theorists thus aim to move beyond mere denaturalization by

---

[38] Nancy Fraser, *Unruly Practices: Power, Discourse, and Gender in Contemporary Social Theory* (Minneapolis: University of Minnesota Press, 1989); Habermas, *The Philosophical Discourse of Modernity*; Martha Nussbaum, "Professor of Parody," *The New Republic*, February 22, 1999, pp. 37–45.

bringing a normative dimension back into critical theory, whether this is based upon the norms implicit in discursive practice itself, a model of democratic citizenship, or an appeal to the liberal impulses underlying the denaturalizers' own projects. In what follows, I attend to one such approach – that proposed by Axel Honneth – though it should be noted that the targets of this critique are by no means empty-handed in response to it (as Honneth himself argues in his *Kritik der Macht*).

While I have some reservations about his project as a whole, Honneth proposes a helpful way of dealing with the objection in question. His suggestion, simply stated, is to take experiences of disrespect (*Mißachtung*) as critical theory's explanatory primitive, since these experiences make explicit the patterns of recognition (and misrecognition) implicit in the way one is treated, and provide a standpoint internal to the recognitive order by means of which it might be criticized – a kind of "immanent transcendence," in other words. To understand how the present account could bring this proposal on board, we will begin by briefly reiterating some points about the way norms circulate through practice and how this circulation renders normative social arrangements invisible, and then explain how experiences of disrespect provide critical resources with which to get some leverage on these arrangements.

On the broadly Schleiermacherian-pragmatist account defended here, norms are implicit in attunement, attunement is an internalization of that which circulates in custom, and this circulation is explained in terms of an ongoing process of recognition. As mentioned above, this account faces a serious problem, namely, that insofar as norms circulate non-inferentially, they come to seem natural, and can accordingly serve to reinforce certain social arrangements without anyone noticing that they are doing so – and without anyone having to engage in explicitly coercive acts in order to enforce these arrangements. So, for instance, numerous studies have shown that persons respond differently to women than to men, to those who appear poor than to those who appear rich, to black persons than to Asian persons than to white persons, and so on, that the vast majority of these differential responses operate at the non-inferential level, and that the differences among these responses are far from innocuous: to take just one among many well-documented examples, white persons in the United States are often treated far more respectfully than black persons, even when controlling for factors such as education and social class.[39] Importantly, though, those who treat white and black persons differently tend to think that race has not played a role in their behavior, and may in fact think that such treatment is unjust. In other words, these persons may have been taught, and earnestly believe, that all persons are equal, yet the norms implicit in their treatment of certain persons run contrary to this belief. It may be that those whom they perceive as "us" – their parents, teachers, peers, etc. – respond differently in circumstances involving black persons than white persons – they tense up a bit when passing a black person on the sidewalk, they use "outsider" language when speaking with or of black persons, they spend little or no time commenting on a black person's contributions to a discussion, and so on – and these persons have, to some degree, at least, become reliably disposed to respond in these ways, too. And because these responses operate without one's having to think about them, it follows that the norms implicit in one's treatment of others may actually betray the norms to which one is explicitly committed. This explains the phenomenon sometimes referred to as "aversive racism" or "racism without racists," and there are precise parallels

[39] On these points, see, for instance, Samuel L. Gaertner and John F. Dovidio, "The Aversive Form of Racism," in *Prejudice, Discrimination, and Racism: Theory and Research* (Orlando, FL: Academic Press, 1986), pp. 61–89; "Aversive Racism and Selection Decisions: 1989 and 1999," *Psychological Science* 11:4 (2002), pp. 315–19; "Aversive Racism," *Advances in Experimental Psychology* 36 (2004), pp. 1–52; and "Aversive Racism: Bias Without Intention," *Handbook of Employment Discrimination Research*, R. L. Nelson and L. B. Nielsen (eds.) (New York: Springer, 2008), pp. 377–93; and Eduardo Bonilla-Silva, *Racism Without Racists: Color-Blind Racism and the Persistence of Racial Inequality in the United States*, second edn. (London: Rowman and Littlefield, 2006).

all along the line: sexism without sexists, classism without classists, ableism without ableists, ageism without ageists, and so on. That is to say, because norms circulate implicitly, at the level of non-inferential responsive dispositions (or "attunement"), and not just explicitly, it follows that one's thinking and acting can be inflected with racism, sexism, classism, and so on, even if one does not realize it – indeed, even if one is strongly and explicitly opposed to racism, sexism, and classism.

Several consequences follow from this. First, because these norms circulate non-inferentially, one seldom notices that norms are even in play; as a result, these norms come to seem natural. Certain norm-laden patterns, having been reproduced over and over again through generations, and having been reinforced by a vast network of responsive dispositions each point of which coheres with this pattern, are no longer perceived as such; they come to be seen as simply the way things are. Patterns of non-recognition are thus covered with a cloak of self-evidence, in consequence of which they need no justification, partly because they are no longer noticed *as* patterns of recognition (which have a history and could therefore be otherwise), and partly because challenges to these patterns are undercut in virtue of their appearing *un*natural. Norms which circulate non-inferentially can thus serve to reproduce the prevailing order without anyone's having to lift a coercive finger, since (a) these norms go largely unnoticed; (b) they are reinforced through a network of countless reiterations; (c) those who resist these patterns are the only ones seen as doing anything, since power which circulates non-inferentially is not seen at all, much less as doing something; and (d) insofar as persons have been attuned in these ways, they are likely to find plausible almost any argument in favor of the prevailing order.

One further consequence deserves special mention: due in part to the fact that they circulate non-inferentially, those who are treated unjustly within these normative patterns may nevertheless internalize them and therefore implicitly recognize the very norms by which they are oppressed. Those who are not recognized by the prevailing order, in other words, may internalize their non-recognition, may implicitly or explicitly recognize that non-recognition, and may therefore play a tragic role in reproducing the conditions of their oppression. Here too we can look to research as well as anecdotal evidence of women internalizing sexist norms, persons of color internalizing racist norms, "common" persons internalizing elitist norms, and so on.[40] Oppressive patterns of recognition can thus be perpetuated by the (mis)recognition of the oppressed, and this (mis)recognition seems in fact to be crucial to these patterns' effectiveness, for without it, these patterns could remain in force only insofar as they could be forced upon those oppressed by them.

the natural produced being explicitly otherwise

So then: because norms circulate implicitly, the prevailing order is able to reproduce itself without being seen or even explicitly affirmed, and can thereby come to seem natural. And because this is the case, persons may accept and reproduce these norms without realizing that they are doing so.

3 *Disrespect as explanatory primitive*

The need for critique should thus be obvious, but this brings us back to one of the points I made at the outset, namely, that it is necessary, but not sufficient, to strip these norms of their apparent naturalness, since, in order to change them, one also needs to be able to stand apart from them, so to speak, in order to see the prevailing order as wrong and to envision different possibilities. The difficulty is this: how can one stand apart from the prevailing order if there is no transcendent standpoint that one can occupy? The rest of this subsection responds to this problem by taking experiences of disrespect as a point of departure. By means of this concept, it should become clear that one's choices are not limited to appeals to a transcendent exteriority, on the one hand, or leaving the prevailing order intact,

---

[40] See here the literature cited in the previous note.

on the other, since experiences of disrespect manifest fissures *within* the prevailing order.

"Disrespect," in the sense I am using it here, is "a matter of the disappointment or violation of normative expectations of society considered justified by those concerned."[41] To experience some treatment as an act of disrespect is thus for one's expectation of recognition to go unmet. To see what this means, consider a simple (if unflattering) example: on more than one occasion I have gone to a particular clothing store in order to look for professional attire or to buy a gift. On those occasions when I have not been *wearing* professional attire, something curious has happened: those who work at the store have been noticeably slower to greet me (if at all) and show me their wares, even when not occupied with other customers. Now, I certainly understand if someone would prefer to do something other than help me, but because the store workers had treated me a certain way when I had been wearing professional attire, and because they were treating other customers that way, I expected that I would be treated that way, too. Interestingly enough, I had not realized that I had come to expect such treatment until that expectation was not met, just as I did not see this sort of treatment as an act of recognition until I failed to receive it. To be sure, there is something problematic in my expecting this sort of treatment, as I hope to make clear in a moment; for now, the point is that I experienced their treatment as an act of disrespect: on the basis of certain precedent acts of recognition, I expected that I, too, would be recognized, and when this expectation was disappointed, their behavior appeared to me as an act of disrespect or non-recognition.

On the account to be defended here, such experiences of disrespect or of unmet expectations play a crucial role in manifesting implicitly circulating norms and in opening up a fissure between

---

[41] Honneth, "Redistribution as Recognition: A Response to Nancy Fraser," in Nancy Fraser and Axel Honneth, *Redistribution or Recognition? A Political-Philosophical Exchange* (New York: Verso, 2003), p. 129.

the way things are and the way they should be. First, on the present
account, one experiences some act as disrespectful only on the basis
of a normative trajectory implicit in precedents which has led one
to expect recognition. Because this is the case, when such an expectation is unmet, the normative trajectory upon which it depends
steps out into the open; it is no longer invisible.[42] I was not conscious
of the fact that there was anything normative about the way I had
been treated in clothing stores, nor did I realize that a kind of recognition is involved in this practice. It was simply how one was treated.
But although I had not realized it, previous practice had led me to
expect that I would receive a certain sort of treatment, such that
when I was not so treated, the experience of an unmet expectation
led me to see that there was indeed a normative trajectory implicit
in this treatment. An experience of disrespect thus made manifest
that which led me to expect something different, namely, the norm
implicit in a particular practice, thereby rendering it explicit *as a*
norm. Moreover, cases where a reasonably expected recognition is
not conferred can lead one to see that what gets recognized is itself
a contested (and contestable) matter, and so not simply an order of
nature. One can realize, that is, not only that there is a normative
trajectory implicit in a pattern of actions, but that the carrying-on of
that trajectory is itself susceptible to normative assessment. Patterns
of recognition, then, can be seen as something more than simply
the way things are; they can be seen as a product of – and contribu-
tor to – our normative attitudes and actions. One tends to see them
as such, however, only when that which would carry them on in a

---

[42] As Axel Honneth argues, "subjects only experience disrespect in what they can grasp
as violations of the normative claims they have come to know in their socialization as
justified implications of established principles of recognition" (*Disrespect* [Cambridge:
Polity Press, 2007], p. xii); experiences of disrespect thus disclose "the normative
constraints embedded in such processes," precisely because "subjects face them
with certain expectations of recognition" ("The Point of Recognition: A Rejoinder
to the Rejoinder," in *Redistribution or Recognition?*, p. 250; cf. "Redistribution as
Recognition," p. 137).

particular circumstance – namely, an expected recognition – fails to materialize.

This brings us to a second point: to recognize non-recognition *as* non-recognition is to open up a fissure between the way things are and the way things ought to be, and thus to be equipped with a ready-to-hand concept of justice.[43] To be led by the normative trajectory implicit in precedent recognitions to expect a particular recognition is implicitly to see such recognition as due one, such that if the expected recognition is not conferred, one may experience it as an injustice. An ad hoc notion of justice thus precipitates out of experiences of disrespect: by experiencing some treatment as disrespect, one perceives that treatment as unjust, and likewise perceives how the trajectory which led one to expect recognition could be carried on in a more just manner. What is crucial here is that the norm implicit in these trajectories can outrun its current application, such that there can arise a kind of normative surplus by appeal to which one can criticize the prevailing order. Rather than invoke clothing stores again, consider a different example: back when I was teaching high school, a group of black students told me about a peculiar phenomenon they had noticed. It seems that one of my colleagues consistently forgot or confused the names of black students, but seldom forgot the names of white students. Once they noticed that this was the case, they realized that there was something disrespectful about it and decided to confront the teacher. Happily, the situation turned out well: once students brought the matter to his attention, the teacher in question offered them a heart-felt apology and worked hard to get *every* student's name right. For our purposes, the important point is that the teacher had not lived up to the norms implicit in his own precedent-setting performances,

---

[43] For further theoretical and empirical defense of this point, see Barrington Moore, *Injustice: The Social Bases of Obedience and Revolt* (London: Macmillan, 1978), and Mary McClintock Fulkerson, *Places of Redemption: Theology for a Worldly Church* (Oxford University Press, 2007).

since his treatment of black students did not carry on the trajectory established by his treatment of other students. The black students expected that they would be treated similarly, yet their expectation was unmet; they accordingly perceived this as an injustice, and tried to rectify the injustice by appealing to the teacher's own normative commitments, since, given the trajectory established by the relevant precedents, his treatment of black students could be seen as unjust *by his own lights*. A distinction between the way things are and the way things ought to be thus emerged from norm-carrying practices, and an ad hoc notion of justice arose out of experiences of disrespect – it precipitated, that is, directly out of the experience of those affected by injustice.[44] So then: experiences of disrespect disclose the normative commitment implicit in certain practices, and this commitment may outrun the current state of its outworking, such that a standpoint is opened up by means of which to critique the status quo and to advance a more just state of affairs.

As it turns out, then, the prevailing order is not as complete as one might think. It may appear that way insofar as it has come to seem natural, but the fact is that the prevailing order contains within itself fissures and normative surpluses by which it can be criticized and changed. On the present account, moreover, the success of any such critique can fund still further critique, since the normative trajectory implicit in a series of precedents changes every time something new is recognized as carrying it on. So, for instance, rights-talk was used to thematize the American colonists' experience of disrespect at the hands of George III; the success of this critique opened up a trajectory in which rights-talk could then be used to thematize the disrespect experienced by women and persons of color; the latter opened up the space within which certain treatments of animals

---

[44] On the importance of this point, see Honneth, "Moral Consciousness and Class Domination: Some Problems in the Analysis of Hidden Morality," in *The Fragmented World of the Social: Essays in Social and Political Philosophy*, Charles W. Wright (ed.) (Albany, NY: State University of New York Press, 1995).

and the natural environment could be criticized, and so on. When a particular pattern of recognition is challenged, accordingly, the normative trajectory implicit in that pattern can itself change, such that still other patterns can be experienced as disrespectful, challenged as such, thereby changing the trajectory again, and so on. Recognition can thus beget recognition, and critique beget critique. Moreover, disrespect, too, is something to which one can become attuned: after one gets some practice in spotting patterns of non-recognition, one can become reliably disposed to do so, such that one will be less and less likely to reproduce injustices which would ordinarily circulate beneath one's conscious awareness.[45]

The virtue of spotting injustices

Experiences of disrespect contribute to the possibility of critique, then, since (a) they render visible norms that have been circulating implicitly, and (b) they manifest the normative surplus within current patterns of recognition, thereby providing a means of criticizing those patterns. Such experiences can thus play a role in achieving that which Mary Daly identifies as crucial to the struggle for emancipation: Daly urges that since oppressed persons "are dealing with demonic power relationships, that is, with structured evil, rage is required as a positive creative force, making possible a breakthrough, encountering the blockages of inauthentic structures. It rises as a reaction to the shock of what has been lost – before it had even been discovered – one's own identity. Out of this block can come intimations of what human being (as opposed to half being) can be."[46] What Daly describes here as "rage" bears strong affinities with what I have been discussing in terms of disrespect, which means that my proposal may shed some light on the process through which Daly's hoped-for breakthroughs become possible.

begins here

---

[45] For a further outworking of this claim, see Jeffrey Stout, *Democracy and Tradition* (Princeton, NJ: Princeton University Press, 2004), pp. 217–24; Iris Murdoch, *The Sovereignty of Good* (London: Routledge, 1970); and Simone Weil, *Gravity and Grace* (London: Routledge, 1947).

[46] Daly, *Beyond God the Father*, p. 43.

4

A clarification, concerning the Spirit's role in such struggles, may be in order. In view of earlier claims about the Spirit's being carried on by the normative trajectories implicit in series of recognized precedents, it should be straightforward enough to see the Spirit as continually opening up (eschatological) possibilities of emancipatory critique, since it is precisely in virtue of the Spirit's outrunning the prevailing order that that order can be challenged. This approach can be further clarified and defended by contrasting it with its two main competitors, which might be called, following Kathryn Tanner, the "institutional-hierarchical" and the "immediate-interior" approaches.[47] (For convenience, I will refer to the present approach as "social-practical.") The institutional-hierarchical approach is a familiar target of Protestant polemics, which claim that such an approach identifies the Spirit's work too closely with certain Church offices; on such a view (whether or not it should be ascribed to Roman Catholicism), a hierarchy is the final arbiter of what counts as a work of the Spirit, such that all other alleged movements of the Spirit (including those which would call the hierarchy itself into question) must be subjected to the hierarchy's authority. The Spirit thus serves to insulate the hierarchy from critique, thereby further entrenching its power. The immediate-interior approach can be seen, at least in part, as a reaction against this institutional-hierarchical view: on this approach, as Tanner summarizes it, "the Spirit is thought to work immediately – both instantaneously and directly, without any obvious mediating forms – in exceptional events, rather than in the ordinary run of human affairs, upon the interior depths of individual persons, apart from the operation of their own faculties, in ways that ensure moral probity and infallible certainty of religious

---

[47] I am here following Kathryn Tanner, "Workings of the Spirit: Simplicity or Complexity?" in *The Work of the Spirit: Pneumatology and Pentecostalism*, Michael Welker (ed.) (Grand Rapids, MI: Eerdmans, 2006), pp. 87–105, as well as Chapter seven of *Christ the Key* (Cambridge University Press, 2010).

thought." This view is attractive, Tanner notes, not least because it opens up the possibility of criticizing the institutional hierarchy: "Appeals to the direct working of the Spirit are proffered as a means of prophetic dissent against otherwise entrenched scripture-based religious views or traditional church teachings. They also work as a defense against the persecution of dissenting religious opinion when such persecution is authorized and fomented by the idea that the majority view has divine sanction of either scripture or church teaching behind it."[48] The immediate-interior approach thus seems to provide critical leverage against an institutional hierarchy that claims to have a monopoly on the Spirit, since the former insists that the Spirit has provided persons with direct guidance, thereby contravening the hierarchy's claim to final authority and sole mediatorship of such guidance. As Tanner notes, however, the immediate-interior approach may end up reproducing some of the very authoritarianisms it seeks to overturn, since such an approach "tends … only to solidify the association of the highest forms of religious authority with simple self-evidence of an uncontestable sort. The Spirit trumps all those other purported authorities because I cannot doubt it; my experience of the Spirit speaks for itself in an indubitable fashion." Hence, "far from countering fanatical zeal and a dogmatism of religious viewpoint that excludes all possibility of criticism from the outside, appeal to the direct workings of the Spirit in one's personal experience would in this way simply reinstate fanaticism and dogmatism on new grounds."[49] That is, by claiming direct inspiration of the Spirit, immediate-interiorists may end up insulating their own views from criticism, thereby not only repeating one of the baleful characteristics of the hierarchy, but also rendering themselves empty-handed to adjudicate among competing claims to inspiration. To avoid this result, accordingly, without sliding back into a hierarchical view, a third approach emerges, namely, what I am

---

[48] Tanner, "Workings of the Spirit," p. 98.
[49] Tanner, "Workings of the Spirit," pp. 102–3.

calling a "social-practical" account. On this account, as Tanner summarizes it, "the Spirit is thought to work gradually, and without final resolution, in and through the usual fully human and fully fallible, often messy and conflict-ridden public processes of give-and-take in ordinary life … [T]he workings of the Spirit emerge from out of the whole of those ordinary operations, in and over their gradual and apparently meandering course, to surprising, indeed unpredictable effect."[50] Such an approach thus seeks critical leverage not by attacking the status quo from the outside, as it were, but by "loosening up the usual sources of religious authority by increasing their flexibility, tolerance for diversity of opinion, and openness to change. By talking about the Spirit at work in them, one would be trying to increase the complexity of the usual sources to bring about their greater inclusiveness and internal diversity. More open-ended processes of religious formation would ensue, with stability no longer secured, in a top-down fashion, through enforced redundancy and mechanical repetition of a linear sort."[51] It is beyond the scope of Tanner's argument to explain how such a social-practical approach would work, but it seems clear enough that the account defended here would count as an example of it: on this account, the Spirit is publicly mediated, yet cannot be identified in advance with the authority of any person or the configuration of any prevailing order; rather, the Spirit's work is continually reconfiguring that order from within. The account defended here thus aims to support Tanner's suggestion that a social-practical approach may be better suited to accomplishing that which the immediate-interior approach aims to do, namely, to "attack dogmatism and fanaticism in claims for divine sanction."[52] On the present account, the emancipatory Spirit of Christ works for increasingly just social arrangements precisely by exploiting the normative surplus implicit in those arrangements,

---

[50] Tanner, "Workings of the Spirit," p. 87.   [51] Tanner, "Workings of the Spirit," p. 102.
[52] Tanner, "Workings of the Spirit," p. 101.

and this differs in crucial respects from either an institutional-hierarchical or an immediate-interiorist approach.

5

There are some obvious objections to which this account is liable, as well as some obvious complications that require consideration. I cannot do justice to all of these here, but I will deal with a few of what I take to be the most serious.[53] The first problem has to do with the fact that an experience of disrespect may not in fact point to an injustice: so, for instance, a wealthy businessman may be used to a certain kind of privileged, deferential treatment, such that he experiences non-deferential treatment as disrespectful. (Call this the "don't you know who I am?" species of disrespect.) In such cases, we might grant that the person actually experiences disrespect, yet we would not – should not – grant that there is anything unjust about his or her expectation going unmet, since the expectation is itself the product of an unjust social arrangement. It seems evident, then, that experiences of disrespect do not necessarily correlate with injustice, which poses a serious problem for a proposal which appeals to such experiences as the basis of an account of justice. To address this problem, it is important to recall earlier remarks about "givenness": the normativity of a candidate perception of disrespect, like the normativity of what nature or Scripture says, still depends upon one's application of norms to it. By means of these norms, persons can adjudicate among candidate experiences of disrespect by determining which pattern of precedents produced the expectation in question and whether this pattern itself carries on the normative trajectory implicit in other patterns that they recognize as just. The point is that by setting a particular

ennering

---

53 A further objection, to the effect that one's expectation of recognition may in fact be mistaken, is easily addressed: if it turns out that a certain store worker did not greet me because, say, he or she had a terrible migraine, then my perception of disrespect would turn out to be an obvious *mis*perception.

trajectory against a background of other trajectories, one can perceive that trajectory as itself unjust, such that one need not confer recognition upon experiences of disrespect which depend upon it. In other words, experiences of disrespect which depend upon a trajectory of injustice need not be taken as injustice-indicating, and one's ability to draw the relevant distinction among trajectories is easily explained in the terms proposed here.

This is related to a second objection: if the prevailing order reinforces the non-recognition of certain persons to the extent that these persons internalize their non-recognition, how can they possibly experience some treatment as disrespect (rather than as what they deserve)? Two responses are relevant. First, there is reason to think that persons are never wholly unrecognized even within communities by which they may be oppressed, since (a) there is evidence that such non-recognition – sometimes termed "reification" – is in fact dependent upon a prior, "primordial" moment of recognition;[54] and (b) non-recognition is seldom uniform; it is far more common for persons to be recognized in certain respects (as, for instance, one of those created in the image of God) and not others (as a candidate for certain positions of authority). In many cases, one's being thus recognized in certain respects is sufficient to enable one to perceive non-recognition in others, and so to perceive the latter as disrespect. A second response is to note that the objection depends upon a rather elitist conception of the prevailing order. To wit: if one were to consider only the conception defended by Pierre Bourdieu, one might come to the conclusion that there is a single prevailing order, with a single dominant class and a single dominated class, and that the norms which circulate in this order always and only reinforce the power of the former at the expense of the latter.[55] On this picture, it would indeed be hard to see how

---

[54] On this point, see Hegel's *Phänomenologie des Geistes* as well as Honneth's *Reification: A New Look at an Old Idea* (Oxford University Press, 2008).

[55] For evidence of this charge, see "La formation des prix et l'anticipation des profits," in *Ce que parler veut dire*, pp. 59–95, where Bourdieu can explain the recognition

someone from a dominated class could experience some treatment as disrespect rather than as what he or she deserves, since it is hard to imagine where such a person would derive the resources by means of which to experience it as such. It would appear that Bourdieu's picture is a drastic simplification, however, and may in fact be tacitly complicit in maintaining the prevailing order, since it seems to take for granted that order's interpretation of itself. Contrary to this picture, we must remember that the prevailing order is neither monolithic nor all-encompassing. It turns out, in fact, that there are all sorts of prevailing orders, and that the order which prevails in one context may not prevail in another. One who is recognized in one context, accordingly, may not be recognized in another, and vice versa: a person who is recognized in an academic seminar may not be recognized in, say, a sports bar, or may be recognized for different characteristics in each setting – so, for instance, the ability to identify relevant objections tends to earn approval in the academy, yet may seem irritating to persons in a bar; the ability to out-joke one's peers, on the other hand, may earn one recognition in a bar, but may seem inappropriate in an academic setting. This strikes me as a fairly obvious point, yet many social theorists fail to account for it. Be that as it may, and besides the good reasons for doubting whether anyone is ever wholly unrecognized in any context, the fact that a person may be unrecognized in a particular context does not entail that he or she is unrecognized full stop, since he or she may be recognized in other contexts, and the latter recognition may

conferred at, say, a sports bar as, at best, a suspension of normative (i.e., for Bourdieu, "market") constraint, rather than as a shift from one set of norms to another, because he equates the realm of the normative with the interests of a single, monolithic dominant class; cf. the essay "Vous avez dit 'populaire'?" in *Actes de la recherché en sciences sociales* 46 (March 1983), pp. 98–105, which gets off to a good start, claiming that non-elite groups may administer their own discursive norms, but then falls back to familiar claims to the effect that such norms are mere parodies of those of the elite, that such persons are freed from the norms of the dominant only so long as no members of the dominant class are around, that the dominant norms condemn them any time they enter into society with any member of the dominant class, and so on.

provide him or her with the resources necessary to perceive a particular treatment as disrespect.

A final objection could be raised on the basis of Stanley Hauerwas's assertion that "Christians think we are creatures that beg. Prayer is the activity that most defines who we are. Through prayer we learn the patience to take the time to beg, to beg to the One alone who is the worthy subject of such prayer. Through prayer Christians learn how to beg from each other. Christians, therefore, can never be at peace with a politics or economic arrangement built on the assumption that we are not fundamentally beggars."[56] It seems to me that Hauerwas here moves much too quickly from a claim about prayer to one about begging from other creatures, but even if I were to grant these claims, I could respond by pointing out (a) that there is an important difference between begging that counts as one's own and that which is either forced upon one or strictly accidental to oneself, (b) that the New Testament seems to call persons only to the former sort of vocation, from which it follows (c) that if the possibility of identifying with some status depends upon one's participation in a community characterized by mutuality and openness, then those who contribute to the achievement of such communities are contributing to the possibility of true begging.

***

Experiences of disrespect can thus be called upon to fund emancipatory critique, since (a) they exhibit the norm implicit in a pattern of recognition, thereby stripping it of its sheen of naturalness, and (b) they make explicit various normative surpluses with which to call the prevailing order into question. On this account, then, the emancipatory Spirit of Christ can be seen as working within ordinary social practices to fund critique and to loosen the bonds of oppression,

---

[56] Hauerwas, *Performing the Faith: Bonhoeffer and the Practice of Nonviolence* (Grand Rapids, MI: Brazos Press, 2004), p. 241.

thereby cultivating the sort of communities which would enable persons to identify fully with their beliefs and actions.

Conclusion

As noted at the outset, theologians have been trying to avoid metaphysics for two centuries, and the present generation is no exception. By contrast with the current trend toward apophaticism, this book has defended a therapeutic approach to metaphysics. One of the key difficulties facing any attempt to overcome metaphysics, I have argued, is that certain metaphysical commitments have become common sense, such that we operate within their bounds without realizing it. In order to do without metaphysics, then, one must first render these commitments visible *as* commitments. On the present approach, this was accomplished by setting another picture alongside the metaphysical one. Not just any picture will do, however; in order to free one from the metaphysical framework, it is crucial that the alternative picture deal with the nostalgia one may feel for that which has been left behind. The key mark of such nostalgia is a sense of alienation: someone long in the grip of metaphysics may feel as if the loss of correspondentism leaves him or her out of touch with the world, or as if the loss of essentialism entails that he or she experiences only the fleeting shadows of things themselves. Such feelings indicate that one is still haunted by the ghost of metaphysics, since it is metaphysics' inflationary claims about reality and about being in touch with objects which make one feel as if something is *missing* once one rejects it. The therapeutic strategy, then, is to immunize one against such homesickness – to exorcize the ghost – by explaining that which metaphysics purports to explain – what an object is like, what it means to be in touch with objects, and so on – in terms of ordinary practices and experience, thereby deflating these notions and demonstrating that one need not appeal to metaphysics in order to do them justice.

Given the current intellectual landscape, the most serious problem facing such an approach is the claim that language is itself metaphysical, such that unless one maintains distance between it and God, one necessarily (if inadvertently) treats God as an idol. Preceding chapters responded to this problem, first, by elaborating and defending a therapeutic account of language: the strategy was to explain semantical notions such as meaning, truth, and reference in terms of pragmatics – in terms, that is, of the norms implicit in what we do with language – and explain pragmatics, in turn, in terms of intersubjective recognition. We thus arrived at an account of concepts that do not "contain," of meaning without "meanings," of reference without "presence," and of truth without "correspondentism." We arrived, in other words, at an account according to which ordinary language might be fit for theological use. With this account on board, we then explained how language could be used to speak of God. The key to this explanation is an understanding of the Holy Spirit's work, according to which the normative Spirit of Christ is carried on from person to person by a process of intersubjective recognition. When this account of the Spirit was brought together with the account of language just mentioned, a novel, non-metaphysical theology of God-talk emerged, a theology in terms of which the "supernatural," namely, one's ability to speak of God, could become "natural." The present proposal thus provides a non-essentialist, non-correspondentist account of God and language which frees us from thinking that one has to choose between metaphysics and alienation.

One of the goals of this project, accordingly, was to chart a course between the idolatrous pretensions of essentialist-correspondentist metaphysics, on the one hand, and the idea that God must stand at a remove from human language, on the other. This chapter made a second goal explicit, namely, the project's commitment to emancipation. Toward this end, I have tried to demonstrate, first, that this proposal funds a kind of *expressive freedom*: since the norm by which one's practices are judged is itself authorized, administered, and shaped by one, and since such norms are continually authorizing novel ways of carrying on these practices, it follows that one can see one's engagement in these practices as one's own. I then turned to experiences of disrespect – themselves explained as a normative surplus implicit in certain precedential trajectories – as a way of explaining how emancipatory critique could gain leverage on the prevailing order, since such experiences render explicit the norms which circulate invisibly in social practices and provide a ready-to-hand principle of justice by which to criticize these norms. Another of the project's goals, then, was to insist that the Spirit of Christ enters into ordinary practices not only to enable one to speak of God, but to contribute to the achievement of justice and liberation.

These goals turn out to be mutually reinforcing: on the one hand, one's liberation from essentialist-correspondentist metaphysics enables one to identify more fully with one's beliefs, words, and actions, since the latter, no longer contrasted with something which stands at a remove from ordinary life, are freed from the suspicion of being somehow second-rate. And on the other hand, one's ability (and inclination) to turn away from metaphysics – and to construct alternative frameworks out of that which is ready-to-hand – seems to grow precisely to the extent that one can experience one's life as one's own. My hope, then, is that by exorcizing the ghost of metaphysics, one may contribute to the achievement of social justice, and vice versa.

Index

Palmer, Humphrey, 131
Pannenberg, Wolfhart, 125, 143
  on resurrection as the end of history,
    142
perception, 186–9
  of God, 189–91
  role of concepts in, 151–3, 208
Pickstock, Catherine
  as recent defender of metaphysics, 1
  critique of Bruce Marshall, 229
  on truth as isomorphic, 206
Pinkard, Terry, 40, 154, 248
Pippin, Robert, 40, 62, 77, 247, 260
Plato, 7–8, 206
pluralism, 178–80, 197, 237–8
Popkin, Richard, 75
postmodernism, 12, 28
pragmatics, 37, 292
  pneumatological, 53, 86
pragmatism, 29, 40
precedents, 61–3
  fulfillment and judgment of, 133–4,
    175–8
  normative trajectory implicit in a series
    of, 38, 49, 63, 66, 68–9, 84, 94, 105,
    107, 133, 193, 232, 257, 281
  responsibility for, 93
predication, 25
  as basic to concept use, 48
  as fitting objects into predetermined
    categories, 15, 47, 52
  of truth, 223
  on the irreversibility of God's
    relationship to, 135
  praise as distinct from, 17–20
  proper vs. derivative, 140
Preller, Victor, 42, 50–1, 130–1
Principle of Charity, 119–20, 123
propositions, 43, 201, 239–41
  de re vs. de dicto elements of, 211
prospective vs. retrospective
  recognizability, 68–9, 85, 133–9
Protestant Reformation, 4, 74–5, 248
Proudfoot, Wayne, 79
Putnam, Hilary, 40, 157
  on a non-descriptivist theory of
    reference, 169

Quine, W. V. O., 40, 106
  on disquotationalism, 204
  on meanings as essences, 105
  on observability as relative to a
    community, 188
  on the demise of foundationalism, 44
  on the inscrutability of reference, 161
  on the truth predicate, 223

Radical Orthodoxy, 1
Rahner, Karl, 33
Ramberg, Bjørn, 40, 196
Ramsey, F. P., 223
rationality, 120
reason-giving, 40, 77, 235, 248, 250–2
recognition, 38, 61–5, 253–9
  and non-recognition, 110, 264–72,
    275–8, 290–1
  and possibilities of individual
    expression, 255–8
  and responsive dispositions, 79–81
  as Christ-following, 89–93, 263
  implicit in practice, 64
  mutuality of, 258–9
reference, 38, 157–66, 171
  and concepts, 22
  apparent impossibility of reference to
    God, 149–51
  as pointing, 168
  change of, 167
  God as identifying with anaphoric
    chain of reference, 172–5
  grammar of "refers"-talk, 166–7
  inheritance of, 164–6, 177–8
  inscrutability of, 161
  Jesus Christ as fulfillment of chain of
    reference, 175–8
  reference to God carried on by
    anaphoric chain, 170–2
  referential vs. attributive descriptions,
    179, 185
  relation of identification to, 171
  speaker's vs. semantic, 164, 167
  theological, 39, 168–80
reification, 288
representationalism, 5–6
Richards, Jay Wesley, 129